ADVANCE ACCLAIM FOR *HOW TO CATCH A PRINCE*

"A stirring modern-day fairy tale about the power of true love."

—CINDY KIRK, AUTHOR OF
LOVE AT MISTLETOE INN

"*How to Catch a Prince* is an enchanting story told with bold flavor and tender insight. Engaging characters come alive as romance blooms between a prince and his one true love. Hauck's own brand of royal-style romance shines in this third installment of the Royal Wedding Series."

—DENISE HUNTER, BESTSELLING
AUTHOR OF *THE WISHING SEASON*

"*How to Catch a Prince* contains all the elements I've come to love in Rachel Hauck's Royal Wedding Series: an "it don't come easy" happily ever after, a contemporary romance woven through with royal history, and a strong spiritual thread with an unexpected touch of the divine. Hauck's smooth writing—and the way she wove life truths through-out the novel—made for a couldn't-put-it-down read."

—BETH K. VOGT, AUTHOR OF *SOMEBODY LIKE YOU*, ONE OF PUBLISHERS WEEKLY BEST BOOKS OF 2014

ACCLAIM FOR PREVIOUS BOOKS

"Rachel Hauck's inspiring Royal Wedding Series is one for which you should reserve space on your keeper shelf!"

—*USA TODAY*

"Hauck spins a surprisingly believable royal-meets-commoner love story. This is a modern and engaging tale with well-developed second-ary characters that are entertaining and add a quirky touch. Hauck fans will find a gem of a tale."

—STARRED REVIEW PUBLISHERS
WEEKLY ON *ONCE UPON A PRINCE*

"Both books, *Once Upon a Prince* and *Princess Ever After* are a good blend of uplifting entertainment with a mystery twist—not too heavy, not too light, just right! Five plus stars awarded to these most excellent books by Rachel Hauck."

—LAURA PALMORE

"A completely satisfying read. I've read *A March Bride* 3 times!"

—J. GOLDHAHN

"Upon entering the world of Brighton and now Hessenberg (*Princess Ever After*), my mind was awash with the colors, sounds, sights, and even smells of this delightful, fictional city. So much so, I wish it were real so that I could schedule a visit! All in all, this was a world I did *not* want to leave."

—THINKING THOUGHTS BLOG

"I just finished my ARC of *Once Upon A Prince* and I LOVED IT! I don't say that often because I do so many book reviews and it's hard to find a real gem, but this one fit the bill!"

—LORI TWICHELL OF *RADIANT LIT*

"*The Wedding Dress* is a thought-provoking read and one of the best books I have read. Look forward to more . . ."

—MICHELLE JOHNMAN,
GOLD COAST, AUSTRALIA

"I thank God for your talent and that you wrote *The Wedding Dress*. I will definitely come back to this book and read it again. And now I cannot wait to read *Once Upon A Prince*."

—AGATA FROM POLAND

"Rachel Hauck writes with comedic timing and dramatic flair that underscore the stirring theme of God equipping and legitimizing those He calls to fulfill a purpose. Her portrayal of the supernatural presence and intercession of the Holy Spirit is artfully executed and a powerful testimony. Hauck illustrates Reggie's spiritual awakening with a purity that leaves little doubt to its credibility."

—*FAMILY FICTION* ON
PRINCESS EVER AFTER

How to Catch a
PRINCE

ALSO BY RACHEL HAUCK

NOVELLAS FOUND IN A YEAR OF WEDDINGS
A March Bride (e-book only)
A Brush with Love: A January Wedding Story (e-book only)

THE ROYAL WEDDING SERIES
Once Upon a Prince
Princess Ever After

LOWCOUNTRY ROMANCE NOVELS
Love Starts with Elle
Sweet Caroline
Dining with Joy

Nashville Sweetheart (e-book only)
Nashville Dreams (e-book only)

WITH SARA EVANS

Sweet By and By
Softly and Tenderly
Love Lifted Me

How to Catch a
PRINCE

❧⋆❧

RACHEL HAUCK

THE ROYAL WEDDING SERIES

ZONDERVAN

How to Catch a Prince

Copyright © 2015 by Rachel Hayes Hauck

This title is also available as a Zondervan e-book. Visit www.zondervan.com.

This title is also available as a Zondervan audiobook. Visit www.zondervan.com.

Requests for information should be addressed to:
Zondervan, *Grand Rapids, Michigan 49546*

Library of Congress Cataloging-in-Publication Data

Hauck, Rachel, 1960-
  How to catch a prince / Rachel Hauck.
    pages ; cm. -- (Royal wedding series)
  ISBN 978-0-310-31554-4 (softcover)
  1. Married people--Fiction. 2. Man-woman relationships--Fiction. I. Title.
  PS3608.A866H69 2015
  813'.6--dc23

2014033423

The author is represented by MacGregor Literary.

Interior design: Mallory Perkins

Printed in the United States of America

15 16 17 18 19 20 / RRD / 20 19 18 17 16 15 14 13 12 11 10 9 8 7 6 5 4 3 2 1

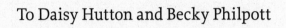
To Daisy Hutton and Becky Philpott

ONE

With each passing day, she remembered she had a secret. She'd lived in the fog of death until six months ago, when she crawled out, reaching for the first glimpse of life and light she'd encountered in five years. It came in the form of a simple telephone call. A refreshing-breeze offer.

But clearing the fog meant the memories surfaced. Ones she'd long since regarded as lost. Now they rattled around the empty corridors of her heart.

And recently, in the faintest ting or ping, like when elevator doors opened just outside her office, Corina remembered how she loved the glorious, rolling chimes of cathedral bells pealing through a crisp Cathedral City dawn.

And she ached. Deep in her soul. With a longing she couldn't reach nor remove.

With an exhale, she slumped in her chair and closed the news video she'd been watching. Two of the *Beaumont Post*'s staff writers entered the bull pen with a nod toward her, a late lunch of McDonald's swinging from their hands.

Corina's gaze followed them as they crossed the wide, boxy room, cutting through the muted afternoon sunlight that spilled through the dirty, rain-splattered windows.

She should go to lunch herself. It was nearly two. But she was waiting for her boss, Gigi Beaumont, to return from lunch. Corina had a proposition for the founder of the online mega newspaper, the *Beaumont Post*. A bold move, even for her, but she felt confident in her idea.

In the meantime, she had work to do. Corina sorted through her e-mail inbox, organizing stories that came in from the *Post* staff writers and stringers from around the world. Gigi's journalism-tabloid-media fingers had a very long reach.

Opening a story that had just come in though it was due last week, Corina started reading but lost her concentration after the first sentence.

What bothered her? *June*. Of course. It was the third of June. Being out from under the *fog*, dates and days had meaning again.

Okay. Fine. It was June third. Just recognize the day had once been significant and move on. But dealing with everything she'd buried more than five years ago proved challenging.

"Corina, hey . . ." Melissa O'Brien perched on the edge of Corina's desk, angling toward the computer screen. "What has you so engrossed? A story by Chip Allen?" She curled her lip.

"Yeah, um . . . it's good." Corina cleared her throat, sat up straight, and gathered herself into business mode—despite her rambling thoughts and rumbling stomach. "He's got a great piece on Hollywood and violence."

"Did you talk to Gigi yet?"

"Not yet." Corina peered down the long, wide center aisle of the bull pen, which ended at Gigi's office. Through the glass panel beside the closed door, she saw her boss pacing, cell phone to her ear. "I thought she was still at lunch."

"Nope, she's back in her office. With that appendage she calls a cell phone. It's going to kill her brain cells."

Corina laughed low. "They'd never have the nerve to die on her."

Gigi Beaumont, who crawled her way out from the poverty of the Blue Ridge Mountains to become a pioneer in the online journalism world, was a force to be reckoned with. No death, sickness, mayhem, corporate lawyers, hostile takeovers, sloppy reporters, lazy editors—nor husbands one through five—could conquer her.

"Are you saying you don't have the nerve?" Melissa let her purse slide from her shoulder to Corina's desk. "We need an editorial director. You've been doing the job since Carly left four months ago. And you're the new girl yet. Come on, be *brave*."

Brave? Courage wasn't the issue. It was timing. All about the timing. "Gigi's a mentor and friend, and I'm here because of her. But if she wants me for the job, why hasn't she asked?"

"It's Gigi." Melissa shrugged with a *pffftt*. "It's a miracle she offered you a job at all. Usually folks have to come begging."

"True." Corina stood, squaring her shoulders and shoving her chair under the desk.

"She's on her feet, ladies and gentlemen." Melissa hissed a faux crowd noise. "I think she's going in."

But Corina didn't move. When Gigi, a long-time family friend of the Del Reys and Corina's first employer after college, called after Thanksgiving last year with a, "Come on down to Florida and work for me," Corina began to wake up from the stupor of grief.

At twenty-nine, she'd spent the last five years in grave clothes. Alive but not living.

"Well?"

"I'm going."

"Doesn't look like you're going."

Corina moved toward Gigi's office with beauty-pageant stride. "You see me walking, don't you?" Her heels thumped against the tight carpet weave.

"Yeah, I do." The melody of Melissa's laugh fueled Corina's courage.

After all, she was a Del Rey, a daughter of great fortune, a steel magnolia, a former Miss Georgia, a summa cum laude college graduate, a writer . . . and twin sister.

She pressed her hand to her heart, slowing her steps and breathing deeply, remembering her brother. Carlos's death in Afghanistan had cost more than she'd have ever imagined.

Arriving at Gigi's door, Corina gathered her scattering thoughts—*forget the past*—and formulated her pitch. *Gigi, I've been doing the job of editorial director . . . formally give me the position . . . value to the team.*

Peering through the glass, Corina knocked, smiling when Gigi waved her in. The media mogul was still on her phone, pacing, speaking with voluminous animation.

"Fantastic, darling. Can*not* wait. You're going to love it here. Splendid family environment. Yes, we're right on the Atlantic. And the Indian River. On the famous U.S. 1." Gigi motioned for Corina to have a seat on the chocolate-colored suede sofa. "Sure he can learn to surf . . . Well, of course. We have our very own East Coast surfer's hall of fame to boot . . . Exactly. Listen, I've someone in my office. See you next week." Gigi ended the call, cradling her phone in her lap, and flashed her snow-white smile while cracking her ever-present Wrigley's Spearmint between her teeth. "Gorgeous Corina Del Rey, to what do I owe this pleasure?" Gigi's gleaming blond hair curled and floated about her face.

"I wanted to talk to you about—"

"I've been thinking." Gigi jumped to her feet, tucking her phone into her skirt pocket, circling the room, snapping her fingers. The riverscape behind her, beyond the windows and through the trees, was lit with the sun, threading diamonds of light into the water's calm surface. "We need a spectacular celebrity piece. You know, something to juice up our front pages." The *Post* started as a series of blogs Gigi chained together, written by

Washington insiders, Hollywood experts, gossip columnists, and the occasional royal watcher. She had boots on the ground in New York, L.A., Dallas, Miami, Atlanta, Toronto, London, Madrid, Cathedral City . . . to the ends of the earth.

"We have the Hollywood violence piece Chip Allen wrote."

"Snore bore, Corina. No one cares about the violence in movies, and if they do, they already agree with Allen. I told him I'm not sure we're going to run that piece." For an "international" newspaper, Gigi was hands-on, involved. She considered the world her backyard and believed sharing news was as simple as talking to her neighbors over the backyard fence. Even if that neighbor was thousands of miles away. "We need something *wow*." Gigi swirled her hands through the air with animation.

"Why do we need something *wow*?"

Gigi stopped treading between the windows and the sitting area, her gaze steady on Corina. "You know why I hired you?"

"Because I'm a good writer. Professional, organized. I'm a hard worker." But in truth? She had no idea why Gigi hired her. Because the last five years of Corina's resume contained a big fat blank. What had she done? Become a professional griever, a professional liaison between her parents. Traveling with Daddy when he asked. Otherwise, living at home, in the shadows of what the family used to be.

But *yes*, she was a good writer and hard worker. Which Gigi knew.

Being an heiress meant nothing to Corina's wealthy but hard-working father who made sure she and Carlos never counted on the family name and fortune to make their way in life. Her high school friends curled their lips in disgust when Corina had to tend to household chores and work a summer job to earn money for her own car. *"But your dad's a millionaire a hundred times over."*

Tell that to Donald Del Rey.

"Good at what you do?" Gigi's furrowed expression as she sat back down on the sofa inspired doubt in Corina. "Well, of course you are. And by the way, splendid of you to step up after Carly left. The bull pen loves you. Who knew you were so good with details?"

"Me."

"But of course."

"That's why I think you should just give me—"

"Corina, I hired you to spice things up."

"Excuse me?"

"Girl, you used to pal around with Paris Hilton, and I bet if I snagged your iPhone, you'd have a Kardashian or two in your contacts."

"Hello, do you not remember my life for the past five years?"

"Yes, I realize . . . all the grief." Gigi pressed her hand on Corina's knee. "I am so sorry about Carlos. He was an amazing young man. Too handsome for his own good and twice as kind." The fiftysomething drew air between her teeth. "He reminds me of my third . . . no fourth . . . yes, fourth husband. Desi." She closed her eyes and drifted away. "Should've never divorced him."

"We can put *that* on the front page," Corina said.

Gigi snapped from her daydream. "Very funny, you clever girl. No, what we need is an exclusive."

"What sort of exclusive?"

"Something no one else is reporting. Contact your celebrity friends, get some sort of inside scoop. Be inventive. Maybe you could sit down with Bill Clinton's daughter. Or one of the Bush twins."

"Gigi," Corina said, standing. "If you want to run a salacious story on a former president's daughter, you're going to have to find someone else to do it. I came in here to ask you for the editorial director job. When you want to talk serious, let me know." She started for the door. Celebrity chums, presidents' daughters, high school friends? She'd spoken to practically none of them since Carlos's funeral.

But she didn't blame them. Everything changed the day he died. Then with such finality the afternoon she helped her daddy shovel the first mounds of dirt over her brother's coffin, Mama weeping and collapsing into the reverend's arms. And the loving, close-knit Del Rey family fell apart. She'd lost her brother, a constant in every tender childhood memory. Then she "lost" her parents, the Del Rey traditions, the closeness, and laughter.

"Editorial director?" She laughed. "Darling, back to my original question. Why I hired you. To go after the rich and famous, the salacious celeb gossip. To travel the world, to spice up our readers' drab little lives with a look at how the one percent lives. Come on, surely you've some lead on a hot story."

"No, and if I did, I'd not betray my friends by giving the story to you."

"Tsk, tsk." Gigi shook her head. "Did you not learn anything from me when you worked with me before?"

"Yes, which is why I'm asking for the director job." She'd lost so much time when she'd holed up at home, trying to comfort herself, her parents over Carlos's death, all the while waiting for her life to begin again. Now that she was free, she wanted to get things moving.

Though Daddy worried a bit about her being out on her own. Something he'd never done in the past. Corina suspected it had to do with losing his son.

"An heiress without any security? Let me hire someone for you, Corina."

But she refused, just wanting to *be*. To find her bearings and destiny. She still felt poor and weak, broken—the furthest thing from an heiress.

In the end, though, she yielded to Daddy's request to buy an apartment in a secure building, finding a lovely spot on the river with hefty security.

"I filled the position today." Gigi sat back, arm propped on the back of the sofa. "Just got off the phone with Mark Johnson."

"Mark Johnson?" Corina paused her exit and stepped back into the room. "*The* Mark Johnson who worked with me after college? The man the rest of us pulled out of the fire *daily* because he partied every night and missed most of his assignments? *That* Mark Johnson?"

"Yes, *that* Mark Johnson." Gigi's laugh mocked Corina's concern. "He might not have been a stellar employee when he was younger—"

"He's so much older now? It's been what, seven years?"

"Certainly he's older and more accomplished, married with a child. He's built an impressive résumé."

Corina heard the subtle innuendo. *You did not.* No, because she was pasting her life together and holding on to her crumbling family.

"He's worked in London, New York, L.A., and is currently the managing editor for Martin Looper Media." Gigi raised her brows. "Our competition."

"Gigi, you called me. You asked me to come work for you. So let me. I can do the job. I've been on the weekly calls with New York and London. I've Skyped, Facetimed, and Google Plused with our bloggers, stringers, and photographers. I know the bull pen."

"Do you want to know the real reason I called?"

It *had* been rather out of the blue. Corina thought perhaps God was answering her pleas to "do something." How could she love and support her parents yet move on with her life? She felt like she was drowning, dying her own special death in the shadow of her brother's. And Carlos would've never wanted it.

"Because your mama said you were driving her crazy."

"Excuse me? I was driving *her* crazy?"

"Said you never left the house."

"Me?" Mama! Frustrating, incorrigible Mama. Corina scrunched her hands into tight fists, digging into her palms with her fingernails. "*She* was the one who never left the house."

"Well, you're here. I thought it was a good idea when she proposed it. You're moving on. I'm glad for it. But editorial director? Shug, please." Gigi stood and crossed over to her desk, her attention to the conversation waning. "I want you to find you the *big* story." She tossed Corina a saucy smile. "The biggest story of your life."

"Yeah?" Corina held open the office door. "And what would that be?"

Back at her desk, Corina sat with a sigh, shaking her head at Melissa, who frowned and stuck her tongue out at Gigi's door.

Story of her life? Corina had a story all right. Of her own life. An *amazing* story, one she'd never told anyone. It was her secret.

And his.

On days when the fog still clouded her heart and thoughts, she imagined it might have all been a dream. Then she'd hear a bell or the ping of the elevator doors and know it was real.

But it was a story she could never tell. Ever. Because it was an incredible secret. Though why she showed *him* any loyalty was beyond her.

With a sigh, Corina sat forward, facing Chip Allen's dry Hollywood piece.

Why *did* she keep their secret? One small thought ricocheted in reply. Because in some small way, maybe she still loved him.

TWO

Brighton Kingdom–Cathedral City

THE LIBERTY PRESS
4 June
PRINCE STEPHEN NAMED THE WORLD'S MOST ELIGIBLE BACHELOR

THE INFORMANT
5 June
KING'S OFFICE CLAIMS PRINCE STEPHEN NOT
LOOKING FOR LOVE, HAPPY WITH RUGBY LIFE

6 June
PRINCE STEPHEN, PATRON OF YOUTH RUGBY,
TO OPEN SUMMER TOURNAMENT

Stephen snapped off the telly, grumbling and muttering to himself about the antics on *Madeline & Hyacinth Live!* Who did they think they were, trying to find him a bride?

To think, he used to consider them friends. But today they went too far, jumping in on the media speculation about his love life. What spurred this? He'd not been out with a woman in ages. And his blasted ankle injury had remanded him from the rugby field and the public eye for the past three months.

What gives?

Nevertheless, at this very moment, men and women around Brighton Kingdom were watching their show and tweeting to the hashtag #howtocatchaprince. Thank you, Maddie and Hy.

He should tweet his own answer. If he had a Twitter account. *Leave him alone #howtocatchaprince.*

Hobbling from his media room toward the kitchen, his belly rumbling for tea and puffs, he paused at the hallway window and gazed through the swaths of shadow and light into the palace gardens.

So lovely and green. Made him miss the pitch. But he was stuck inside, healing, his high ankle sprain fortified with a walking boot. He sustained the injury during the spring 7 Nations matches, just as his career crested into a new high. The Rugby Union had listed him as the top winger in the league.

He, a royal prince, accomplished such an acclaim all on his own.

Yet the injury lingered, not healing as quickly as Stephen would have liked. Day by day, he sensed his achievements slipping away while the younger, more hardy lads gunned for his position. Number 14.

In the kitchen, the tea service and a plate of cinnamon puffs were already set for him. Good man, Robert, his valet, butler, and aide.

Sitting at the island counter, set with linen, china, and silver—a royal etiquette Robert refused to abandon—Stephen poured a steaming cup of tea and took a long, hardy sip, then dipped in the tip of a puff.

The light, sweet pastry melted on his tongue. Pure delight.

Staring across the steel-and-granite kitchen—a remodel overseen by his mum while he played in the World Cup a few years back—Stephen sorted through his emotions.

What bugged him really? The headlines about his love life? Maddie and Hy and the whole of the Twitter universe advising him? Perhaps it was his lack of a love life that bothered him.

In truth, Maddie and Hy didn't bother him much. The hashtag was kind of clever. The girls were good chums, really, and simply doing their job. Entertaining Brightonians each weekday afternoon.

No, *no*, what truly bothered him were the nightmares. The flooding memories. The times and events he'd run a thousand miles up and down the rugby pitch striving to forget.

Put it all behind me.

But the arrogant things demanded his attention now that his mind and body were not consumed with the game.

Surely he'd be back in command by summer's end. Since his surgery in the spring, he'd been faithful with physiotherapy. He'd be in tip-top shape, ready to play in the fall Premiership.

Stephen picked up another puff, and another one of his distant memories drifted to the front. Why did puffs make him think of *her*?

But he knew. They'd eaten puffs together, that night, at Franklin's Bakery. And it was forever lodged in his psyche.

Robert entered, a set of tea towels in hand. "Sir, there you are. How was your therapy?"

"Fine. Did you see the headlines again today?"

"Ghastly business, speculating on your love life."

"They didn't ring round here, inquiring, did they?"

Robert made a face, folding the towels neatly into a drawer above the cabinets. "They'd be foolhardy if they did. Wasting their time."

"As I thought. I can't imagine what sparked this sudden interest."

"Perhaps a slow news week." Robert smiled and Stephen laughed.

"I'll take that as a compliment."

"As it was intended." Robert bustled about the kitchen, preparing for supper. "I trust you'll be on the pitch for the summer internationals? After all, the Brighton Eagles need their star winger." The older gentleman, with a thick coif of pale red hair, was lean and fit, an ardent rugby enthusiast. "The whole city is electric with excitement over the upcoming tournament."

When Stephen took Robert on in the spring, his love for the game was the one quality that set him above the rest of the royal household staff. That and the fact he was the son of a valet who was the son of a valet. His father had also served in the palace.

"No summer internationals for me," Stephen said. *Thanks to his blasted, stupid injury.* He should've taken more care with his weak left side. With these international games, he'd have earned another cap. So far, he'd collected twenty-eight in all, on his way to a goal of fifty. "The ankle is not ready."

'Tis a shame, sir, what with the new stadium and all. They say we're poised for a good show opening weekend."

"I'll be cheering from the bench."

"I'm sure the lads will love the support of their prince and team leader."

Stephen shifted in his seat, gently stretching his left ankle, silently dealing with the pain. Why wasn't it getting better? The throbbing seemed to be a constant. Even more bewildering to him was how the pain leaked upward toward his chest and drilled into his heart.

Ever since he returned from his tour in Afghanistan and demobbed from the Royal Air Command, he'd been on the pitch, consumed with the present, fashioning his future, grateful for every training session, every test that excised his dark demons, the painful past, and his doubts about a kind, loving God.

Okay, so it was only June. He'd miss the summer games, but Dr. Gaylord predicted another month in the walking boot along with physiotherapy and Stephen would be ready to train at 100 percent again.

As he stuffed his sixth puff into his mouth and washed it down with tea, door chimes pealed through his palace apartment.

Robert wiped his hands on a towel. "Are you expecting someone, sir?"

"Perhaps it's someone who's figured out how to catch a prince?"

Robert's small white smile sparked in his eyes. "Shall I let them in?"

"Please, I'd like to know the answer myself."

Stephen poured another cup of tea. Just how did one catch a prince? An American, Susanna, had captured his brother, the king, with a single glance.

As for him? He'd been caught. Once. And he was certain he'd never want to be caught again, despite all of Mum's not-so-subtle hints about grandchildren to *both* of her sons.

"Sir, your brother is here to see you."

Stephen glanced around to see Nathaniel enter, a large white envelope under his arm. "Come join me, Nathaniel, for puffs and tea. Your favorites." Stephen reached over, shoving the second stool away from the island, intending for his brother to sit.

"May I see you in private?" Nathaniel said, serious and deep voiced, and without a nod to the puffs.

"Um, sure, what's up?" It wasn't like Nathaniel to pass up puffs. Stephen motioned again for him to sit. "Robert, can you give us a moment?"

The valet-butler-aide set out another tea service, then left without a word, drawing closed the kitchen doors with multicolored stained-glass centers.

"At least have some tea?" Stephen reached for the china pot and filled the cup Robert left for the king.

"I guess I could use a cup." Nathaniel sat, still holding the envelope.

"Why so glum? You and Susanna have a row?"

"No, we're fine. More than fine. Trying for a baby."

Stephen grinned. "Then why the long face, my brother?" Then he pointed to the envelope. "Please, don't tell me you're here about the Prince of Brighton argument again."

Nathaniel set the envelope on the counter, patting it with his palm as if to make sure it stayed in place. "Not today, but the argument is moot. I don't understand your resistance. As my brother, you are the Prince of Brighton. The coronation only makes it official."

"Precisely, and with the official setting in, I become patron of what? Fifteen charities and organizations . . . including the War Memorial and Remembrance Day."

"I would think you'd consider it an honor to patron the War Memorial and Remembrance Day. You fought for and were wounded for your country."

"Don't, Nathaniel. *You* know why."

"I know what you tell me, yes, but I'm not quite sure I understand it all."

"Shall I recap my final days in Afghanistan for you?"

"No, I remember the tragic details and the lives lost—which is all the more reason I think you'd want to honor those men by being a voice to the people, reminding them of the price paid for their freedoms."

"I remember the lads by being on the pitch. I play for them."

Stephen understood the pressure Nathaniel faced. He was a king with royal duties and responsibilities, expectations. The press had all but given up on inquiring when the king would coronate his brother into the office of Prince of Brighton.

The King's Office always answered the same. *"His rugby is his focus for now. We're giving him room to pursue his interests."*

The Prince of Brighton served as a patron, humanitarian, and defender of the weak. The peerage had been created by King Leopold IV for his brother in 1850, citing him as a chairman and spokesman for the poor and the aging vets.

The peerage was inherited by the oldest sibling of the ruling royal. The last Prince of Brighton had been their great-great-uncle Prince Michael, also a rugby player and an RAC colonel, who died on D-Day.

"I'd think you'd want to honor Uncle Michael, the men who died, and their families by being the War Memorial patron. Especially for those from other countries who were a part of the Joint International Coalition, men who were not Brightonian but gave their lives. Those men were your mates and your—"

Stephen shoved away from the counter, stumbling over his stool, his booted foot caught. "I know who those men were and how they died. I don't need a lecture, Nathaniel." The tea and puffs soured in his belly.

He couldn't do it. Don his uniform and stand before the nation, the world, with his holier-than-thou royal title and pretend to be someone he was not. Someone worthy.

Besides, he'd created his own memorial at the Parrsons House and paid his respects every Remembrance Day. Or whenever he traveled to the country.

"Listen, I'm sure I don't understand, but . . ." Nathaniel picked up the envelope.

"No, you don't understand. Not really. So give me a break. General Horsch has been doing a grand job of patroning Remembrance Day and the War Memorial. He's a great man, a stalwart warrior, and was the commander of the Joint International Coalition."

"You're giving in to your fears, mate."

"Giving in?" *Ha!* "You think this is giving in? I've earned the right to choose, Nathaniel." Stephen slapped his hand to his chest, bridling his fears. "But don't ever say I've given in. I get up *every* day and face life, remembering what happened that day in Torkham."

His voice dropped, and the silence reverberated against the tile and plaster.

"I'm sorry," Nathaniel said after a moment. "But I am here for another reason. We can talk about the coronation later." Nathaniel passed Stephen the envelope. "I need you to explain this."

Stephen flipped the envelope over. "It's a white, legal-sized envelope. Used to mail papers or perhaps store files."

"Very funny. My brother, the comic. Inside. Look at the contents inside." Nathaniel angled forward, flicking the edge of the envelope. "I've not said a word to Mum about this because it would crush her."

In his thirty-one years, he'd crushed his mum many times. But as a young man. Not since his university days. At least not to his knowledge. He'd worked hard to erase his reputation as the screw-up prince. The one who had tried but failed.

"Crush her? What are you talking about?" Dread iced over Stephen as the paper inside slipped into his hand. He swore softly under his breath. "Where did this come from?"

"So it's true?"

Stephen stared at the gilded certificate with the embossed calligraphy letters. "Sort of. Not really. I mean, yes, we went to Hessenberg, and . . . Where did you get this?"

Memories, feelings, a longing he thought he'd divorced sauntered through him.

"Archbishop Burkhardt had it sent to me by special courier. He's most concerned." Miles Burkhardt was the most recent leader of the Church in the Grand Duchy of Hessenberg, Brighton's North Sea sister island nation. "He came across the certificate in his office, found it in some secret compartment Archbishop Caldwell never mentioned to him. He was sorting things out for a remodel and there it was, presenting itself."

"Then don't worry about it." Stephen returned the certificate to the envelope, his head reminding his heart this was *no big deal.* "I never filed with the Court. It's not legal. And we ended things when I came back from my tour."

"Ended?" Nathaniel's furrowed brow irritated Stephen. Did he not understand? "How did it end?"

"I don't know." But oh, he did. *Liar.* "She went her way and I went mine." He'd reasoned this out so many times to convince himself he did the right thing. To convince himself he didn't care. Either way, it had to end. So he ended it.

"Stephen," Nathaniel said, rising and snatching the envelope, "you're married."

"No, I'm not. I never filed with the Court."

"Did you file an annulment with the Church then? Because according to this . . ." Nathaniel waved the marriage certificate like it was some kind of you-messed-up-again banner. "You're still married."

"Annulment? How could I? No one knew. You said so yourself . . . This thing," Stephen flicked the edge of the envelope, "was tucked away in some secret compartment. The marriage was never official."

"Are you so daft? A marriage performed by an archbishop is automatically on file with the Church. That's as good as the Court, if not more so."

"But Archbishop Caldwell never filed it." Were they to continue this circular argument? It was so clear to Stephen. He was not married. He returned from Afghanistan with a mission to play professional rugby and end his relationship with his wife.

"Are you so naive? You are a member of the royal family. If this certificate says you married Corina Del Rey"—Nathaniel pulled out and examined the certificate—"on three June, six years ago, then you are married, little brother."

"Impossible." Stephen paced around the island, thinking, his thoughts colliding with his palpitating emotions. "I've not even seen her since—"

"That doesn't change this signed and sealed certificate. You are married before God and the Church. Unless you petitioned for disillusion. Did you?"

"No!" He cut the air with a wide sweep of his arm. "It was a secret. The archbishop promised to hold the certificate until I came for it."

"Well, he proved to be trustworthy. Unfortunately, he didn't pass the word along to Archbishop Burkhardt. Didn't Caldwell tell you this certificate marries you whether you file with the Court or not?"

No. Maybe. Yes. Stephen scooped his fingers through his hair, leaving his locks to stand on end. Impetuous. It had been a spur-of-the-moment, *impetuous* decision. They were in love. He was about to deploy. They had four weeks to be man and wife before he left. They'd keep their secret for the six months he was away, then tell his family and hers, and finally, the world.

He was good at impetuous, on-his-feet thinking. It was when he hesitated that things went wrong. Like that day in Torkham. Like that day on the pitch during 7 Nations, when he hesitated on his sidestep around an England Lions defender.

"Did you love her?"

"I suppose . . . yes."

Nathaniel exhaled and ran his hand over his hair. "You married an American heiress and told no one?" Fire flamed in his eyes. His nostrils flared. Stephen resented his tone.

"Yes, I married her. What of it?" He snatched the envelope back from his brother. He might be his brother and king, but he was not his father, his conscience, or his God. "As I recall, you liked her."

"Where is she now?" Nathaniel glanced about the kitchen with exaggeration, hands on his belt. "I see no photographs. No mementos. No evidence she was ever in your life."

"Because the relationship is over. As for where she is, I don't know. The States, I assume. With her family. She went home after her brother died." He wanted to resent his brother for bringing this to light. "Look, we'll just tear it up and forget about it. No harm, no foul."

"The archbishop, rightly so, made a copy. And we can't just tear up a marriage certificate, Stephen. Corina is not your pet. She's your wife."

"Whom I've not seen in five years." Stephen returned to his stool at the island, picking up a puff, then dropping it back on the plate.

"I didn't realize marriages had statutes of limitations on physically *seeing* someone. Unless, of course, she's passed on. Has she? Died?"

"Don't be morbid. And it's rude because you know what happened to her twin brother." Stephen paced again, his adrenaline spiked, making it impossible to sit still. "And don't talk down to me."

"You're right. I apologize. I'm just put out by this business. I'm not sure where to land. Stephen, what were you thinking? You willingly risked the Brighton throne? This marriage was entirely illegal six years ago. A royal in line to the throne was forbidden to marry a foreigner. What if something had happened to me?" The steam of anger curled Nathaniel's words. "You are second in line."

"Please, I was the one shipping off to war. You, the crown prince, were not allowed to go."

"I could've slipped and fallen in the bathtub, hit my head."

"You cannot be serious." Stephen accented his mocking laugh with a sardonic edge.

"No, I guess not." Nathaniel noticed his tea for the first time and took a sip. He made a face. "It's cold."

"I'll freshen the pot—"

"Leave it be, Stephen." Nathaniel perched on his stool. "Tell me, what happened? Why the secrecy? What was the plan when you returned—"

"I don't know, Nathaniel. You with your twenty questions. All right, I was in love." Stephen fell against the kitchen's counter, crossing his booted foot over his healthy one, a dull ache gripping his ankle. "It was the night of the Military Ball. Corina and I had gone to the top of the Braithwaite Tower. No one was there—it was just the two of us. We were looking out over the Rue du Roi, surrounded by the lights of the city, and in that moment life was perfect. It was nine o'clock. The cathedral bells had just started to chime."

The wind swept along the avenue, bringing with it the fragrance of the River Conour. Stephen anchored his hands on the upper railing of the Braithwaite, capturing Corina between his arms.

Her hair brushed against his cheek, and he felt as if he were drowning in the pleasure of her.

Turning her to him, he delicately traced his finger along the curve of her jaw, then raised her chin and touched his lips to hers. So soft, so sweet. It awakened a deeper, more powerful hunger. Stepping back, he knew what had been whispering in his heart for the last few months was real.

He loved her. He wanted to marry her. But he was shipping out in four weeks for a six-month tour in Torkham with his RAC flight.

Behind him, beside him, before him, the synchronized cathedral bells began to ring out.

One, two, three . . .

Then she said it first. The words his heart burst to share. "I love you, Stephen. You are my prince." Her light laugh wound around his heart.

Four, five, six . . .

Then he knew what he wanted more than anything. He didn't think or hesitate, because he knew what was right. Dropping to one knee, he gazed into her hazel eyes with the flecks of gold.

Seven, eight . . .

"Marry me, Corina Del Rey, because I love you so very much."

Nine.

"What? Marry you?" Her voice resounded in the silence. The June air swept around them, scented with honeysuckle.

"Yes, tonight. We can catch the ferry to Hessenberg."

"Hessenberg? But why? How? Brighton law forbids you marrying a foreigner." Her voice quivered as she exposed the truth.

"But yet, here you are in my arms."

"I love you and I don't understand the law, but Stephen, I won't be responsible for toppling any part of the House of Stratton."

"Indeed not. I am capable of that all on my own. Darling, I'm going to war in thirty days' time. If that is not a threat to the House of Stratton, I don't know what is. Certainly not a prince marrying the woman who has captured his heart. So marry me. Please. The archbishop there is a good bloke. I'm sure he'll marry us." Or at least he believed so.

"You really want to marry me?"

"Is that a yes?"

"If you want to marry me, then—"

"Yes, you'll marry me." He gathered her into his arms, swinging her round, kissing her in the first of many intimate kisses.

"Stephen? Did you hear me?"

He leveled on his brother, bringing his thoughts about. "Say again?"

Nathaniel poured a cup of tea. "Why did it end?"

"Why are *you* doing this? Take a guess. You know her brother was one of the men killed *that* day." Nathaniel, along with the defense minister, the RAC general counsel, and his dear departed father, were the only ones who knew the whole truth.

"Ah, you ended the marriage because of her brother." Nathaniel knew Stephen and Carlos had been friends. And he knew Stephen had been somewhat smitten with his mate's twin sister, Corina.

"She went home to be with her parents when she got the news . . . about Carlos." Stephen shook his head, a shallow, simple way of expressing what his words could not. "Those five days I was in the hospital, after the blast, I knew every time I looked at her I'd remember and—"

"Then what? You just rang up and said, 'It's over love'?"

"No . . . she returned to Brighton after Carlos's funeral. I couldn't tell her why I'd gone missing on her, why I didn't return her calls or e-mails, why I missed her brother's funeral. Since the RAC didn't know she was my wife, naturally they didn't contact her when I was wounded."

"Nor did the family. Good grief, Stephen." Nathaniel's sigh more than scolded. It affirmed. *You messed up.*

"We lost contact for about two weeks. First with me in the hospital, then with me . . . well, dealing with the whole mess. She didn't know Carlos had been transferred to my crew. She flew back to Brighton to try to find out what had happened to me and to tell me about Carlos in case I hadn't heard. I was at her flat when she arrived, getting my things. We lived there after we married . . . to keep the press away from us."

"And you sent her away?"

"I told her the marriage was a mistake. It sounded reasonable since marrying a foreigner was illegal. I had the law on my side."

"So you didn't really love her when you married her?"

Stephen glanced at his brother. "I loved her very much."

Their phone calls, e-mails were his lifeline. Her care packages of biscuits and cakes, little drawings and poems, set his heart ablaze as much as her kisses and love making. She wasn't a grand baker—he and the lads had to wash her cookies down with big gulps of water—but Stephen loved that she tried.

So his time in Torkham had passed quickly. The unit had engaged in some intense fighting, and day after day, his love for her kept him going. But July to January seemed like an eternity to a thirsty man dwelling in the desert.

Then four weeks from the end of his tour, an enemy they

never anticipated blew up the mess tent, killing the six men on Stephen's crew. Including his wife's brother.

Stephen survived, spending a week in a field hospital, before special forces transported him home on New Year's Eve. All under cover.

"You must have crushed her, Stephen."

"Crushed seems like such a hard word." Lately, there were nights when he dreamt of her tears. All the more reason he needed to return to rugby. To exert his physical power over his emotional weakness.

"I'm sure it does." Nathaniel sighed his disappointment. "However, it's fitting. Did she ask what happened? Where you'd been? Why you lost communication? Did you tell her you knew about Carlos? That he was with you?"

"I couldn't tell her why Carlos was with me, could I? It's classified. So I just avoided all detail. PTSD makes a good excuse." Even now, the truth was buried so deep it hurt if he even thought of it. "Well, I did tell her there was an explosion. Nothing more. All that nonsense is classified anyway. I said it made me realize I had a responsibility to the Crown and the House of Stratton. If word got out I'd married an American, there'd be chaos. I'd have to step out of line to the throne, and frankly, I couldn't do that to Dad. Or you. God rest his soul."

King Leopold V, Stephen's father, had succumbed to leukemia two years ago. And Stephen never missed him more.

"Blimey, you're a piece of work."

"Nathaniel, I don't need your judgment. Even now, I still believe I did what was best. Besides all of the legal ramifications, which didn't change until you wanted to marry Susanna, I needed to forget everything about Afghanistan and move on. And that included Corina. How could I look at her and not remember?"

"I can't believe she gave in without an argument."

"She didn't until I told her I'd have to renounce the throne. She embraced the end of things then."

"But you never told her you were with Carlos when he died?"

"No." The pain on her face when he told her he wanted out of the marriage nearly did him in. It was forever etched on his heart. He refused to add the image of her tears when he told her Carlos died needlessly. That he died because of him.

So Stephen blotted out the day he ended their marriage. Yet this conversation with Nathaniel dragged through the depths and crevasses of his mind, raising bits and pieces of that horrid day to the surface.

She'd been weeping so bitterly, reminding him of their love, how she needed him in the wake of Carlos's death. Stephen had nearly relented and scooped her in his arms, telling her everything would be all right.

But then he heard the phantom explosion, the echoing screams. He saw the blood on his hands. And it was all he could do not to run from her presence.

Stephen closed the blinds on those memories, fingers pressed to his forehead.

"Tell me this—how did Archbishop Caldwell not challenge you?" Nathaniel said.

"He protested at first, but then his wife brewed him a spot of tea and he seemed rather cordial afterwards. I think he was persuaded we were in love and knew what we were doing." Stephen caught Nathaniel by the arm. "I did love her. Truly. But Torkham changed everything."

"You realize you need to fix this." Nathaniel shoved the envelope toward him.

"There's nothing to fix. She thinks it's over. It is over. Toss it in the trash."

Nathaniel reached inside his pocket, producing a folded piece of paper. "I told you. We can't do that. Archbishop Burkhardt sent this note along with the certificate. Shall I read it?"

"Be my guest." Sarcasm. He was at the end of his patience.

"He writes, 'I'm unsure of the meaning of this certificate. Prince Stephen does not presently have a wife to my knowledge, but I pray that whatever has become of their relationship, the prince will handle it with honor before God and men. While I suspect he married her in secret, he cannot put her away in the same fashion. A proper annulment must be filed with the Church.'"

"I didn't put her away in secret. She knows. I told her to her face."

"You're going to have to file an annulment. Let's pray she's not moved on and remarried already. There hasn't been much in the media about her lately, nor her family, which, I suppose, if Corina Del Rey married, it would be quite the society affair."

"W–what?" Stephen scoffed. She'd not have married again. Would she? A whip of jealousy stung his heart.

"She's a beautiful, intelligent woman. Surely you've considered that another man might want her. That she'd want to move on, have a family." Nathaniel glanced at his watch. "Sorry to cut this off, but I've a meeting. Ring Jonathan in the morning. He'll help you locate her. Then you can fly Royal Air One to meet with her."

"Pardon? Nathaniel, I'm not going to 'meet with her.' We can courier the proper papers to her."

"Stephen, she's your wife, deserving of your respect and honor. Especially since she's been lied to for the past five or so years, thinking she's a freed woman when she is not. Not to mention, she married the royal Prince of Brighton. I'd say she is deserving of a princess honor." Nathaniel made his way through the kitchen doors. "If you argue any more about it, I'll haul out the big guns."

Mum! "You wouldn't."

"Don't test me."

He felt twelve again. Under his father's disapproving scrutiny when he brought his mates into the throne room and set up a bowling lane. "I meant to handle it, Nathaniel." Stephen walked with his brother to the front door. "But I ended up playing in the summer internationals. Then I realized I didn't have the marriage certificate, so I just let it go."

"Did you forget your way to the good archbishop's office?" Nathaniel opened the door and the scent of an evening rain swept into the apartment. "Make this right, Stephen."

Blimey. He'd not truly encountered brother-king Nathaniel before. But he was right. Stephen had to see her. Tell Corina face-to-face. With a giant, weight-bearing exhale, he sank into the nearest chair and stared out the window.

Rain splashed down, bouncing off the warm summer sidewalk, and in the distance he heard the first choreographed chimes of the city's six o'clock bells.

One . . .

Two . . .

Three . . .

THREE

$\mathcal{I}$t was late. She was tired and ready to go home, but since Mark Johnson had arrived Monday afternoon, walking the bull pen with political candidate gravitas, shaking hands, pledging hope and change, Corina's workload doubled.

She'd been assigned to bring him up to speed on the writers and the way of the bull pen. She spent her days introducing him to the Melbourne, Florida, staff as well as the writers scattered across the country and around the world via the wonder of the Internet.

In the evenings, after everyone left, she stayed to answer e-mails from stringers, edit articles, check on the bloggers, and make sure deadlines were being met.

She tried to show Mark their online assignment board so he could take some of the load, but he remained in *campaign* mode, schmoozing with Gigi and the staff, distracted, taking calls from his old job as well as his wife, his Realtor, and some dude designing a custom surfboard.

Yeah, Gigi, Mark's just perfect for this job.

With a sigh, Corina slumped in her chair and stared at the Indian Harbor Beach lights reflecting in the river.

Tonight Gigi was throwing a "Welcome Mark" party for the

entire staff at River Rock. On a Thursday too. Half the staff would call in tomorrow, claiming to be "working from home." She should go, be a part of the team, but she couldn't motivate herself to move away from her desk.

Adjusting her lamp, Corina pushed back a bit of the bull pen's darkness and stared at her computer screen. Nine o'clock. Really, she should head home. Pull on her comfy clothes and watch a *Mary Tyler Moore* DVD.

Or if she could stay awake, she'd sit in the peace of her condo and wait on God. If there was a silver lining to the last five and a half years, it was the discovery of truth. Despite her pain and grief, she found comfort in a God of love and peace, who was everything he claimed to be.

But the off-site staff needed attention, awaiting assignments and answers. They didn't know or care about Mark tying one on at his welcome party.

Truth? She struggled with the idea of Mark being her boss. The guy who partied his way through his first stint at good ole *Beaumont Post.*

"Darling, are you still here?"

Corina glanced through the low light to see Gigi making her way down the aisle, her svelte figure wrapped in a pale blue designer dress. What was she doing here? Corina thought she'd left with the last of the bull pen.

"Aren't you going to Mark's party?"

"I've spent enough time with Mark this week." Corina closed e-mail and turned off her computer as Gigi perched on the side of her desk, laughing softly. She'd made up her mind. Time to go home.

"Come now, be a team player."

"I'm the epitome of a team player. Save this speech for Mark. It's not too late to change your mind," Corina said. "He's only been here a week. You can send him packing."

"I see. Is this how you're going to play it? I thought more of you, darling." Gigi took a tube of lipstick and a mirror from her orange Hermes Birkin and traced her lips with a dark red. Then she clicked off Corina's desk lamp. "Work is done for the day. Let's join the others, shall we?"

"Give them my love." Corina took her handbag, a Prada she'd had for years and still loved, and walked with Gigi toward the door. "I'm heading home. My sweet condo is calling me."

She'd never really lived on her own. Not even from the womb, which she shared with Carlos. After high school she went to college and roomed with her best friend, Daisy, all four years. She did a year in Melbourne with Gigi right after college. Lived with her friend Tammy. And Daisy came down at least once a month for girls' weekends.

Then Carlos joined the Marines and was selected for a joint international task force in Brighton. She tagged along to be with him, did freelance work for Gigi, and studied creative writing at Knoxton University.

And that's how she met him. Her prince on campus.

Corina sighed.

"What's this?" Gigi, always paying attention. Always watching. Listening. "Such a sigh."

"Nothing." But it was something. Recalling Stephen reminded Corina of the vast emptiness in her heart.

Gigi pushed the elevator button. "Never you fear, we're going to find you a hot, hot story. You know, I don't have a solid stringer in London. Nor Cathedral City, come to think of it. They all left me to have babies. The nerve of some women."

"Yeah, what's up with that? Women wanting to have babies, raise a family?" The elevator door pinged open and Corina stepped in to the melody of Gigi's chortling.

"What am I going to do with you, Corina Del Rey?"

"Love me, I guess." She laughed and pressed her hand on

Gigi's arm. "I'm not sure I ever said it, but thank you. Your call with a job offer saved me."

Gigi squeezed her hand as the doors slid closed, and they rode in silence down to the glass-and-tile lobby with the high, exposed, steel beam arches.

They waved good night to the night security guard, Jones Parker. "Night, Ms. Beaumont. You too, Miss Del Rey. Take care out there. They say a tropical storm is heading our way."

"And only the tenth of June," Gigi said. "Well, it's the price we pay for our Florida sunshine and glorious winters."

"Yes, ma'am. They say she's bringing lots of wind and rain. Calling this one Anna. She's coming ashore on the weekend."

Corina stepped outside, into the warm, dewy evening, into the stiff breeze channeling down U.S. 1 from the Indian River.

"Let's be ready, Corina. We might want to close the office early tomorrow."

Corina started across the parking lot toward her classic '67 black GTO sitting under the amber-glowing lamp. "Be sure to tell your editorial director."

Gigi laughed. "You're keeping me honest." Then she reached for Corina. "You know I want all the best for you. Your mother and I go way back, but I—"

"It's okay, Gigi. I know, I know."

"Good." Gigi started off around the building for her car. "Then stop busting my chops."

"Never. You'll be telling me, 'You were right,' within six months." If not before.

"Whatever, darling, whatever."

At her car, Corina unlocked the door, tossed her bag across the red leather bench seat, and faced the wind. She loved storms. Natural ones, not emotional. She'd had enough of those for a lifetime.

A tropical storm would be new for her. Besides the security

features of her penthouse, the builder guaranteed the construction could withstand a Category 4 hurricane.

Tipping back her head, Corina scanned the sky. So clear and beautiful, fresh and breezy, with no hint of a tropical storm among the glittering stars.

"Corina?"

She turned at the familiar voice, her heartbeat cresting. *Stephen?*

Sure enough, standing between the glow of the parking lot lights and the shadows of royal palms was Stephen Stratton, Prince of Brighton, hands in his jeans pockets, his dark hair twisting above his crystalline eyes with every gust of wind.

"Oh my gosh . . ." She caught her trembling breath as she collapsed against the car. "What are you doing here?"

"I tried your flat but your doorman said you'd not returned for the evening. So I came here." He stepped closer. "How are you?"

"How am I? You flew four thousand miles to ask me how I am?"

"You look well." The end of his comment dropped low, a husky resonance soaking his voice. "Beautiful as ever."

"Five and a half years." She gripped her hands into fists. "Not a peep out of you. No call, no letter, not even a text or an e-mail." She caught a shift in the shadows, a broad, burly figure, inching his way toward them. "You have a protection officer?"

"Thomas." Stephen motioned over his shoulder toward the man.

"What are you doing here?" She crossed her arms and squared off with the man she used to love. Wholeheartedly. Without reservation. With a passion she never knew she possessed.

"I'm here on a private, sensitive matter."

"You flew four thousand miles to talk to me about a sensitive matter? What happened to Brighton's telephone service? Is the palace still denying you e-mail? The ability to text?"

"Brighton Telephone is in fine order. And all of Brighton

royalty is current with the world's technological standards. But the matter for which I stand here now was not one for a long distance call or a by-the-by e-mail." Stephen glanced around and hobbled closer, his left foot bound up in a walking boot. "Is it possible to sit in your flat with a cup of tea?"

Corina motioned to the palms. "I think the parking lot can handle whatever you have to say. As I recall, the last time we talked it was outside the rugby stadium with you wearing a sweaty kit."

He sighed, leaning to check his fingers in the light, and her bravado faded. Her knees weakened, and her heart smacked her head with a one-two, demanding a more cordial response.

He's here.

In my parking lot.

For five and a half years she'd waited for him to call. Now here he stood, three feet from her. He was as handsome and confident as ever, and try as she might to boil up some righteous anger, she felt like putty in his presence. And all she wanted to do was throw her arms about him. Kiss him. Adore him with everything she'd stored up in her heart.

But he'd tossed her off. He was not worthy of her.

"Yes, I'm sure the parking lot and the surrounding trees and brush will be tender with our conversation, but I'm asking for mercy. We just arrived this evening and are a bit jet-lagged. If not for me, consider Thomas." He motioned to his booted foot. "And my poor ankle could use a prop."

Corina regarded him for a moment, drawing on the courageous Del Rey blood that flowed through her veins. "This is unbelievable. I don't hear boo from you in years, but you have the gall to make demands. Once a prince, always a prince."

"Once an American heiress, always an American heiress. I appeal to your mercy and charm, and your good southern graces."

She wanted to laugh at his attempt to placate her. But he'd

always been quick with his replies, cheeky and clever. Except when he was dark, sullen, and battle weary.

"How did you find me?"

"It wasn't hard. You're not exactly hiding."

"Miss Del Rey?" Jones stepped into the night, calling from the lobby. "Is everything all right?"

"Yes, Jones, thank you."

"Are you sure?"

Corina surveyed the contours of Stephen's face, highlighted by the glow of the streetlights. His chest and arms were thick and broad, more developed and taut than when she said yes to his proposal. She turned her attention to answer Jones.

"Yes, I'm sure."

What she wouldn't give to have Jones call the police. But what good would that do? Stephen had diplomatic immunity. And there was no law against talking to a friend, er, an ex-wife, in the parking lot.

Stephen glanced toward the Beaumont Media building as Jones stepped inside, then faced Corina for a long, quiet moment.

"So?" she said. "Why are you here?"

"I guess there's no use bandying about." He drew a long inhale, striking a buzz through her nerves. What bothered him so much? "Corina," he said. "We are still married."

Her arms fell limp at her side, her courage draining. "W– we're what?"

"We're married. The Grand Duchy of Hessenberg has a new archbishop, and he discovered our marriage certificate hidden away in his office when he was preparing for remodeling. I suppose Archbishop Caldwell stuck it there for safekeeping. In turn, the new archbishop sent the certificate to Nathaniel."

"You said the one we signed was never filed with the Court, therefore invalid. We could just walk away."

"I–I was mistaken. Apparently, since we were married in

the Church by an archbishop, and I'm a royal, the Court was not needed. Our vows are legal and binding."

Corina dropped against the car. *Married?* "I asked you, remember? How the marriage was legal for us to go on a honeymoon but not legal when you wanted the marriage to be over. You said, 'It just is.' You lied? So blatantly? To get your way? Why?"

"I didn't lie. I thought we could walk away, as if it never happened."

Never happened? His words twisted deeper today than they did five years ago. "But it did happen, Stephen."

The scents and images of his romantic proposal possessed her. The windy ride on the ferry. Rattling the archbishop awake. Their honeymoon, stowing away in her flat, hiding from the world, even Carlos, knowing their days together before his deployment were coming to an end.

Of sharing intimate love. Their first night together.

She needed to think. To drive. To open up the GTO down the dark lanes of U.S. 1. "I have to go." Corina slipped behind the wheel and fired up the engine, gunning the gas.

"I've brought annulment papers." Flat. Calm. As if nothing in this conversation stirred his emotions at all. Well, she'd long suspected he'd lost his heart somewhere in the Afghan desert.

"You have the papers?" She wrapped her hand around the steering wheel. "Why thank you. How convenient." She stepped out of the car, slamming the door behind her, leaving the engine in a soft rumble. "Stephen, what if I'd met someone else? Gotten married? Had children?"

"Why do you think I'm standing here now? To tell you the truth."

"And have me sign annulment papers?"

"I'm sorry," he said, soft, low with a hint of tenderness.

Corina glanced up at him, catching the whites of his eyes. "What are you not telling me?"

"I'm telling you we're still married and I have the annulment papers." He jerked his thumb toward Thomas and the dark car parked by the front of the building.

"Just like that?" Corina snapped her fingers in the dewy, warm air. "Hey, Corina, I've not seen you in forever, sign this paper."

He stepped away from the car. "I didn't want to tell you in the car park, but you didn't want to leave."

She felt sick and weak. "Stephen, this is not about the parking lot. This is about you showing up and ramming that annulment at me. When I'm still not sure why our marriage ended in the first place." Corina got behind the wheel and gunned the gas, shifting into reverse. But she could not hit the gas. With a fast glance up at him, grounding down the whisper of regret, she said, "You know where I live?"

"I do."

"Then I'll see you there." She fired out of the parking lot, powering down the convertible top, gunning down U.S 1 toward home, the GTO, her entire world, rumbling beneath her.

FOUR

His ankle was killing Stephen as he hobbled across the parking lot with Thomas to the front entrance of Harbor's Edge, a luxury condominium on the bank of a river.

The doorman greeted them with a dubious once-over. "Here to see Ms. Del Rey?"

"She's expecting us, yes."

The man stepped back with a nod. "Top floor. Penthouse on the right."

In the elevator, Stephen rode in silence, grappling with his thoughts, sorting his feelings. She awakened something in him he thought he no longer possessed.

"She's very beautiful," Thomas said, staring straight ahead.

"She is."

"Rather decisive too."

"Yes, rather."

"I like her."

Stephen faced his protection officer as the elevator slowed, delivering them on the top floor. "We're not here to like her." While Thomas was an employee of the Royal Guard, he'd also become Stephen's friend over the years. He'd been a near constant companion when Stephen traveled with Brighton Eagles for every international match.

"I'm merely saying—"

"Well, don't say it." Stephen patted the messenger bag slung over his shoulder. "I came here to ask her to sign the annulment papers. End of story."

"All business?"

"Yes, all business."

But he lied, making himself feel better by wrapping it with some thin ribbon of the truth. He did come for the annulment, but more lurked beneath the surface. The moment he spoke her name and she turned toward him, his feelings for her awakened and butterflied in his chest.

He liked her. Still. Very much. But his feelings did not change why he came. Nor the secret about Afghanistan he harbored.

He could not tell her the real truth as to why he ended their marriage. For the sake of national security, his personal safety and that of the family, and for the welfare of his country, the Crown, and the four-hundred-and-sixty-year-old House of Stratton, the details of that day in Torkham were sealed under "Top Secret."

The elevator eased to a stop and the doors opened. Stephen walked with Thomas through the corridor to Corina's door. He paused, inhaling deep, before knocking, then glanced at Thomas. "Listen, mate, can you give us a moment? An audience seems a bit inappropriate."

Thomas backed away with a single pat on Stephen's shoulder. "I'll be right out here." He pointed to a plush settee against the wall, holding up his phone. "I can catch up on e-mail."

"Thanks, mate." Another breath or two and Stephen knocked lightly. Then a third time with more vigor, listening for sounds from the other side.

When he first returned from Afghanistan with a heart

of stone, he'd convinced himself Corina had to go. One, he couldn't give his heart to her because if she knew the truth, she'd despise him.

Second, every time he saw her, he'd remember what he wanted to ardently forget.

Third, she could not be trusted with the truth. The Defense Ministry determined the incident to be one of national security. Corina and the Del Reys were a powerful family with access and influence.

With the truth in their hands, they could have exposed everything. And Stephen's plan to excise his demons on the rugby pitch would've come to ruin.

The door flew open, startling him. "Come in," she said with a sweep of her arm.

He hesitated, then stepped inside. "Thank you." Was it possible she still took his breath away? He wanted to push Pause and simply stare at her for a moment, refilling his cup with the light of her hazel eyes. He itched to weave his fingers through the long silky flow of her dark hair.

He'd first noticed her as she walked across Knoxton's campus, her long locks flowing behind her as if baiting the breeze to follow.

"Where's your protection officer?"

"In the hall, waiting." Stephen remained just inside the door. The sprawling loft was very much Corina. Elegant and classic with hardwood floors, cathedral ceilings, arched doorways, and ornate crown molding, yet lived in, cozy and homey. "Your place is lovely, Corina."

"Thank you. I like it." She switched on a kitchen light that spilled a golden glow down the walls. "Can I get you a bottle of water?"

"Water would be lovely." Stephen spied a pile of newspapers by the rocker-recliner and a familiar twist tightened in his chest.

Their honeymoon month had been the last time he had known real peace and true comfort.

"Here you go." Corina handed him the water and remained standing.

She wasn't going to invite him farther in, was she? He pointed to the newspapers. "I see you still enjoy the printed news."

"I do," she said without looking at him.

His memories congealed, forming a soft reminiscence in his heart, but there was no wisdom in strolling down memory lane. He had a task to do.

"So what do you need from me?" Her crisp, sharp voice sliced into his thoughts.

Their gazes locked for a moment, and Stephen's resolve wavered ever so slightly. Breaking from her visual hold, he moved inside and set his water on the kitchen table, retrieving the documents from his messenger bag. "Just need you to sign these." He spread the papers on the table.

She didn't move, just stared. "I was sorry to hear about your father's passing. I'd planned to send a card, but . . ." She picked at the paper label on her water bottle.

"Don't mention it. I–I understand." Stephen slid the papers toward her, sweat beading under his arms and down his back. He ignored the pressure mounting in his ankle. He could sit when he returned to his beachside condo. But for now . . . "We all miss him."

"I miss Carlos." Her unexpected honesty ignited an inferno in Stephen, charring his personal rules of engagement for this exchange. To be businesslike, frank, saying nothing intimate or personal. Just tend to the task.

Her hazel gaze swept across his face, inspiring sweat beads on top of sweat beads. He twisted the top from his water bottle and gulped a long, undignified swig. The cold did little to cool his hot sand soul.

"You'll see the papers are all here." He pushed the annulment documents nearer to the table's edge. She wanted a response, didn't she? But blimey, he could never bring himself to speak of her brother in her presence. "Read them over. See if you have questions."

He smiled as if to convince her this was going rather well. Wasn't it? But she didn't move toward him, the table, or the papers. He cleared his throat, shifted his weight, breathed through the twinge in his foot. "Have you lived here long?" Mundane, superficial, but he yielded to the temptation to chip away at some of her ice.

"Six months." Corina tipped her water bottle to her lips. "But you didn't fly four thousand miles to chitchat." Moving to the kitchen table, she snapped on a nearby lamp and glanced at the documents. Stephen waited. What was going on behind her amber and green eyes? She gave no real clues. A moment later, she glanced up. "If you want me to sign these, I'm going to need something from you."

He lowered his arms. Stiffened his back. How did he not anticipate a counterplay? He was a sportsman, running offense and defense. *You're losing your wits, chap. Pay attention.*

"So, state your request. But I make no guarantees." She couldn't want money. The Del Reys most likely had more wealth than the Strattons. In fact, he was sure of it. He'd not given her a ring, nor any other gifts of worth, so she'd not ask to keep anything. Did she want a princess title? He bristled at the idea. Nathaniel would heartily object.

"Find out what really happened to my brother."

"Pardon?" But he'd heard her. The room darkened, and in Stephen's ear he heard the mocking of his demons. His blood flowed like molten lava, burning him from the inside out. His ankle shot shards of pain through his leg. "You give me more credit than I'm due, Corina. I—I've no access to your brother's records. He was in a different unit, which deployed six weeks before mine. How am I to find out? I'm but a lowly prince." He could not control the tremor in his voice.

"A lowly prince?" Her expression matched her sharp tone. "You're the Prince of Brighton, or you're supposed to be. You have access to the Defense Ministry, to top clearance."

"You mistake me for my brother."

"Then ask your brother." She stepped away from the table, her eyes blazing. "My twin, Stephen. My best friend, my Carlos, went to war and never returned. The only answer we got from the Pentagon is that he was under the command of the Joint International Coalition out of Cathedral City, and if we wanted answers, we had to inquire with your Defense Ministry."

"Then inquire. Surely your father has connections."

"He meets with silence and steel doors. He can't get answers. We're told only that he died in a firefight. A hero, they say, but we've no medals. No accolades. No honor ceremony."

The drumming in his ears muted her words. *Corina ... What are you asking of me?* "Believe me, I'm limited in my executive privileges."

"Then find a way. Speak to Nathaniel. Hire a private investigator, a skilled thief who can break into the Defense Ministry, I don't care. Just find out what happened. Nothing has been the same since he died. I lost everything. My family. You." She bit her lower lip and fell silent.

Stephen wanted to pace, but his ankle revolted. He pulled out a chair and sat down hard, his thoughts churning, his heart raging. *Tell her. Just tell her.* But he could not. His confession lay so deep, not even the earthquake of her request could raise it to the surface.

After a moment, he peered up at her. "And if I can't find out what happened to him? Are you going to just leave the papers unsigned? Surely you want to move on with your life, marry again."

Her laugh pierced his soul, inspiring a mocking chortle from his demons. *You fool. You're not worthy.* "My life stopped the day Carlos died. My parents still grieve. They've had no closure. Our house, once alive with laughter, is weighted with sorrow. My father can't stay in the house for more than five minutes. My mother can't leave. They weep for Carlos as if we'd just covered his grave with fresh dirt. For the past five and a half years I've straddled my heart between the two of them, trying to be a bridge, to create some sort of happiness, trying to be the family we used to be. But they are not healing, Stephen. They want to know what happened to their beautiful boy, their star, the heir to the Del Rey name and dynasty."

Corina leaned toward him, placing her hands on the arms of the chair, boxing him in. "If it means I stay married to you in an effort to help my parents, then I'll pay the price. The question is, do *you* want to pay that price? No truth, no signature."

Oh, didn't she seem puffed up and pleased with herself. "You must be joking." He fired back, mounting his own resolve.

"Am I laughing?"

"Corina, our relationship has nothing to do with your brother's death. We can't remain in limbo—"

"Sure we can. In fact, we've been in limbo for five and a half years. We just didn't know it." She squinted at him with a curled lip, and his heart trembled. "Since the day I saw you after you returned from Afghanistan, bruised and cut up, silent and sullen, I knew something was up. Something you were not telling. And I can't figure what or why. But you know things and I think you can find out about my brother."

"I told you. After the explosion I realized I couldn't put the House of Stratton at risk. I would've had to give up my rights to the throne if our marriage had gone public. I was wrong to marry you in secret, breaking Brighton law and risking the Crown. Nothing more, nothing less."

"So you were madly in love with me during your entire deployment until . . . when? I hear nothing from you after Carlos was killed. I was worried sick, wondering if something had happened to you too. I called and called, flew back to Brighton. I was about to go to the King's Office when I found you in my flat that New Year's Day."

He knew all of this. Why did she feel compelled to recap it? "Corina, there's no need—"

"Oh, there's a need. I want to see if I have my facts straight." She paced around the kitchen and then into the living room before going on. "I fly over to Brighton, my heart in my hands, seeking the solace and comfort of my husband after losing my brother, hoping and praying you are all right, wanting to comfort you and be with you. But what greets me? A man of steel, and not of the Superman variety. Cold, hard eyes like polished blue stones. I go to kiss you and you push me away."

The details dug into his dry, fallow ground. He'd wanted to take her in his arms that day. Hold her, make love to her, feel alive again. But all he saw was blood and death. "Corina—" Stephen shoved to his feet, the past all too present.

"I asked what was wrong, what happened in Torkham. You said an explosion. I touched the cuts on your face, on your hands, your arms, but you pulled away, telling me without any warning that we were through. The whole marriage had been a mistake." She gripped his shoulders and shook him. Hard. "I was madly in love with you. I gave you my heart, my soul, my body. And you crushed me without reason."

Crushed. Nathaniel's word. He trembled at her confession, avoiding her eyes, drawing his rugby-trained shoulders back and breaking free of her. "I'm sorry." He swallowed his confession. "But it must be this way."

"Why?" She leaned to see his face, but he'd had enough.

"Because, Corina . . ." His voice boomed through the expansive loft, "I said so. Enough. Will you sign the annulment papers or not?" He braced himself with a hand on the table.

"You know my stipulation."

"I don't accept your stipulation."

"Too bad. You can't have everything your way, Stephen. I've had too much time to think about this. No news, no signature. Find out what happened to Carlos and you're a free man."

FIVE

er condo echoed with their argument long after Stephen left. Weak with ebbing adrenaline, Corina shut off all the lights except the ones glowing from her glass-front kitchen cabinets.

In her bedroom, she shoved open the balcony doors and stepped into the night, into the stiff breeze off the brackish river and the song of crickets. Long angles of light fell over the waters from the homes and businesses across the way on the barrier island. Draped in a strand of Christmas lights, a small sailboat drifted toward the high, arching causeway.

Stephen. He'd come to see her. But not to claim her as his own, to confess his love, but to reject her all over again. Corina leaned on the rail and dropped her head, vivid emotions churning through her, tears sailing down her cheeks.

Her marriage. Carlos. Her family life. So much loss. When she'd arrived home after Stephen's parking-lot confrontation, she was determined to sign the papers. After all, wasn't the move to Melbourne about starting over, carving out a life for herself?

How could she do it if she were chained to *him*? She prayed for courage as she waited for him to knock on her door. But when he walked in, the idea about Carlos sparked and she couldn't let it go.

Wiping her cheeks with the edge of her top, she had no regrets over her request. Her little speech to Stephen flowed straight from her heart, and it felt good to cleanse herself of her burden.

She didn't need Stephen's mercy. He needed hers. So what if her demand hitched her wagon to his for the next few weeks, months, or even years? Her family would finally have closure. Peace. The chance to be *the* Del Reys again. Always together, always laughing.

Corina eased down into the wooden Adirondack chair. In moments like these, she missed her brother's wise, albeit saucy counsel. She missed his robust confidence. His booming laugh.

But tonight she also missed what should have been with Stephen. Carlos had always been her best friend. She never imagined anyone could take Carlos's place. Until she met Stephen.

His bold, brash confidence won her over . . . Well, eventually. Corina smiled at the picture of Stephen sitting behind her in a postgraduate leadership class, leaning over her, whispering his questions in her ear. As if he sincerely needed her help. But he was a flirt. An unabashed, charming flirt.

When she relented to his persistent chase and agreed to a date, she lost a piece of herself to him. He became her soul mate, her true love. More than a best friend.

But life decided to have its way with her.

Corina pushed up from the Adirondack, leaving her thoughts on the balcony, and headed inside. Snatching her phone from her handbag, she dialed Daisy, her best friend since junior high, married with two gorgeous little girls.

But she hung up before the first ring. She didn't feel much like talking. And conversations with Daisy were peppered with dialogue to her daughters.

Tossing her phone onto the bed, Corina walked over to

her wardrobe in the corner of the bedroom, cutting through a mysterious, lingering scent of Stephen's cologne. Or was her imagination playing tricks on her? When he was deployed, she'd keep his pillow case unwashed so she could breathe him in as she drifted off to sleep.

But that was a long time ago. A story from the fairy tales. Corina faced the antique wardrobe that had once belonged to her great-great-grandmother Thurman on her mama's side, purchased in France in 1910.

Turning on the corner lamp, Corina opened the carved oak doors and shoved aside her sweaters, finding the iron ring on the back panel that let her into a secret compartment. Didn't she put something in here after her last trip to Brighton? When Stephen had rejected her?

In the muted light, she found the envelope. The one she'd stuffed in there when she came home from Brighton that fateful January over five years ago.

A month before she'd been so happy, anticipating a joyous, happy Christmas at home, her secret of being a married woman adding a bit of private fun to the season.

Presents had been shipped to Carlos in plenty of time. And Corina's private gifts had gone out to Stephen.

She was to Skype with him in the early hours of Christmas morning. Oh, how buoyant and warm she was with the treasure of their secret. A lovers' dream.

But the Skype call went unanswered. As well as the family's call to Carlos.

What seemed perhaps an innocuous, minor thing—after all, they'd missed calls before—became a heinous nightmare from which Corina thought she'd never wake up.

Reaching in, she took the envelope from the compartment and headed to the balcony, thinking she should throw the darn thing in the river. Never mind the water's edge was about a quarter mile away. The toss would be symbolic. A metaphor for removing the last bit of Stephen from her heart and head.

She drew back her hand, wondering how far she could fling the lightweight envelope. Just her luck, it would get caught in the wind and fall to Mrs. Davenport's balcony below.

Corina returned to her bed and dumped out the contents.

One greeting card. One newspaper clipping. One soda bottle cap. And one thin, silky red ribbon.

Corina picked up the card, tracing the image of a beautiful, demure 1900s bride wearing a gown with a high neck collar and a long, flowing veil. Her burnished ringlets curled about her porcelain cheek as she smiled at her dazzling, dark-haired groom with blue eyes.

And she slipped into the memory.

"He looks like me." Stephen said, plucking the card from the rack.

"Yes, but she doesn't look like me."

"Perfect, this card is for you. To remember me." He gathered her to himself and kissed her, passionate and loving, not caring one whit that the shop owner looked on. "I'll have my own memories of you." His wicked grin told her exactly what kind of memories he'd treasure, and she blushed.

"Stephen, shhh . . ."

"What? You're my wife. My memories will carry me through my tour. I love that they'll be mine, all mine. No one knows to ask, 'Ow's the missus?' When I get a goofy grin on my face, they'll just think I ate too much succotash."

"My, my, such high praise. I equate with your love of succotash." Corina popped his shoulder gently, laughing, blushing. "I'll have my own private memories too. But I'll take the card. It's so lovely. And a souvenir from our Hessenberg wedding night."

"Sorry we can't do more, love," Stephen said. "But when I'm back from my tour, we'll sort our marriage out with Dad and the Parliament. You'll select a ring from the royal jewels. Then we'll have a proper party. Fit for a prince and his princess."

"Stephen, I don't care. You know that, don't you? As long as I'm yours." She kissed him with ardent love. "Is it real? You're all mine?"

"Very real. You've captured my heart, love, and we've our whole lives to make memories." He blessed her temple with a brush of his lips. "But until then, you have this as a reminder." Stephen held up the card, walking toward the sales counter.

If the shop owner recognized him, he said not a word. Now Corina opened the card, tears pooling in her eyes as she read the simple verse.

To say I love you is more than mere words.
'Tis a truth in my heart.
I love you, my darling, and you've married me.
And we will never be apart.

Beneath the rhyme, they each signed the card. Their signatures represented their final pledge to one another.

Corina tossed the card across the bed. What a crock. It was all a lie. Stephen only loved when it was fun, easy, and convenient. When some mysterious obstacle arose? *Bam*, he was gone.

She reached for the ribbon and roped it around her ring finger. Since they didn't exchange wedding rings, Archbishop Caldwell offered Stephen the ribbon to tie around Corina's finger as he repeated his vows.

Stephen was so apologetic he'd not planned more thoroughly for his proposal. *"But I promise ... any jewel you want when I return."* He'd held her face in his hands and kissed her over and over.

Truth was Corina had her own family heirlooms to bring to their union. Her great-grandmother Del Rey's diamond engagement ring had once been on display at the Smithsonian. But how Corina loved the ribbon and the tender, sweet, romantic moment it represented. She held up her hand and listened ...

"I pledge to you my love and fidelity, my honor and trust, to cherish you until death parts us."

The heiress and the prince. They were meant to be. In love. Forever. They were going to make it, defeat the odds of wealth and power pulling a modern couple apart.

Both of their parents had a loving relationship. Well, hers did until Carlos died.

Corina tucked the ribbon back in the envelope. How could she have been so fooled by him?

The third memento rested inside the envelope. A large color photo of them at the Military Ball, the night of Stephen's proposal. One of Corina's friends had taken the shot with her iPhone and texted it to her. *"Save to show your grandchildren. The night you danced with a prince."* Oh, little did she know . . .

Corina had printed it out and framed it, setting it by their bed in her flat, treasuring all the image represented.

Now, out of its frame and folded into quarters, Corina smoothed the picture on her bed. The image, bent and creased, caught her in Stephen's arms, in their element, the emotions of their hearts all over their faces. Relaxed, laughing, in love.

She was surprised the press didn't catch on that night. But Stephen had a clever and keen way to stay out of the media's eye.

Lying back on her pillow, Corina held up the photo, allowing some of her sentiment to remind her how she felt that night.

Stephen was striking and swoon worthy in his dress uniform. She looked free and happy, wearing the heck out of the white, feathery Luciano Diamatia. Mama had moved heaven and earth to have the gown made for Corina's society debut when she turned eighteen, using every wily prowess in her vast arsenal to lure the world's most exclusive and reclusive designer out of hiding to sew her daughter a *little ole dress.*

But the designer failed to deliver the gown on time for her

debut. Mama was fit to be tied. Corina almost wore it in the Miss Georgia contest, but Mama feared it'd start a riot with the other girls.

But five years later, when Corina moved to Brighton to be with Carlos as he trained for the international peace task force, she packed the dress, obeying the still small voice telling her she might need it.

The rare, precious gown was one of Corina's most prized possessions. Because the first and only time she'd ever worn it, she wed her true love.

Corina lowered the photo and stared at the ceiling. Maybe they *had* just been caught up in the moment, swept away in the romance, the drama of being able to marry simply because they wanted.

She sat up. But no, when he proposed atop the Braithwaite Tower, Corina had absolutely no reservations or doubts.

"Yes, of course I'll marry you. Yes!"

In that moment, they were the only two in the world. No media. No rules. No traditions. No two-hundred-year-old laws. No expectations. No aristocratic loyalties on either side of the ocean. No pressure. No deployment. No war. No obligations.

They were free to follow their hearts. And so they did.

She glanced at the photo, staring for another moment. The face smiling at her from the photo paper was hers. But the emotion of *that* Corina was a lifetime away from *this* Corina.

And her prince? He was more handsome than ever, confident and full of swagger, his physique rugby-muscled and disciplined.

But that was on the outside. He still carried pain in his eyes. The same look she saw when she flew to Brighton that New Year's Eve.

"What happened in Torkham, Stephen?"

His crystal blues were dull, lacking life and merriment. Something ate at him deep down. But instead of telling her what it was, he ended their marriage.

Enough. Memory lane was fraught with peril. Returning the

picture to the envelope, Corina spied the ferry tickets lodged in the bottom. They'd barely made the last boat to Hessenberg, their feet landing on the deck just as the vessel was about to pull away from the dock.

Laughing, they tripped their way to an inner cabin.

"Are we doing this?"

"We're doing this."

"Are you sure, really sure? I can wait—"

His lips covered hers, stealing her breath and her confession. "Corina, I've loved you since the moment I saw you. Walking across campus."

She pressed her hand against his chest. "And I didn't give you the time of day."

What was she to do with her unrequited love? The man wanted an annulment.

Corina stuffed the envelope back into the secret compartment of the wardrobe and slammed the door shut. When and if she ever met a man to marry—should God be so kind to her—she'd find the courage to toss that envelope, with all of its treasures, into the river.

SIX

Gigi

Even when she was a girl running barefoot through the hills of her Blue Ridge, Georgia, home, Gigi Beaumont had a nose for news.

She'd collect all the best gossip by sneaking around the wizened mountain women—who had a knack for telling a yarn or two—as they talked in the Mast General or strolled the town square. Then she wrote their stories and mimeographed them on the machine she found in the church basement, producing her first newspaper at the mature age of ten.

When Mama read it, whoa doggies, she gave Gigi a walloping for the ages on account of what she printed about the mayor's wife. But when it turned out to be true—an affair with the sheriff—Mama became her chief distributor and fact finder.

Forty-six years later, she still crawled around behind the storytellers and gossips, hoping for the scoop. The scandalous story that would turn the world on its ear.

Mercy knows, Beaumont Media needed a break. A big one.

Hiring Mark Johnson was just one stealth move to reignite her newspaper's faltering brand.

Twenty years ago, she was a pioneer in the online news game.

Fifteen years ago, she was the lead dog in the ever-growing pack of Internet news outlets.

Ten years ago, the bigger, old print dogs jumped off the porch with the power and might of their long traditions and stocked bank accounts and edged past her.

Last year, her books ran with red ink.

She was failing. Losing. A place she'd never been in all her adult life. Things were so bad she'd almost, *almost*, prayed this morning as she showered, dreading the morning meeting with her CFO.

What she needed was a scoop. A big story. Get her back on top in the reality, gossip news business. That's where Corina was worth her heiress weight in gold.

So were Gigi's thoughts as she entered the Beaumont offices eight thirty Friday morning, a latte in one hand, a brown bag containing a scone in the other. The place was quiet. The party for Mark ran late last night. When Gigi left River Rock at eleven, most of the staff was still there.

She didn't mind a quiet Friday as long as everyone got their work done before Monday.

As she crossed the lobby, Jones, still on security, *psst* her over. Gigi had a good mind to keep going, but she yielded with a telling exhale. "Yes, Jones, good morning. What can I do for you?" Admittedly, he was a great source of information and gossip about the Melbourne staff. Gigi leaned over his security desk, listening with a keen ear. She was suspicious her director of IT was stealing from her. Seems she was signing for an awful lot of new laptops lately.

"I thought you'd like to know that a gentleman met Miss Del Rey in the parking lot last night after you left."

That's it? His *psst* news? "You don't say? What kind of *gentleman*?" Corina was a goody-two-shoes. How? Gigi would never know. The girl ran with the likes of Paris Hilton when they were teens and never once got busted for drinking, smoking, or sex taping.

Gigi raised her latte for a sip, already bored with this conversation, just as the edge of her nose twitched. *Well, well . . .*

"Can't say what kind of gentleman. He seemed like an all-right dude, though Miss Del Rey appeared a might tense. I called out to her, asking if everything was all right. She assured me it was, but Ms. Beaumont, I think they was arguing about something."

Gigi gave Jones an approving smile. "Did you hear any of their conversation?" *So Corina, what are you hiding?*

"No, can't say as I did, but I'm thinking something serious was going on between them."

"Thank you, Jones. You're a good man. Remind me to give you a raise."

"Yes, ma'am. Anytime."

He nodded in a way that told Gigi he was more delighted that he *knew* how to fit into her scheme than over the idea of a raise.

As she turned to walk away, Jones offered an oh-by-the-way. "Did I mention there was another man too? Big and burley, reminded me of my brother-in-law in the Special Forces. He waited for the man by their car. Being in the security business, I knows a bodyguard when I see one."

"A bodyguard? Are you sure?"

"Would wager that raise you promised."

"Hmm . . . See what else you can find out, Jones."

He flashed his large, white grin. "You can count on me."

At the elevator, Gigi pressed the Up button. How-do, but if the plot didn't thicken. She'd not planned on working a mental puzzle this early in the morning, but Jones's news fascinated her.

"Then the roses came."

Gigi spun toward Jones. "Roses?"

"Up on her desk. A man delivered them at eight this morning. Can you believe that? Eight a.m."

"Really, Jones?"

"My bet, someone fancies her a great deal."

"You'd probably win that bet." A man in love? Gigi rubbed the tip of her nose. Yep, love. She'd bet her fortune on it. "Thank you very much, Jones."

"Anytime, Ms. Beaumont."

"I'll have accounting put that raise through for you."

"Why, thank you very much. Very, very much."

This was how she expanded her empire, won folks over. By paying them what they were worth. Paying them for their knowledge, loyalty, and on occasion silence.

Gigi rode the elevator to the second floor, mulling over this development. Typically, she'd not give a second thought to one of the women talking to a man in the parking lot. But Corina Del Rey was no ordinary woman.

Gigi entered the bull pen, aiming for Corina's desk, where the most beautiful bouquet of red roses captured the sun falling through the skylight. Two dozen if there was one.

She snapped Melissa's arm as she slunk past. "Who sent these?"

"You tell me, *boss*. You're her lifelong friend."

"What do you know about Corina's love life?" Gigi's nose itched like a flea-bitten dog.

"Uh, that she doesn't have one?" Melissa leaned across the desk and sniffed the silky flowers. "I've never seen roses that shade of red."

"Get on her Facebook," Gigi commanded, leaving no room for disagreement. "See if she's posted anything about a date or an 'old friend' coming into town."

Melissa balked, trying to walk off. "I'm not going to spy on her, Gigi. Even for you."

"If she posted on Facebook, darling, how is it spying?" Really, she was going to have to break down and join the Facebook generation. She'd be done already if she just surfed the site herself, but this was her MO. Using, rather, *working* with people. Getting them on her team. Gigi motioned for Mel to sit at her computer. "Just take a quick look. Is she on Instagram? Twitter?"

"I don't know, but if you want to know, ask her when she comes in."

"She won't tell me the truth."

"Then leave her alone." Melissa dropped her bag on her desk and sat, waking up her sleeping Mac with a jiggle of the mouse. "And just so you know, she rarely posts on Facebook."

"Fine, then this exercise should leave you guilt-free. Come on, aren't you curious?"

"A little."

Gigi peered over Melissa's shoulder as she brought up Corina's Facebook profile.

She had a feeling, a gut instinct, that she was onto something. But what? How big?

Since the day Corina walked into the bull pen, Gigi sensed she hid a story in her heart. A secret. But in the last six months, Corina had been nothing more than a faithful, *boring*, steady writer and editor.

What good was it to hire one of the wealthiest young women in the world if she wasn't going to provide any fodder?

Ooh, maybe the man was the boyfriend, or perhaps husband, of one of Corina's friends? And the roses were a bribe. Gigi was cooking with gas now.

"Nothing," Melissa said, sitting back, slapping her palm on the top of her desk. "She's not posted since last week, and then it was just a repost of a Remembrance Day fund in Brighton Kingdom." Melissa clicked on the link and popped open to a *Liberty Press* article on a new War Memorial and the defense minister's plans for a grand Remembrance Day next spring.

"Thank you for trying, Mel. Remind me to give you a raise." Gigi started toward her office with her scone and latte, her Gucci bag swinging from her arm.

"Didn't Corina do some postgrad work at Knoxton University? In Brighton?" Melissa said, almost as a by-the-by. Gigi stopped and backed up.

"Indeed she did. When her twin brother, Carlos, was stationed there for military training. She did some freelance work for me back then. Reported on their art show, film festival, fashion week."

"She has a twin brother?" Melissa peered up at Gigi.

"He was killed in Afghanistan. Apparently in a shroud of mystery." His death had to be the source of the clouds in Corina's eyes. The root of her secret.

Was the man from last night connected to Carlos? Perhaps a gay lover? Oh, wouldn't that be a headline of all headlines? Gigi imagined all the black ink returning to her accounts.

"She never mentioned him to me." Melissa scrolled farther down the Facebook page. "Seems she has an affection for Cathedral City. She's posted a picture of King Nathaniel on his wedding day. But that was two years ago. Can you believe he married an American?"

"You're going somewhere with this? Where? What are you thinking?"

Mel clicked out of Corina's profile. "Nothing, Gigi. Just that maybe the flowers are from someone in Brighton. I mean, she did live there."

"But why would someone send her flowers? Are you thinking perhaps an old flame?" Gigi stepped back around to Corina's desk, set down her latte, and peeked into the roses. Sure enough. A card. Why didn't she think of that before? Carefully she slipped it from the bouquet. The envelope was white. Plain. With absolutely no intel whatsoever. Not even the name of the floral shop.

"You're giving this a lot of energy, Gigi. It's just roses."

"There's where you're wrong, sugar." Gigi snatched up her latte and started for her office. "Those roses are a statement. And I want to know what they are saying."

In her office, she closed her door, set her breakfast aside, her blood pulsing with the thrill of a news story, and fired up e-mail.

Deanna Robertson was her girl on the ground in Brighton. She worked at the *Informant*, but Gigi had launched the woman's career when she came begging to write for the *Post* right after college. Deanna was well connected too.

Then there was Madeline Stone. Goodness, how could she forget Maddie? She was the cohost of the popular *Madeline & Hyacinth Live!* show—Gigi caught an episode on YouTube now and then—but ten years ago, Maddie was a *Beaumont Post* intern.

If Deanna and Maddie came up empty, Gigi would widen her reach to London and New York, but for now these two carefully selected, well-paid informants would serve nicely. She sent a private e-mail to Deanna, then Madeline, with her clandestine subject line.

Subject: Love this recipe!

On the DL. Corina Del Rey, an international socialite, is also a *Beaumont Post* staffer. She attended Knoxton University, you may recall, and freelanced for me.

I would love some stories or tidbits about her. Where she lived, who she socialized with, how she got on in the aristocratic world of Cathedral City.

Any ideas, connections, thoughts? I believe there's a story here. Just can't get a thread to pull. Your help is greatly valued and will be well compensated.

Sincerely,
GB

SEVEN

riday morning, Stephen walked the beach, his phone pressed to his ear, waiting for his brother to come on.

He leaned into the stiff breeze and listened to the rumble of waves crashing down on the shore. The storm—Anna, was that it?—was making her way ashore.

He wanted to leave this afternoon, before the storm locked them in, and had Thomas on the telly with the pilot to lay a plan, but he must get Corina's signature before he left or he feared he'd never get it.

Corina. This jaunt to America was to be simple with a defined task. *"Please sign these annulment papers."* But whatever possessed him to believe such a thing would be simple? Without complications?

Careful of his ankle, freed from his walking boot, Stephen's footsteps sank into the cool wet sand, the wind pressing his Brighton Eagles T-shirt against his chest. *Blimey, Nathaniel, did they have to track you to the loo?*

"Stephen?" Finally!

"What took you so long?"

"On another call. So how're you getting on with Corina?"

Stephen ran his hand through his hair, facing the wind. "They're predicting a tropical storm here."

"Is that some kind of sign? You're experiencing a storm with Corina?"

"She won't sign."

"She what? Why not?"

"Said she wants me to find out what happened to her brother." Stephen sank a little deeper as the waves washed the soft sand from under his feet.

Nathaniel whistled. "What did you tell her?"

"I told her I don't know anything. She argued my brother is the king and I have access to the Defense Ministry, so I can find out."

"Stephen, the events of that day are sealed. You know what's at risk. Mum doesn't even know the details."

"Don't preach to me. I'm giving you an update. Besides the details being a matter of national security, and I dare say my future in rugby, I don't want to tell her. If she hates me now, she'll despise me with the whole truth." And rightfully so. He believed that with his whole being.

"Not to mention she's a member of the media. Didn't you say she works for *Beaumont*?"

"She'd not betray us, Nathaniel. She's not the sort."

"Perhaps, but we've seen trusted reporters and presenters breach trust before. Intentional or otherwise. Be very leery, Stephen. On your best guard. I don't want to see the palace gone up in smoke and lives lost."

"We don't know that will happen, Nathaniel."

"We never believed it would happen in Torkham, either. One whiff of the whole sordid thing and we'd have more copycats on our hands."

"So what do I do?" The question wasn't rhetorical. He needed his brother's advice and wisdom. "I'm not even hinting at how her brother died. But she won't sign the annulment without information."

Over the years, in the quiet hours, Stephen tried to imagine telling Corina the truth, but when he visualized her expression, heard the cry in her voice, saw the disdain in her eyes, he'd cringe, thanking the good Lord the event had been sealed.

It was the only thing he thanked God for these days. Otherwise, he had no understanding of how a good Lord could allow such trials and travesty, such as war, in the world.

"Convince her. You charmed her into marrying you, so you must have some kind of sway with her. Charm her into signing the papers.

"You didn't see her face, Nathaniel. Resolute. Determined. She's nothing to lose. She's already lost it all." The pulse of the salty breeze drove Stephen's confession to the center of his heart.

A lesser woman might have gone mad, crazy with grief. But not Corina. She carried on. For herself, for her parents. He might not be free to love her again, but he admired her.

"Then figure a way. Tell her the Defense Ministry won't allow you at the records."

"And for what reason? I was a commissioned officer in the RAC. I'm second in line to the throne. My brother is the king. Why would they not allow me to see the records, to put a grieving family at ease? She'll see right through it, I tell you. She's suspicious, Nathaniel. When a man like her father, Donald Del Rey, cannot get answers with his power and wealth, something is amiss. And I can't stay here forever, wearing her down. My diary is rather full this month."

"Then find a way round. Talk her into it."

"I'll do my best, but, Nathaniel, I must leave on schedule Sunday morning, if not before. Save this storm doesn't ground us. Besides a full diary, I have to keep up with my physiotherapy."

"Then get cracking."

Stephen hung up, shoving the phone into his shorts pocket and facing the churning ocean. The day promised to be warm and stormy. How fitting.

Heading back to their rented condo, Stephen saw Thomas watching and waiting on the balcony.

"What's going on with this storm?" Stephen said as he entered the cool condo foyer. "High winds, gobs of rain, power outages?"

Brighton, a North Sea island, experienced her share of shore-crashing storms, but Stephen had always lived away from the worst of the turmoil on a Cathedral City hilltop.

Thomas nodded. "Or worse. Some people came round while you were on the phone. We're to leave the beach and barrier island."

Stephen squinted up at him, the wind tugging at his shorts. "And go where?"

"You've business with Miss Del Rey. Why not there?"

"Blimey, mate, no. Holed up with her for a night might be the death of us all."

"Or you might get what you came for."

Stephen made a face, then stared toward the Atlantic, the waters churning. Of all the protection officers, he had to get one with keen insight and a clever barb.

The idea of spending an evening with Corina shook him to the core. He preferred distance. An ocean between them. And five plus years.

Stephen glanced at his ankle and the perfect up and down scar. A faint dialogue played across his mind.

"What do you want to do with your life, Prince Stephen?"

"Play for the Brighton Eagles." He'd confessed his heart's secret desire on their first date. When she didn't laugh at the idea that a prince wanted to play professional rugby, he knew she was special.

"Then you should go for it."

"With my royal title and expectations, I've my time in the RAC to complete." Voicing his doubts highlighted the shadows and greys of his life.

"Blah, blah, excuses. If you're scared to try, just say so. No one will blame you."

"Pardon me, but did you say 'blah, blah'? And I'm not scared. Please."

"Well, we know there's nothing wrong with your hearing."

He'd laughed, scooping her into his arms, swinging her round. And nearly kissed her. "Americans. You think you're so wise."

Her eyes narrowed into a golden, hazel-tipped spear. "Think? My dear Stephen, we know."

"Stephen." Thomas came onto the balcony. "I rang Miss Del Rey. She granted permission to stay at her flat."

"You what?" Was this a conspiracy? "No. Find other accommodations."

Thomas shook his head. "I'm head of security and I make the calls. Miss Del Rey's place is secure and private. Her flat is the easiest and safest."

Stephen sighed. Thomas maintained strict control when they traveled. Even with the team, if Thomas didn't feel safe, he'd move Stephen to another hotel. Since Torkham, the palace demanded certain security requirements. Stephen could never be "one of the lads." But he'd made concessions to do what he loved.

He narrowed his gaze at Thomas. "Are you sure she doesn't mind?"

"I didn't ask her if she minded. I asked her if there was room for us. How she feels about the situation is second to your security."

Stephen sighed and started for the stairs. "When do we meet up with her?"

"She's on her way home now, making a stop along the way. We'll meet her there in an hour."

Up the stairs and in the shower, a wave of panic slipped through him, soaking through to his heart as warm water ran down his neck and back.

How could he convince her? He could be a brute about the

annulment, make her hate him. But he wasn't sure he could bring himself to do that. Or if it would break her resolve to find out what happened to her brother.

Regret. He wore it like a winter scarf. If he could go back and change the events leading up to that night, he would. But he couldn't, and six men had died. For him.

Stephen hammered the shower tile with his fists. He didn't know. *He did not know!*

What did it matter what he told her? He'd just make up something. Because whether or not she signed the papers, he'd never be a free man.

And that was the reality he'd live with for the rest of his life.

At her condo building, Corina stepped out of the elevator to the sound of the familiar ping, Publix bags swinging from her fingertips and a vase of red roses cradled in the crook of her arm.

Gigi had just dismissed the staff to take care of their homes and families when Thomas rang, asking for shelter in his kind voice, catching her off guard.

"It's just that we don't know anyone else and we do need a secure location."

"Well, I–I don't know . . ."

"Please, Corina, you're our quickest and safest option."

Sigh. *"Only if he behaves."*

Thomas laughed. "You've my word."

But really, what was she to do? Tell Thomas no? *"Let the son of a gun get washed out to sea."* Or *"Weather it out at the Sea Joy Motel"*?

As she pushed her cart through a crowded Publix, she found the silver lining. Spending eighteen or so hours locked in her condo while a storm raged might just get the truth out of Stephen.

As she entered the building lobby, Corina nodded at Captain, the doorman, as Stephen and Thomas came in behind her.

"I hope we're not imposing."

She glanced around to see Stephen striding, so confidently, toward her.

Balancing the roses, she adjusted her grip on the plastic bags. "I said yes, didn't I?" She pushed the elevator button, her heart beating with a thousand emotions.

At her apartment, Corina invited the men in, pointing them toward the bedrooms down the short, dark hall, feeling sure she'd lose the grip on the flowers. "There are fresh towels in the bathroom linen closet." She exhaled when she set her packages on the kitchen island.

"Corina, the Crown thanks you," Thomas said, his bass voice resonating sincerity. "We'll reimburse you for any expenses—"

"Please, expenses." She dug a bag of peanut M&Ms from a Publix bag. "You mean the whopping five dollars I paid for these?"

"Those are my favorite," Stephen said with a casual, flip air that didn't sound at all like him. "I might as well give you five quid now."

She didn't laugh. Only because she wasn't sure what he was doing. Humor? Deflection? Embarrassment?

He glared back at her. "Just a joke, Core."

Core. He'd used the pet name on their second date. After a semester of enduring Stephen's flirting three times a week during a leadership course—had there been an inkwell on his desk, her hair would've been in it—they were at once friends. Companions. As if they'd grown up as the boy and girl next door. Everything was easy. Conversation. Laughter. Even the moments of silence.

"You can help yourself to anything. For *free.*" Because that had always been the Del Rey kitchen policy.

While Stephen and Thomas set up in the guest room, Corina

emptied the Publix bags, arranging the Oreos, M&Ms, grapes, cherries, and apples with caramel on the kitchen island. Then she shoved the water and Diet Coke into the refrigerator.

In her bedroom, she changed into shorts and a top. Only now did she realize how subliminal it had been for her to choose peanut M&Ms. Plain were her favorite. But peanut were Stephen's.

She'd hardly considered her action as she strolled through Publix.

During their honeymoon month, Stephen had eaten peanut M&Ms by the gallon. Or so it seemed.

"I might not get any more until I come home."

"Darling, I'll send you a bag every week."

"Promise?" His kiss tasted like chocolate.

"Promise."

She kept her promise. Stopping by the sweet shop every week for a large bag of peanut M&Ms, then heading straight to the post office. Her routine became so regular after a while that the post mistress had the shipping box addressed and ready to go before Corina arrived.

She returned to the kitchen–living room the same time as Stephen. A block of wind hammered the penthouse as Corina poured the M&Ms into a crystal dish.

"I remember how you sent me a box of peanut M&Ms every week."

"Yeah, so I did."

Stephen tossed a few of the candies in his mouth, seeming lost, uncomfortable. "Oh yes, Thomas is catching a quick wink."

"He can sleep through the wind hitting the condo?"

"He was Special Forces in Afghanistan. He can sleep through rockets, mortar rounds, explosions. I've seen him sleep at attention."

"Isn't he blessed."

Their eyes met, and Stephen's demeanor was humble and contrite. "Thank you for letting us come."

"Have you thought more of my request?" She set out a cutting board and rinsed the apples, his presence soaking into her reality.

She was *married*. At the moment. *To him*. Where did a girl go after marrying a prince? After saying "I do" to the love of her life?

A bang resounded from the balcony door. Corina leaned away from the sink to see the Adirondack smashed up against the glass. "Rats. I forgot to bring in the balcony furniture."

She dried her hands, but Stephen was already moving toward the doorway, opening the double doors, dragging in the chairs and the wobbly wooden planter with its dying ivy.

"Anything else need tidied?" he said with a glance around.

"That's it. Thank you, Stephen."

"It's the least I could do."

Their eyes met. It had never been like this between them—formal and awkward. Even when he was flirting and she was ignoring.

Back in the kitchen, she found a cutting knife and commenced slicing up apples, the task giving her a chance for stealth peeks at her prince. She wanted to kiss him. *Why do I still love you?*

With another fistful of M&Ms, Stephen wandered into the living room and peered out the window, standing in the storm's grey light. "To answer your question, I rang Nathaniel, Corina. There's nothing to tell. Your brother died in a firefight."

"In Torkham? He was stationed in Peshawar." She drove the knife through the sweet apple. "What was he doing in Torkham?"

"Troops get moved about all the time. There are any number of reasons for him to have been in Torkham. Short-term assignment."

"But you know exactly why he was in Torkham, don't you?" She was reaching. Poking. Trying to draw it out of him.

"What do you want?" Stephen crossed the room and leaned against the island counter. "For me to make up something? Construct some grand story that sounds believable? He was in

Torkham doing his job. Keeping the peace. The purpose of the Joint Coalition." He motioned to the roses. "Those are lovely."

Corina glared at him. "They're from you."

"Me?" He slapped his hand to his chest. "I didn't send them."

Now he was just being rude. "Then why is the card signed with your name?" Corina snatched the white envelope from amid the blooms and tossed it to him. But Stephen wasn't one to play games. When he sent her flowers before, he'd call almost hourly until she got them. Though she did find it strange for him to use the initials PS. Prince Stephen.

"Anything new? Interesting?"

"No, just working on a story."

"Ring if anything, you know, happens."

"Like what?"

"Like anything at all, love. Just ring."

He held up the card, making a show of reading the text. "I treasure our memories. Love, PS." With a scoff, he peered at her. "I treasure our memories? PS? Does that even sound like me? First of all, the initials would be SS. Second of all, I'd say something like, 'Be well, love.'"

Corina snapped the card from his hand. "Then who sent them?"

"I've no idea, I assure you. Perhaps your boyfriend."

He was flirting "I don't have a boyfriend."

"So you've not dated since you—"

"Got kicked to the curb by you?" Corina brought the knife hard through another apple. "Yes, a few times. I thought I was single."

"How'd you get on?"

"Well enough." *Not like you and me.* "He was an old friend from college. But he lives in New York. Every now and then he had business in Atlanta." Why was she telling him this? "He'd call and I'd meet him for dinner."

On those nights she'd shed her mourning clothes and pretend life was full of splendor and opportunity. Death and heartache were a million miles away. She'd always be grateful for those nights of reprieve.

"What happened?"

She sliced the quartered apples into pieces. "Why do you care?"

"Making conversation." Stephen reached for an apple slice, then opened the caramel cup and dipped in his slice.

"He lives in New York and I live here."

Stephen slipped a quick blue gaze past her. "I know this business between us is not pleasant, Corina."

"Not pleasant?" She rammed the knife through another crisp apple. Not pleasant was a speck in her rearview. "Not pleasant is a toothache, a paper cut, losing your iPhone. This between us is horrid. I wanted to hate you, you know. By the way, whoever sent the roses, shouldn't have. Gigi Beaumont hovered over my desk like a hungry hawk all morning, wondering who sent them."

"Tell her they're from your ole chap."

"I'm not going to lie to her. And I'm not going to give her one tiny wink into my life. Who do you think sent them?"

"I've no idea. But believe me, I'll inquire when I return home. It could've only been one of a very few people."

"When do you leave?"

"Sunday."

His answer hung between them.

"My condition still stands," she said.

"As does my answer. I don't understand why you can't see reason—"

"Reason? Nothing in the past five and a half years has made a lick of sense. Not you leaving me, not my parents falling apart. In some ways, Carlos's death is the only thing that does make sense. He went to war and men die in war. But how he died? That doesn't make sense. Why the secrecy? And this dealie between

71

you and me? It's my only bargaining chip. The only way to understand why I found myself so very alone."

He swallowed and turned away, saying nothing.

"Someday I want to drive home to Marietta and say, 'Mama, Daddy, your son didn't die in vain.'" Corina stared at the bowl of apples, her eyes welling up, the moaning wind driving the storm's first raindrops against the windows.

They'd never eat all of these slices. She tugged open a drawer and took out a baggie.

Stephen pointed to his foot. "I should elevate my ankle."

"Do you need ice?"

"No, thanks. Just elevation."

She pointed to one of the recliners. "Help yourself."

"Corina," he said slowly, hesitating, debating his thoughts. "Your brother died a hero."

She peered at Stephen for a long moment, choosing her words, ready to demand more details, insisting he knew more than he claimed. She felt in her gut that he did. But instead of demanding more, a confession rose from her heart. "Do you know what I think about?"

He shook his head, still standing between the kitchen and living room, his dark hair flying all over, his eyes set, his jaw taut.

"Did I love him well?"

"Love him well?" Stephen said. "What do you mean? I never knew two more devoted, adoring siblings. I'd say you loved him well."

The conversation stirred Corina's hidden, deeper emotions. "But did I really?"

The notion of loving well first came to Corina as she wept on the floor of an old chapel outside Marietta, right after Carlos's funeral, right after she'd called Stephen for the umpteenth time with no answer and her shattered heart feared she'd lost him too.

Lord, how can I live without them?

"There was a night, right before he shipped out," she began, intentional, weighing her words, barely opening the door of her heart to the prince. "Carlos came by my apartment. You were at the base, doing something. We weren't married yet, of course, but in love." She cleared her throat, breathed back the tears. "I was dying to tell him about us, that we'd gotten serious. Carlos and I never kept secrets from each other. Plus, you two were friends, so I thought, why not bring him in on it? You were my first real love.

"But it seemed he had something on his mind, so I made some tea, put out biscuits, and waited for him to get to his point. Oh, that boy could take forever to get it out, you know? So I started doing laundry, cleaning up dishes, answering a text from another freelance reporter . . .

"Then you rang saying you were beat and going to your flat to crash. I sat on the kitchen floor, curled up in the kitchen corner, smiling, listening to you tell me you loved . . ." She stopped. Repeating that long ago conversation was futile. "When we hung up, Carlos asked how things were going. He liked you, you know, ever since you trained together for the Joint Coalition."

"Did you tell him?"

"No, because I could tell he had something on his mind. You had to let Carlos be to get the good stuff out of him. So we watched TV for a while, then he left. He never told me why he came by, if something bothered him or not. He shipped out two days later."

"How is that not loving him well, Corina? He was a big boy. He could've told you what was on his mind if he wanted."

"Don't you see? I was so caught up in my life and loving you, I think he felt like something had come between us. And he wasn't sure how to ask. I should've just told him." Her watered-down words broke her voice. "I felt like I ignored him after you and I started dating. I think he felt the same way. I was so intense with you, I let my relationship with Carlos suffer. Things were weird, different between us, the last part of May before he left."

She snatched a napkin from the basket on top of the refrigerator and blew her nose, wiped her eyes. "I remember one night he called, wondered what I was doing, asked if I wanted to grab a sandwich at the pub. I said no because I was going out with you. But did I invite Carlos along? No, because I wanted to be alone with you. I–I think he missed me, Stephen. I followed him to Brighton to be there with him. But I was all about me and my feelings." She fell against the counter, sobs gathering in her chest. "I didn't see my brother might have been scared, even homesick already, not knowing what he might encounter in an Afghan desert."

Face to her hands, she could not control her tears. It'd been several years since she let her heart wander this dark road.

Stephen's hand lightly grazed her shoulder, then he slipped his arm around her back and pressed her head against his chest. He smelled clean, of fabric softener, of spice and wildwood.

"There, there, love. Carlos knew you loved him. Of that I'm quite certain."

She pushed away from him. "No, don't." Frustrated to be so vulnerable before him, she gathered herself, inhaling all of her emotions, so deeply her lungs ached.

"Yes, he knew I loved him. We had a bond, you know? You were his friend, but did you know him as the consummate listener? Because he was." Talking about Carlos actually felt good. Mama and Daddy didn't like trips down memory lane. "Yet it took hours for him to say what he had to say. In high school, his girlfriend, Kerri, broke up with him at the end of our junior year, but I didn't find out until the end of summer when we'd been at the Hawaii house for six weeks. That night in my flat, I should've drawn it out of him. I knew something was bothering him, but I never said, 'Silence!' to my world so I could listen to his. He left that night and I never saw him again."

"Corina, you're too hard on yourself. Naturally, when someone dies so young and unexpectedly, one becomes introspective."

"Now you know why I must know what happened to him. We have his footlocker, his pictures, and a few letters. The cute little stuffed bear he took with him. The one he had as a baby. And a book of prayers given to us at our baptism. But that's all. No truth. Don't you see? Can't this be your parting gift to me?"

His countenance darkened as he swallowed and turned away from her. "I wish I could give you what you want, but I can't. There's nothing to say, love."

A soft moan reverberated in her chest.

"He was a perfect soldier. A good mate."

"So why the shroud of secrecy?"

"You read too much into the lack of details, Corina."

"Carlos volunteered. He wanted to stand on the wall for freedom, for the weak." She hammered the island countertop with her fist. "That's why I want to know. I'm sorry if it holds you prisoner to me and our so-called wedding vows, but now you know how my family feels."

Then there was nothing left to say. She'd poured out her soul, and it was then she remembered a storm raged outside the penthouse.

"I–I'll do what I can. That's all I can promise."

"That's all I can ask."

Thomas appeared in the kitchen, digging into the candy and cookies, wondering if there was something on the telly, perhaps a movie, and if they could watch. His presence pierced the tension between Corina and Stephen. If he noticed anything amiss, he gave no indication.

The trio settled in the living room with the lights dim and found *Back to the Future* on AMC. Corina sank exhausted into her recliner, grabbing her University of Georgia pillow pet and curling up. The penthouse shook with another wind blast, but Corina found it oddly peaceful, preferring Tropical Storm Anna to the churning in her chest.

She glanced at Stephen before closing her eyes, responding to his reticent smile with her own, hating how he made her soft. How his very presence mined the intimate thoughts of her heart.

The next morning when she woke up, the storm had subsided and Stephen and Thomas were gone. Their beds were made up as if they'd never been there. Thomas left a note on his pillow.

Thank you for your service to the king and Brighton Kingdom!

On the kitchen counter, Stephen left a note along with the annulment papers.

Sign and send them when you're ready. Thanks for the shelter. Be well, love. SS.

EIGHT

Clouds and rain trailed Tropical Storm Anna and covered Melbourne and the beaches all weekend.

Corina distracted herself Saturday by cleaning and running errands through semi-flooded streets, regretting that she'd shared such a tender part of her heart with Stephen. He'd not earned the right, and now he'd carry another part of her away with him.

But as the day passed, she felt his absence and wondered how he and Thomas filled their day.

She also felt lighter. Her thoughts clearer. A melody bubbling in her heart. Maybe that's what she needed all along. An unburdening. A good therapy session. She'd been to grief counseling years ago, but it had taken time for all of her thoughts and feelings to manifest.

She slept fitfully Saturday night but woke Sunday with the need to worship. To fix her heart on Someone greater than herself. Tugging on a pair of jeans and a blouse, she made her way to the House of Freedom in Viera.

Church had been a staple in the Del Reys' home until Carlos's funeral. Afterward, Daddy resigned from the church board and Mama left all of her committees as well as the Georgia Women's Charity she'd founded.

The years of mourning wearied Corina, made her spiritually dull, and she found herself drifting a bit from Truth. She'd spend her Sundays sleeping in, reading the paper, watching movies. Escape of the carnal kind.

But coming out of the fog, she knew she must return to the One who held the answers. He had to be the true solution to her dark years. Because he was the only true light.

She'd visited Freedom a handful of times since she'd moved to Melbourne, so Sunday morning, as she slipped into the back row and the music started, she was instantly caught up in his presence.

She closed her eyes and raised her hands as high as any Baptist girl could do, weeping, and whispered, "Here I am, Lord."

The music changed and Corina moaned, pressing her hand to her heart, feeling as if another door had cracked open. Tears streamed down her cheeks, and she didn't care who saw her.

Her adrenaline surged when she thought she heard cathedral bells. Opening her eyes, she scanned the musicians on the stage for bells or chimes. But there were only guitars and drums today.

With a dry swallow, she repeated her prayer. "Here I am, Lord."

That's when she heard his voice, an echo of the divine guidance she'd heard that night in the Marietta chapel five and a half years ago. The simple phrase vibrated through her.

Love well.

But what did that mean?

Corina pondered it all afternoon Sunday and spent a good portion of the evening reading the gospel of John, seeking, asking, believing.

Now it was Monday morning, raining, and Corina drove to work grumpy and tired after another restless night of sleep. She woke up far too many times thinking of Stephen, then muttering prayers until she slipped back into slumber, only to jolt awake again.

She had a meeting first thing with Mark this morning and wanted to be on her A game.

The GTO's engine rumbled low as Corina pulled into the *Post* parking lot. Slinging her cross-body bag over her head, she grabbed her grande green tea and made her way to the building, dodging the rain, and wishing for sunshine.

And missing Stephen.

No, I can't love him. It was just the residue of the weekend. In a few days it would pass. But the last four days had packed an emotional wallop. Last Thursday morning she had walked into work as a single woman jump-starting her life, and by the day's end, she was married. To a prince.

The idea sparked a zip of electricity through her. On the surface, how many women could say they knew a prince, let alone be married to one? Though that's not why she married him. She rather preferred he was an athlete and soldier to being a prince.

But really, what was the point to this line of thinking? No good, that's what. As of this morning, the annulment papers remained where Stephen had left them, and there they would stay until he coughed up some information.

"Your brother died a hero."

Stephen knew something or Del Rey blood didn't flow through her veins.

Climbing the stairs, Corina entered the quiet bull pen.

Dropping her purse in the bottom drawer of her desk, she sat and tried a sip of green tea. Too hot. Corina peeled off the lid, letting out the steam.

"Hey you," Melissa said, stopping at her desk. "I tried to call you Friday. See if you wanted to join our tropical storm party."

"Really?" Corina yanked her phone from her purse. "It doesn't show missed calls."

"I hated thinking of you home alone. Did you come through it okay?"

"Sort of, y–yes. What fun, huh? All that wind and rain." Melissa made a face. No, she didn't consider the storm all that fun. "I bought all the tropical storm food you suggested—M&Ms, cookies, fruit." Add one prince and his protection officer and she had herself a *par-tay*!

Corina smiled on the inside. It was a rather outlandish situation. Funny in a sad sort of way. *My husband the prince stopped by for a chat.*

"Okay . . ." Melissa moved to her desk. "Just as long as you had *fun.* Some of us are going to River Rock tonight, if you want to come."

"Sure, why not." Corina tried her tea again. Still too hot. So she powered up her Mac and launched e-mail, then the Internet, making her way through her morning list of newspapers. She had a few minutes before her nine o'clock meeting with Mark.

Suddenly Gigi perched on Corina's desk. "How are those roses doing?"

"Blooming." Corina blew over the surface of her tea.

"And you?" Gigi said. "Are you blooming? This business with Mark isn't getting you down?"

"Getting me down? No. This is just a blip in the road. Listen, Gigi, I have a meeting with speak-of-the-devil in nine minutes. Do you need something?"

"You, darling." Gigi floated a gold embossed invitation through the light and onto the desk in front of Corina. "Your first road assignment."

Corina read the script on the heavy card stock.

On behalf of His Majesty and the Royal House of Stratton
You Are Cordially Invited to the Gold Carpet Premier of
King Stephen I
14 June, 8:00 p.m.
RSVP to His Lord Chamberlain

"What is this?"

"An invitation. See right there. 'You are cordially invited . . .' I want you to cover the premier." Gigi was in full-fledged media-mogul form. "I've also spoken to the film's star, Clive Boston, and he's agreed to do an exclusive with us." She grinned with a wink. "He owes me one."

"Clive Boston owes you one?" The boisterous but reclusive star hadn't given an interview in ten years. "Do I want to know why? Or how?"

"No, trust me. Anyway, I want you to—"

"No, Gigi. No." Flat out. No. Corina handed Gigi the invitation. "We've got stringers in London who can go down to Cathedral City to do the job."

"Fine if I wanted a piece on tourism or the opening day of the summer season in Cathedral City, but this is a royal invitation to a movie premier. I'm not sending just any ole body in my stead. I'm sending you."

"You're sending me all the way to Cathedral City to cover a movie premier? That's a mighty expensive junket."

"Don't forget Clive. The fact we're getting an interview, my dear, is what separates the big dogs. Who gets the scoop, the inside story, is the one everyone will turn to for their news. Anyway, I had to sweeten the deal with Clive, so I tossed you into the bargaining. Told him you'd be doing the interview." She gave Corina a hard stare. "You need to leave by the end of the week."

"Gig, did it occur to you to ask me? Clive Boston? He's an arrogant blowhard." Corina had crossed paths with the iconic actor in years past—when she traveled with Daddy to L.A.—but they had nothing more than a "Hello, how are you?" relationship. Certainly not enough to lure the actor to the interview couch. "He's notorious for not showing up."

"He seemed really keen on seeing you. Said he'd always wanted to know you more. He'll be in Cathedral City for the premier next week, so you can do your interview there. Two birds, one stone." Gigi slapped a sticky note to the desktop. "Here's his information. He said texting works best. We need this scoop, Corina. The *Beaumont Post* is due for a scoop, a righteous exclusive." Gigi stood to leave, jerking the hem of her suit jacket. "Don't let me down, shug."

"Corina?" Mark stuck his head into the bull pen from his corner office. "You coming?"

"She's on her way, Mark," Gigi said.

"Just a sec, Mark. Gigi," Corina called after her with a *righteous* hiss, gathering her notes for her meeting with Mark, "I'm not saying yes to this."

Cathedral City? She couldn't go to Cathedral City. *He*, the man she was married to, lived there.

"Sure you are. This is perfect for us. An American heiress on the gold carpet … Everyone will be talking about it. Then we run an exclusive with a major recluse, a star the world wants to know more about, interviewed by *the* Corina Del Rey." Gigi shivered and sighed. "Brilliant. I'm ecstatic with myself."

"Gigi!" A few of the staff lifted their heads above their computer monitors as Corina's call rocketed through the bull pen, "Send a stringer." She dropped her tone. "It's a movie premier. An interview. Clive is a sucker for any gorgeous face. Send … I don't know … He's going to probably be a no-show anyway."

"He'll show. I'm sending you. Why would I send anyone else but you, darling? A stunning, wealthy, intelligent woman. A Del Rey, the South's answer to the Kennedys. I dare say you're as much an interest to the world as Clive."

"I'm nobody, Gigi." Corina glanced toward Mark, who waited for her with his arms crossed, leaning against the door frame. "Why are you doing this?"

Did the woman know something? Did she see Stephen this weekend? Or perhaps one of her spies? Corina suspected Jones from the night security desk was an informant of some kind, and he had seen her with Stephen in the parking lot last week. But Corina had been careful. She felt sure she'd not given Stephen away. Could the roses have tipped her off?

Surely if Gigi had any kind of a story on a royal like Prince Stephen, she would've run it on the front page of the Sunday *Post*, the newspaper's only online and print edition.

Corina assumed her weekend secret remained safe. Yet this sudden go-to-Cathedral-City rattled her. Raised her suspicions.

"It's a royal invitation and I'm sending my A team. Live a little, Corina. Take an adventure. Remember what kind of life you had before your brother died."

"That life is over, Gigi. All that remains is life *after* Carlos died."

"Well then, start carving out your destiny. Goodness girl, don't confine yourself to a life of insignificance."

"Excuse me? What did you say?"

"I said carve out your destiny."

"No, after . . ."

"Don't confine yourself to a life of insignificance. Make Carlos proud. Do something. This?" She flagged her hand toward the corners of the building. "A baby step for you. Now, don't keep Mark waiting."

But Corina couldn't move. Gigi's words, so off-the-cuff and flippant, nailed her to where she stood. Corina's heart cracked open a little bit further. She was uncomfortable with an internal trembling.

"Do I have a say in this, Gigi?" Mark called, finally engaging the conversation.

"Not really."

With a shrug, Mark turned into his office. Oh sure, he was exactly what the *Post* needed. A weak-bellied Gigi Beaumont pawn. He'd be no help in this fight.

"Darling, what are you thinking on so hard?" Gigi waved her hand in the air. "I can almost smell the smoke. It's a simple decision. Yes. Tell you what—you can stay at The Wellington. On me."

"The Wellington?" Cathedral City's luxury hotel. Corina's family had stayed there when they visited Brighton in the summers.

"Corina," Mark said from the far corner, exerting what little backbone he possessed, "any day now."

She made her way to his office, trying to figure out how she could get out of this outlandish assignment. Surely she'd run into someone from the royal family at the premier. Maybe Stephen himself. Then what?

Besides, how was going to a movie premier and conducting an interview with a long-in-the-tooth actor living a life of significance?

Just as she crossed into Mark's office, the peaceful voice from the chapel, from church yesterday, moved across her heart.

Love well.

The simple communication aroused all sorts of ponderings. She still didn't know exactly what it meant. Love well? Love who? Love how?

Shaking off the residue of the divine whisper, she set up at the conference table, preparing to show Mark, again, how the *Post* online assignment board worked. But he was on his phone now, so she paced over to his window, which faced the road and the community beside the *Post* building.

Across U.S. 1 was a Catholic church with a cross perched on the highest point of the pitched roof. The midmorning sun highlighted the icon, sending a long shadow of the cross over the four-lane road. The shadow also fell through Mark's window and across his floor.

When Corina glanced down, the cross also covered her. Shivering, she stepped back. How was that possible? The church was sixty, seventy yards away.

Backing toward the conference table, she felt light and swirly. She steadied herself with her hand on the table.

"Ready?" Mark said, hanging up, coming around to the head of the conference table. "Let's get to it." "I'm meeting my wife at ten to look at a house."

"R–ready." But she wasn't ready. For anything. She couldn't collect her thoughts into anything cohesive. They were buckshot with the events of the weekend. And the shadow of the cross that had just fallen over her.

At that moment, a grandfather clock in the corner chimed the hour, it's tone rich and resonate, coursing through Corina. She pressed her fingers to her temples, her heart palpitating with each bong.

For a wrinkle in time, she was atop the Braithwaite, in Stephen's arms, dancing to the glorious symphony of Cathedral City's nine o'clock bells.

"Stupid clock. Can't keep time." Mark shoved away from the table with an angry huff and opened the clock's glass door, stopping the pendulum on the third chime.

"Wait, it wasn't finished," Corina said.

"Who cares. The time is wrong. My wife insisted I bring this thing in here. Give the office some charm, she said."

Mark returned to the table, but Corina felt robbed, cheated, of the music that flowed from the clock's time.

"Cheap old thing . . . my grandfather made it when he was a kid. In shop or something. I think I'll tell maintenance they can have it." Mark scooted up to the table with a glance at Corina. "Listen, I know you love working with that albatross of an assignment board, but come on, it was designed for Windows 3.1.1. I want to develop a new online board. I have a friend who is a developer and—"

"Give it to maintenance? You are willing to discard your grand-father's clock because 'it's not working'?" Corina didn't mask her emotions. Mark's furrowed brow warned her she danced around crazy.

"It's a clock, Corina. I don't even think my grandfather liked it."

"But it's worth fighting for. You can't just d–dismiss it—"

"Corina, what are you talking about?"

Love well.

Then she knew. She couldn't just *dismiss* it. The door had been opened. Not just her heart, but his. A peace filled the cracks and holes of her soul. For the first time in over five years, she recognized a piece of herself. Until now she'd only been going through the motions.

"Mark, I'm going to do it. Cover the premier." She left the conference table, her thoughts forward. She'd need to book a flight and the hotel. Do some research. Beef up her knowledge of King Stephen I history. And what had Clive Boston been up to lately? She'd need a premier gown. But she had *just the one* at home in Marietta. At the door she turned back to Mark. "I think a new assignment board is a fantastic idea. The staff will love it."

She strode into Gigi's office with her head high, shoulders square. "I'll do it."

"Of course you will." The boss dragged her eyes away from her computer. "But what brings you in here to tell me?"

"The chimes of an old grandfather clock."

NINE

Four days after his return from Florida, Stephen woke up panting, a fire blazing over his skin.

Corina had paraded through his nightmare, a death scene, weeping and wailing, wearing a white wedding gown stained with her brother's blood, her golden-brown eyes wild with pain.

"Did I love him well?"

Stephen rolled out of bed and dropped to his knees, pressing his forehead into the thick carpet.

Rocking from side to side, he pleaded with his soul to end the night memories. He'd petition the Almighty, if he could muster enough faith to believe in the God who allowed bad things to happen.

He'd locked away every memory, his thoughts and feelings with the key of "Why?" If God "so loved the world," then why did he stomach atrocities such as war?

Above all, why did a good man like Carlos Del Rey have to die while Stephen lived?

Either way, answers or not, this *had* to end. And it wouldn't until he was back on the pitch with the rugby ball tucked under his arm, an intense defender the only thing chasing him.

After a moment, he gathered himself and showered. He had a full day ahead with no time to deal with black emotions and haunting, weeping brides.

But his soul was disturbed, tainted, and he felt helpless to do anything about it.

In the dining hall, Robert brought round Stephen's breakfast, then produced an iPad.

"The King's Office asked that I confirm your diary this week."

Stephen nodded, sipping his tea. He'd always kept his schedule in his head, never bothered with a proper diary. Much to the chagrin of the King's Office. Though to be fair, Stephen had, on occasion, missed an event. Which did not go well for him. Thus the need for Robert.

"You've Brighton Eagles Fan Day today at The Wellington Hotel. Thomas will be arriving at eleven to drive over with you."

"Dressed and ready." Stephen smiled, biting into his buttered muffin and picking at the sleeve of his rugby jersey. He'd watched the news while getting dressed earlier, and Channel One reported, " . . . over a thousand estimated to be lining Market Street. Many anxious to meet the team as well as a royal prince."

As much as Stephen looked forward to the event, being with his teammates, meeting the fans, a crowd of thousands would pose security issues. Though five and a half years had passed without incident, Stephen carried a reflex in his body, ready to pounce should another familiar face, a friend—

"Sir, did you hear me? Tomorrow, Friday . . ." Robert carried on, reading from his iPad. "You open the youth rugby tournament. Have you a speech ready?"

"Yes, yes, of course. Right here." Stephen tapped his heart. He didn't need a formal script to speak to Brighton's youth about rugby and the importance of sports.

"Two more items then you're free," Robert said, hiding his smile. He knew how tedious Stephen found all this *i* dotting and *t* crossing. "This coming Monday evening is the *King Stephen I* premier, where you are representing the royal family. Do you have everything you need? The palace will send the limo for you at seven. Thomas will go over the security details with you. There's an after party to which I RSVP'd affirmative, but you're not expected to make an appearance if you do not wish. I informed the hostess if you did attend, it would only be briefly."

"You're a good man, Robert."

"This rather late request came yesterday evening. The *Madeline & Hyacinth Live!* show asked if you could come on as a surprise guest tomorrow, after opening the rugby tournament. The King's Office left it to your discretion, though if you can see your way clear to be on the show, Albert believes it will be 'good PR.'" Robert set down his iPad. "However, it is Madeline and Hyacinth, so no telling what mischief they've planned."

Stephen washed down the last of his muffin with a heady gulp of tea. "Did they say why they want me on?" He leaned toward a yes, even after last week's #howtocatchaprince Twitter campaign. Given time and perspective, the whole bit was rather clever.

Only caveat? He didn't want to be caught in some sort of prank or "Here's the winner of our contest," to which he'd have to be princely and sweet to a woman he'd never met. On national television.

Still, Maddie and Hy were fun, creative, and the heart of Brighton Kingdom's pop culture.

"They say they want to talk about the film," Robert said. "The royal family, the history of the House of Stratton, and your rugby game."

Stephen hesitated. "All right, I'll do it. But I want a contract with a rider. I'll not discuss the war or my love life."

"Very well, sir."

Stephen selected another muffin and reached for the jam.

RACHEL HAUCK

"What's next? The art auction for the Children's Literacy Foundation Tuesday?"

"Very good. Yes. And you've not forgotten your weekly dinner with your family Sunday evening."

"Got it." Though he had forgotten dinner with the family before. Stephen glanced at his watch, shoving the big bite of muffin in his mouth.

Thomas would be here shortly, and he wanted to run through some exercises for his ankle. The bugger hurt more than usual this morning.

"Your brother rang while you were dressing," Robert said, closing the calendar on the screen. "He wanted to know how you were getting on with the task. Said you'd know to what he referenced."

"The task is in limbo." Stephen set aside his napkin and headed out of the kitchen toward the closet on the other side of the foyer. He wanted to take a couple of rugby caps he had made, like the ones professional players earned, to Fan Day for the kids. He'd find one or two he felt especially deserving.

"Is there anything else, sir?" Robert said, trailing behind him.

Stephen paused at the door. "I don't believe so."

"Nothing to follow up from your trip to America? Perhaps this task His Majesty mentioned?"

"Got it covered. Oh, set a late supper. I'm going to the stadium for a walk-through for the youth tournament opening."

"Very well."

Stephen made his way to his office. He had the better part of an hour to do his exercises, clean up his desk, and muse over how to get Corina to sign the annulment.

But Robert's questions about America nagged him. Did he know something? Someone? Did Corina call? He felt exposed and vulnerable. And he didn't like it.

He'd have to be careful. Keep an eye out.

A minute after 11:00 a.m., Stephen met Thomas in the garage.

The man greeted him, folding up his newspaper and shoving down the last of a chocolate biscuit.

Slipping behind the wheel, Thomas detailed the security measures set for the event. "We've a green room set up for you and the team. I've two men at every door, and the hotel security will monitor the entrance and the lobby."

From the passenger seat, Stephen listened. Then as Thomas backed out of the garage and merged into traffic, he said, "Do you think she told?"

"Who?" Thomas glanced sideways at him. "Corina?"

"Who else?" Stephen stared out his window, watching the hustle and bustle of Cathedral City whisk past.

"Who would she tell? Don't see how it could be to her advantage after all these years."

"Spite doesn't always need advantage, Thomas."

"Pardon me for saying so, but Corina doesn't strike me as the vindictive type. Not her way. What makes you ask?"

"No reason." Stephen sat back, stretching his leg, gently moving the kinks from his ankle. Blimey, the thing hurt today. "Robert was just asking if I needed help with anything from America. The way he said it piqued my curiosity."

Besides Robert's comment, remnants from his dream lingered, disturbing him in places he couldn't reach with his thoughts.

If he had his way . . .

. . . he'd reverse his days, go back three months to the game against England and *not* take the sidestep that tore his ankle. He'd go back five and a half years and *not* hesitate that day in Torkham.

He'd go back even further and *not* recommend Asif as interpreter. And *not* recommend Carlos to his commander as a new member of his crew.

He'd go back six years and *not* propose to Corina.

All to save himself from what he wrestled with today. Sigh.

This was *not* fruitful thinking. *Come on, get your head in the game. Be on for the fans.*

The car jerked and Thomas muttered, smashing the horn, ordering a slow-moving car to move out of his Royal Highness's way. "Prince of Brighton on board."

"Steady, mate," Stephen said, exhaling, letting go of his thoughts. Of his regrets.

In another few minutes, Thomas turned down Market, whistling low. "Look at this."

Thousands of fans lined the avenue, creating a giant, waving banner of blue and gold. Stephen's heart warmed. This was what he lived for—the fans. He was their winger, and he was going to do everything he could to get back on the pitch.

Thomas maneuvered toward The Wellington's circular drive, where bell caps swarmed, shoving the hordes out of the way.

"Stay put," Thomas said as he got out, pushing the Audi's door against the throng.

"I've faced Taliban bullets, Thomas. Surely I can manage a few maniac fans." Stephen stepped out, rising to his full height, waving. *This* was his princely element. The fans roared, calling Stephen's nickname, "Strat, Strat, Strat." The noise was deafening under the covered drive.

"Didn't they teach you to obey orders in the RAC?" Thomas shouldered alongside him. "This is a crowd. Have you forgotten the protocol?"

"It's Fan Day. Give them what they want, eh?"

Besides, he couldn't let fear sink in or he'd trust no one. He'd never leave the palace, always worried a rogue with a bomb lay in wait.

"But I'll be the one who answers to the palace if something happens." Thomas cut a path to The Wellington's glass-and-concrete lobby, the shouts under the covering now a heavy, indiscernible sound.

The bell captain and hotel security darted from the expansive, sliding doors, pushing the crowd aside. "Stand back. Be orderly. You'll get your chance to meet the team and the prince."

The prince? The team would give him the dickens if he expected royal protocol.

"Welcome, Your Highness." The hotel manager met Stephen just inside the door with a curt bow. "The green room is just this way."

Suffocated by security, Stephen cut across the marble floor toward an unmarked door, the rise of the steel-and-windowed lobby peeking over him in a dome ceiling.

From his right, a beautiful redhead made a sultry, green-eyed approach.

"Your Highness," she said as she curtsyed, "might I have your autograph?"

Stephen slowed, drawn in by her confidence and husky voice, but remembering he was not a free man. His heart sighed relief. He was pledged. For now anyway, and he liked the security.

Thomas blocked her next step. "Autographs are for the event only. Please wait in line."

Stephen smiled, shrugging. *Got to follow the rules.*

"Then I'll see you in the line." She captured the pout forming on her lower lip and instead, gave him a rather saucy wink.

In the green room, Stephen greeted his teammates, joining in their banter, preparing to meet their fans, relishing in their recent win over Ulster and harassing the event coordinator as he tried to gain their attention. They were worse than schoolboys, and Stephen loved them.

"Please, pay attention. My name is Langley and I'm your *host* for the day. Now, the signing goes until six, no later." Langley popped his hands together, looking as if he might say, "Children, children."

"Gentleman, please focus. *On* me. If you don't know what's going on, I'm not going to tell you when you come round begging."

"Listen up, lads," Stephen said, tipping his head toward the coordinator. The team settled down. As much as he wanted to be just one of the boys, Stephen was ever aware of his royal status. He must be both man and prince.

"Thank you, Your Highness." Langley was prim and neat, too skinny for any adult man, but Stephen liked him. He seemed efficient and passionate about his job. "The hotel lobby has stations with your names. The fans will make their way in single file, receive a souvenir, then pass by the stations for signatures. Do not speak with the media." He jabbed the air with his finger. "They will sneak in and try to trick you, but we've no time for their games."

"You do realize you're talking to rugby men, right, mate?" This from tight head prop Earl Bruce, who never knew a rule or regulation he couldn't break.

"I do, and you realize you're to be goodwill ambassadors for not only the sport of rugby but Brighton Kingdom. Do not forget your prince is among you."

The boys jeered, and Randall Cummings, an Eagle center, slapped Stephen on the back, sending him forward, causing him to stumble and catch his balance with his left, aching foot. A slice of pain gripped his ankle. "Careful Randall, or I'll never be on the pitch again."

Langley snapped his fingers. "Still talking, still talking . . . Do not pause for pictures, or selfies, as they say, lest we be here all day." The man gave them his best stern expression, but it only made the men snicker more and whisper barbs to one another. "There are more than five thousand people waiting to see you."

That shut them up. Stephen peered at his mates. Every jovial rugby face turned to stone. It was one thing to play before tens of thousands in the stadium. The boys were in their element. But it was quite another to greet so many face-to-face.

"It's time." Langley clapped his hands, trying to corral the men and usher them out of the green room. But they'd not listen.

Stephen pierced the din with a sharp whistle. "It's time. Let's go."

The Wellington lobby was crammed and jammed. Literally swimming with kids from ages one to ninety-two—young rugby players, families, fans, and beautiful, stylish women who batted their eyes at the team.

At Stephen.

Thomas walked beside him, just off his right shoulder. "Security is tight. We've a plainclothes team watching the crowd inside and out. A metal detector is working at the entrance. Bags are searched."

"Good," Stephen said. "I wouldn't be here if I thought anyone was at risk. But please, keep vigilant."

Heightened security and keeping war secrets was the only way Stephen could play professional rugby. His admittance to the team only came when the league agreed to a strict security protocol. Otherwise, traveling with the prince put the players and fans at risk.

He was grateful the last five and a half years had been without incident.

He found his name at the table. Blimey. His placard read Prince Stephen, not Stephen Stratton. Grabbing the Sharpie set out for signing, he scratched out Prince and wrote Winger.

And the crowd was let loose. For three hours he never looked up. Boys, girls, mums and dads, fans of all ages, shapes, and sizes offering congratulations for the spring 7 Nations Championship, wishing them well in the upcoming World Cup.

"When do you think you'll be back on the pitch, Your Highness? Brighton needs their Number 14." A tall man with broad shoulders offered Stephen a rugby ball for signature.

"Who's to say?" He signed with a flourish. "We're not answering questions right now."

"Come on, I'm just a fan. All I want to know—"

"You're a reporter. Rich Ackers from the *Sports Guardian*."

The man reddened. "I told them you'd remember me." He leaned over the table. From the corner of his eye, Stephen saw Thomas step up. "We're your biggest fans at the *Guardian*. We'd love a scoop, sir."

Stephen handed back his ball. "Have a nice day, Rick."

"A month? Six weeks? Will you make it to the Premiership?"

But Stephen had already moved his attention to an intense-looking girl of eight or so. "Are you here to watch your brother play in the tournament tomorrow?"

"Me brother?" She stuck out her chin with an air of offense. "Number 6, I am. A good one too."

"Are you now? A blindside flanker. My apologies." Stephen smiled his sincerest, taking the poster she offered. "What's your name?"

"Leslie, and I'm every bit as good as the boys."

"Probably better." Stephen signed the poster, then bent under the table for one of his caps. "Here you go. A special cap for a special girl."

"For me?" Her blue eyes sparked.

"Never hold back. Play hard." Stephen nodded at her dad. "You ever need anything from me, ring the King's Office."

He blanched and stuttered. "Y–you don't say? T–thank you, sir. You're very kind."

"We need more players like Leslie."

"She's a tough one, that she is, Your Highness."

Leslie gave Stephen a nod as if that was that and moved on, addressing Earl Bruce and his duties as a prop.

Langley bustled down the line, whispering to the team. "Quickly, move quickly. We've no time to linger."

Stephen greeted the next fan. A teen boy. Then the next. A young lad. After him was the redhead, who seemed to have little affinity for rugby.

"So we meet again, Your Highness." She giggled as she angled gracefully toward him, exposing the fleshly part of her womanly essence.

"So we do." He signed her poster of the team and was about to shake her hand when he caught sight of a woman moving across the crowded lobby.

"Excuse me." He stepped away from his station, ignoring the redhead's scowl, and ducked under the velvet rope, squinting through the crowd. Corina? He'd know that dark sheen of hair anywhere. What was she doing here?

"Your Highness, Your Highness," Poor Langley, calling after him, his thin voice barely slithering through the crowded lobby. "Your station, please. You must stay behind the rope. Pandemonium, pandemonium."

But Stephen continued to squeeze through the crowd with rugby prowess, his intention fixed. He'd stop for no one if Corina was in the lobby. Did she fly all the way over to bring the signed annulment papers?

"Stephen." Thomas's hand clapped onto his shoulder. "Where are you going?"

"She's here." Stephen shoved around a large man, catching up to Corina at the registration desk. But just as he reached for her shoulder, she turned.

Stephen stopped, hand frozen in midair. It was *not* Corina. His strength weakened as his adrenaline ebbed, his disappointment was palatable.

The woman gasped and offered Stephen an awkward curtsy. "Your Highness . . ."

"W–welcome to The Wellington." He gave her a weak smile then turned, excusing his way through the crowd toward the green room.

"You thought she was Corina?" Thomas said, walking beside him, whispering over Stephen's shoulder.

"Leave me be, Thomas." Stephen found the water bins and

jerked a bottle from the ice, taking a cold, cleansing swig, soaking his parched throat.

"You're still in love with her." Thomas, much to Stephen's discomfiture, did *not* leave him alone. He reached in the bin of ice for a Coke, peering at Stephen with a smirk.

"Don't tell me how I feel, Thomas." Stephen sat on the hard, pea-green couch, his ankle throbbing. He polished off his water and crushed the plastic bottle, tossing it into the rubbish against the wall. In love with her? No, ten times no.

"Let's get back out there." He didn't want to let down the fans. As he stood, Stephen caught his reflection in the mirror on the wall and he knew.

Thomas was right. He was still in love with his wife.

TEN

Thursday morning Corina stepped out of the cab and into the shade of her childhood Marietta home. A one hundred and fifty-year-old white, two-story antebellum with floor-to-ceiling windows and a wraparound veranda that was purchased by her great-, great-, great-grandfather right after the Civil War. In 1867.

Just six months in America from the ancient royal city of Castile, Spain, Grandpa Carlos Del Rey I quickly made his mark in the newly changed South.

Since then, one Del Rey or another had inherited and lived in Casa Hermosa. Home Beautiful. So it had been as Corina grew up—full of life and joy, laughter.

The lovely estate she used to call home, run to for safety, for comfort and love, for acceptance, for laughter, was now a morose mausoleum.

She glanced toward the third-floor captain's deck as the cab driver set her suitcases at her feet. She and Carlos used to climb out there on summer nights and wish upon the stars.

"That'll be forty-two fifty."

Corina glanced at the cab driver, emptying out the last of

her reminiscing, and reached in her bag for her wallet. Without Carlos, would Casa Hermosa ever be beautiful again?

She paid the driver as the sticky Georgia humidity rode the low breeze that brushed her shorts against her skin. Then she found herself alone under the magnolias and live oaks, the Spanish moss waving in greeting.

No one knew she was coming. Her first time back since she went to work for Gigi. For some stubborn reason, she'd not telephoned to let Mama know she was coming.

Probably because she had so much on her mind. The reappearance of Prince Stephen sank deeper into her soul day after day.

During her preparations for the trip to Brighton, and on the one-hour flight from Melbourne to Atlanta, Corina tried to sort out her thoughts and feelings, separating truth from vain hopes, dreams from reality.

She told herself going to Brighton was her job. Gigi insisted she cover the premier, interview Clive. But she wondered if "love well" encouraged her to win back her husband.

Yet Stephen came to Melbourne looking for an annulment. Not reconciliation. Why would she even consider any other possibility? Especially after his cruel rejection during the darkest days of her life. Crazy, right?

But they were still married. Five and a half years after believing they were over.

Honestly, she was practically a ball of weepy confusion. Worse, there was no one to talk to about this mess because no one knew.

Corina nearly broke down and called Daisy, ready to confess the whole secret thing. Though, in the end, she couldn't form the words. Her marriage, her relationship with Stephen felt private, personal, as if something for God's hearing only.

He knew the truth. She could talk to him. He was more than willing to listen.

If God was behind this Brighton excursion, and if she'd

correctly interpreted the grandfather clock chimes and the "love well" whisper, then she wanted to obey.

Or this all boiled down to the fact she was just a foolish girl, desperate to cling to something, anything, she'd once loved and lost.

"God," she whispered now, in the shadow of home, "I trust you, but help me out here, please. Am I even close? Can I win Stephen back? Is that what you want?"

Nevertheless, at this point she was all in, willing to sacrifice her heart, her will, and her pride. Shoot, she wasn't even above begging.

Love had a way of making a girl empty herself.

If Stephen refused her flat out, she'd sign the papers—with or without news on Carlos. The truth, while comforting, would not bring him back, and she felt desperate to deal with this open chapter of her life.

Corina's memories spoke as she made her way to the veranda. Summer evenings of chasing fireflies, the scent of Daddy's grill in the air. The hum of the ice-cream maker. The strum of Daddy's guitar and the beauty of Mama's sweet soprano. Sneaking out with Carlos for a midnight swim in the pool.

Stringing Christmas lights on the railing. Birthday parties and cutting cake. Saturday nights in the porch rocker, quietly talking, listening to the crickets and cicadas, making up lyrics for their music.

Laughing until her side hurt.

All of it ended when Carlos died. Corina understood that. She endured the same pain as her parents. What was her birthday without her twin, her best friend? What were holiday traditions with part of her heart missing?

Yet how could she survive without the laughter, love, and affection? Without new memories and new traditions. She tried for five years and nearly lost her soul.

However, she didn't fly up here just to remember what had

been. She came for *the* dress. The Luciana Diamatia. Perfect for a royal movie premier. For reminding Stephen of the love they shared.

She stooped to gather her luggage when a short horn blast caused her to glance around. Daisy Blackwell. She'd recognize that horn toot anywhere.

"Well, as I live and breathe, Corina Del Rey," Daisy said, pulling her Mercedes SUV alongside Corina.

"Daisy Blackwell, as I live and breathe." Corina forced a bit of cheer in her words as the lovely, tan, and fit Daisy slipped from behind the wheel. She was southern from the top of her blond head to the tips of her pedicured toes.

"Why didn't you tell a body you were coming?" Daisy wrapped Corina in a great hug, the fragrance of Chanel chasing around them.

"I'm only here for a few hours. I'm flying out tonight." Seeing her old friend tied another knot in her tangled emotions.

How many hours they'd spent up in her room giggling, dreaming, getting ready for cheer practice, football and basketball games, homecoming, prom, Saturday night dates, and their first pageant? Thousands of hours. Thousands of blessings.

"I swear to goodness it's been a coon's age since I've seen you. Girls"—Daisy leaned into the driver's side open window—"you remember your Aunt Corina, Mama's best friend in high school."

Corina peeked inside and waved at towheaded little girls buckled into car seats. "Hey, Anna." She was four and cuter than a speckled pup. "And hi, Betsy," Corina said. At two, the younger of Daisy's daughters was the image of her beauty. "They're gorgeous, Daisy."

"I know." She sighed, turning to Corina, arms folded. Dressed like every upperclass Georgia belle, in her pleated shorts and matching top, wearing bedazzled sandals, Daisy was everything she had dreamed of being. A country club wife with a lawyer husband. And a mom of two. "But they'll be the death of me. Travis says we just have to get them *to* college. Then they're on their own." Her chortle flirted with the breeze. "So, how's life with the great Gigi Beaumont?"

"Crazy as usual. She's sending me to Brighton on assignment."

"Well, lucky you. I love Brighton. Wish I could get Travis to go, but he hates long trips with the girls. And he won't go so far away without them. They're so young. If anything were to happen . . ." Daisy raised her blue eyes to Corina. "I'm sorry, I forget sometimes."

"I wish I could forget." More and more, Corina craved speaking the truth. She drank up honest conversation. Mama refused to talk about Carlos. And Daddy never seemed to be around. "You're allowed to talk about your life, Daisy. It makes sense you'd not want to leave the girls." If she had two beauties like Anna and Betsy, Corina wouldn't let them out of her sight.

"So, you've returned to the dark plantation." Daisy glanced toward the house. "Your Mama still hasn't been to a Daughters of Dixie meeting. And Daddy said your daddy has yet to hit the golf course or attend a church meeting." Daisy bit her lower lip. "I'm sorry, I know it's all so painful, but we miss your parents around here."

"You know it's why I had to leave. They can't get out of mourning." Corina scooped her hair off of her neck, releasing the Georgia heat trapped next to her skin. "I've come to grips that life will never be the same."

"But you're the Del Reys. The best family in town. Y'all will come around, I'm sure of it. Horatia will show up at a Dixies meeting one day with an agenda a mile long. Ole Donald will be on the golf course with my daddy and Reverend Pike, ready to talk a new church addition." Daisy squeezed Corina's arm as if she could infuse her with the same enthusiasm.

"You're a bigger dreamer than I am."

"No one will argue with you there." Daisy's laugh brought

Corina around the bend, closer to her journey home. "So tell me what's in Brighton? And why did you come home first?"

What's in Brighton? Perhaps true love. "I came for the Luciano Diamatia."

Daisy slapped her hand to her heart. "Be still. Oh, I *looove* that dress." Then she cocked an eyebrow at her friend. "What sort of event needs the Diamatia? I mean, really Corina, it has to be one of the world's rarest and, may I say, least-worn designer gowns."

"Not my fault he didn't finish it in time for my debut. I'm wearing it to a movie premier. *King Stephen I.*"

"Oh girl, you have all the luck." Daisy shoved her slender hand through her hair. "We saw the trailer last night and it looks fantastic. Braveheart meets King Arthur. And Clive Boston . . ." Daisy closed her eyes and exhaled. "A more gorgeous man never lived."

"I'm interviewing him." Well, supposedly, if he shows, but this was the most fun Corina had had in a while, so why spoil it?

"Get out." Daisy shoved Corina's shoulder. "You're interviewing Clive Boston? Remember when you met him a few years ago at that indie film fest? He was such a snob, but oh, who cares? I could just stare at him for hours."

Corina laughed, unhindered by the hiccup of grief. "He was downright rude until he found out Daddy was one of the film backers. Then he was all like, 'Miss Del Rey, can I call you Corina?'"

The friends laughed in harmony, like they used to, when they held the tiger of life by the tail. The breeze moseyed between them as the Georgia sun eavesdropped through the summer leaves.

Daisy sobered. "I miss you."

"I miss me too."

"I wish you'd tell me what else bothers you." Daisy drilled Corina with her gaze, one friend detecting another's sorrow. "I can't help it, I just see something else in your countenance. Is it because you left a twin? Does that make it worse?"

"Yes, twins . . ." There. Nice and safe. And true. But with no need to expose her journey with Prince Stephen.

"Corina, I cannot imagine . . ." Daisy gripped her hand. "You know I'm always here for you."

"And I love you for it."

Daisy had been patient since Carlos's death, giving Corina space, filling her days with her own life and family. But always, during the dark years of grieving, Daisy popped around the house a few times a year, trying to draw Corina out.

But Corina found it hard to shower Daisy's joy with her dark rain.

"I had a dream about you," Daisy began, slow, staring off, remembering. "You were . . ." She laughed. "You'll love this . . . A princess."

Corina made sure she laughed. Loud and quick. "Oh, that's rich."

"I mean, what made me have such a dream? But it was so real." Daisy's merriment faded as she turned a serious eye toward Corina. "You were so happy. Your eyes radiated this glow . . . of joy. You were married to Prince Stephen of Brighton."

Daisy's last words sucked the air out of Corina. She faltered backward, trying to breathe, chills racing down her arms despite the Georgia heat.

"Oh my!" She jammed her hands on her waist and tried to laugh, but the thin air in her lungs only produced a shallow exhale. "Th–that's something . . . a *nightmare* . . . that's what. Me, a princess? All those photographers chasing you about, blogs and newspapers picking on your clothes and hair. Duchess Kate is a saint if you ask me."

"No, Corina," Daisy said, more somber than before. "You'd be a perfect princess. You're practically one now. But what struck me was how happy you were. I woke up in tears, really."

From inside the SUV, one of the girls screamed while the other called, "Mama!"

Daisy angled down to see through the open window. "Betsy, sugar, I told you not to open your juice lid." Daisy smiled at Corina. "She spilled it all over herself, and she hates being wet. She'll cry all the way home."

"Go, you have better things to do than stand here with me."

"I don't know about better, but . . ." With a smile, Daisy pulled Corina into a hug. And for a fleeting second, Corina cradled her cheek on her friend's shoulder and left a piece of her burden there.

Daisy gave her signature horn toot as she crept down the drive. Corina waved, her bags at her feet, the reality of Daisy's dream the first kiss on her heart that God heard her prayers.

Did it mean she'd reconcile with Stephen? She had no idea, but for now she had an ounce more courage, and that was worth something.

Ida Mae, Mama's maid, with her tan, fleshy arms pumping, opened the door, a smile on her broad face. "Land sakes alive, get in here, girl." She snagged Corina in a bosomy, vanilla-cinnamon hug. "Why didn't you call ahead? I'd have made dumplings."

"I'm only here for a few hours." Corina peered into the aging woman's snappy brown eyes. "How about when I get back? Dumplings and apple pie."

The maid's eyes misted. "I've been missing you." She wiped her tears with the edge of her apron. "Tell me, how's Florida? It's just not the same since you've been gone." She paused for a silent beat. *And Carlos.*

"Florida is fine." Corina looped her arm around her old friend. "I'm here for my passport and the Diamatia. I'm flying out of Atlanta to Brighton tonight."

"T–the Diamatia, you say?" Ida Mae's eyes enlarged and she

angled away from Corina. "W–well, ain't that nice? I–I could've sent it down to you."

"Just found out I needed it on Monday and it's been crazy . . . You okay, Ida Mae?"

The woman nodded, inhaling deeply. "What you be needing the dress for?"

"I'm covering a movie premier in Cathedral City Monday night." *And winning back my husband.*

Ida Mae sighed, folding her hands over her heart. "I sure do miss our summers on Brighton's shores."

The maid had been a part of the Del Rey family since Daddy and Mama were newlyweds. Never married, she traveled with them to their homes in Hawaii, Colorado, and Vermont, and the every-other summers in Brighton. She was family. Mama's best friend, if her mother was honest.

More than the aristocratic society ladies with whom she luncheoned and ran charities. Because in Mama's darkest hour, Ida Mae had been her comfort. Her friends were nowhere to be found. Grief manhandled some folks.

"I miss Brighton too." Truth? She did. "And oh, Ida Mae, you'll like this. I'm working on an interview with Clive Boston."

Ida Mae paused in the kitchen doorway and feigned a swoon, pressing the back of her hand to her forehead. "Clive Boston is one of my favorites. I met him at that premier of your daddy's." Daddy's hobby of Hollywood films benefited them all. "What about him for a beau?" Ida Mae wiggled her eyebrows, taking a tall pitcher of golden brown tea from the refrigerator.

"Clive?" Corina curled her lip. "He's not my type." Dark-haired, rugby-playing princes were more her speed. "And he's like, forty-five."

"Oh I see, a Methuselah, is he? I'll take forty-five. Shoot, darling, I'll take fifty-five." Ida Mae snorted a laugh as she poured

Corina a glass of tea and filled bowls with chips and salsa. "Eat up. You're looking too skinny."

"I don't have you to cook for me." Corina dipped the chips in Ida Mae's homemade salsa and sighed. Simply heaven.

"Got cookies in the jar too." The maid set a blue-and-gold ceramic cookie jar on the counter.

Corina lifted the lid, a surprise splash of tears in her eyes. Since she'd been old enough to shove the kitchen stool across the tile floor, she'd found the ceramic blue-and-gold jar full of cookies. But it was a tradition that got lost amid the grieving and coping.

"I decided it was time," Ida Mae said.

"Does Mama know?" Cookie baking was one of the family traditions she'd discouraged after the funeral.

"She does, but I've never seen her eat one. I eat them or carry them over to my family dinners on Sunday. But once, I'm not sure, I thought I heard the lid clanking one afternoon when I was downstairs tending laundry."

"Wow." Maybe there was hope for Horatia Del Rey after all.

Ida Mae went to the library door. "Horatia, darling, someone's here to see you." The maid sounded more like a kind mother than a lifelong servant.

"Yes, I know," Mama said, her voice coming from deep inside the light and shadowed library. "I saw you outside talking to Daisy. Corina, what brings you here?"

She saw her? And didn't come to the door? When Corina and Carlos came home for Christmas their first year of college, Mama had the high school band waiting for them in the front yard.

"Hey, Mama." Corina washed down her last bite of chips with a sweet swig of tea and moved into the library. The white brick fireplace in the center of the room was where she learned her letters. Where she curled up on winter nights and read her first book, *Little House in the Big Woods*. "I'm leaving for Brighton tomorrow. I came to get a few things."

"I see." Mama looked beautiful, as always, impeccably dressed in her silk blouse, linen skirt, and string of pearls resting at the base of her throat. Any other time she might think Mama was on her way to a luncheon or returning from a charity meeting.

But her gaunt cheeks accented by the dark circles under her eyes told a different story.

"How's Daddy?"

"Off to Birmingham. Overseeing the construction of a new golf course."

"Good for him." As chairman of the Del Rey family fortune, Daddy mostly managed investments and sat on the board of a dozen companies. But when she and Carlos were teens, he developed a passion for designing and building golf courses.

"There's another one after this one." Mama sighed, smoothed her skirt, and sat in the Queen Anne-Marie chair she'd inherited from Corina's great-great-grandmother Thurman. "What's in Brighton?"

"A movie premier. Gigi received an invitation from the palace and decided to send me in her place." Corina inched farther into the room, as if Mama's question gave her permission to do so. Leaning against the couch, she ran her hands over the wool-and-silk upholstery. "Clive Boston is the star, and I'm supposed to interview him. But he's notorious for not showing up."

"Oh? Give Clive my regards."

"Mama, say, why don't you come?" On the spot. Spur of the moment. It *felt* like a good idea. She'd have to figure out how to explain Stephen, but details, details. "I'm staying at The Wellington."

Mama laughed. "Goodness no. What would I do in Brighton?"

"What you used to do in Brighton. Shop. Go down to the shore. Walk the art festival. Have tea with Lady Hutton. Take in a rugby match." *Be with me, your daughter.*

Mama picked up her book. "I don't need to shop. I've got more clothes than I can possibly wear. I've no need for art and I've not talked to Lady Hutton in . . ." Her voice faded. "I'm fine right here."

"Don't you want to—"

"Corina," Mama said with a sharp sigh and warning glance. *Don't push.*

"I'm going up to my room. I need my passport and the Diamatia. I want to wear it to the premier."

Mama swept imaginary lint from her skirt. "Ida Mae, Corina came for her passport."

The faithful maid came to the library door, her expression dark. "Horatia, you might as well tell her."

"Tell me what?" Corina said. "Mama?"

Mama pursed her lips, exchanging glances with Ida Mae. "I made over your room."

"You what?"

"I needed a project, so I turned your room into a quiet room."

"A quiet room? This whole place is a morgue." Corina's voice carried, and her words were sharper than she'd intended. "How can you possibly want quiet?"

Mama didn't respond but sat in her chair, staring out the window toward the garden.

Corina knelt next to her. "Mama, I'm sorry, but why my room? We have a ton of spare rooms to make over."

"Yours was across from Carlos's." What little light lived in Mama's eyes shone when she said his name. "I don't want to argue with you. Ida Mae can take you to your things."

"Mama." Corina squeezed Mama's thin arm, fearing she was losing more of her every day. "For the life of me, I—"

"You know what your problem is, Corina?" Mama said, chin resting in her fingers, her gaze cold and vacant. "You don't know when to give up. When to realize life has you beat."

"I'm thirty, Mama. You had Carlos and me by my age. I can't believe that life defeated me at twenty-five. What would I do with myself otherwise?" She'd hung around, trying to draw Mama out, get her to live again. "Mama, don't give up. You have so much to live for yet."

"I lost my son, Corina. And for what? A war that our government made sure we could never win. Killed in a firefight? What does that even mean?" Shaking, Mama pressed her hand to her forehead. It was as if the news of Carlos's death had just arrived. "My baby . . ."

"You're not alone, Mama. I lost my brother, my twin." Corina ached to draw Mama into a hug, but she would only shrug her off.

"But yet, look at you, moving to Florida, attending movie premiers."

"I couldn't sit around here another day, Mama. Five years, just existing and not living. You know darn well Carlos would hate it."

"We don't know what he would think or want, do we? Because he's not here." Mama shot to her feet and paced to the window, the southern light accenting her dark hair and narrow frame so she appeared angelic. "By the way, the Diamatia is not here."

"Not here?" Something in Mama's tone carved a dark pit in Corina's belly. "Where is it then?"

"I donated it," Mama said, brushing her hand up and down her arm as if she were chilled.

"You *donated* it?" A ticklish heat flashed over Corina and flared her temper. She thudded toward Mama, taking hold of her arm. "To whom? When? And might I ask, why?"

"We no longer had need of it."

"We? No longer . . . had *need* of . . . it? Who's we, Mama? It was *my* gown." Anger fueled Corina's tears, but they were too hot, too thick to slip down her cheeks.

"Which I purchased for you." Mama turned from the window, hands on her hips. "By hunting down the most elusive, exclusive designer in the world."

"So you have the right to give it away? You moved heaven and earth to convince Luciano to design a gown for me. How did you suddenly feel the need to give it away?"

"Livy Rothschild was auctioning items for charity at Christie's and she wondered if I had any items to sell."

"Livy Rothschild? She just suddenly called up and said, 'Hello, Horatia, got stuff to sell? How about that Diamatia?'"

"Don't be smart. She called to see how I fared. She's been one of my true friends through this ordeal."

Corina fisted her hands, pressing them over her eyes. Livy was a fair-weather friend like the rest of them. Grief made her uncomfortable and she avoided it like a ten-dollar skirt from Walmart. Corina could remember only a handful of short calls from the aristocratic Bostonian after the funeral.

"What about me, Mama? Huh? I stayed here with you. Gave up my career, my social life. Most of my friends are married, starting families. But I stayed with you and Daddy." Corina demanded an answer with her posture and tone. "So why would you even think to give away my dress?"

"Do not badger me. It's done."

Corina stepped back. "Has it sold? 'Cause I'll get it from Livy."

"Yes, it sold. The money went to help foster girls who were too old to stay in the system but had no place to go."

"Mama, that's fantastic, but why not just write them a check?" The black hole in her middle widened, and Corina struggled not to fall in. "Don't sell my stuff." It was as if little by little, Mama was removing all signs of Corina. "We were going to give that dress to my daughter for her debut, remember? And if I didn't have a daughter, we'd give it to Carlos's. Then one day, she'd hand it down to *her* daughter."

"Carlos is not going to have a daughter now, is he? Nor a son." Mama faced Corina, arms folded, back straight. "And are you planning on marrying anytime soon?"

Steam. Could Mama see the steam rising from Corina?

"I thought not," Mama said. "So I gave up the gown. It was the right thing to do."

"Mama." Corina took her mother by the arms, her legs trembling, her heart exploding. "I. Am. Not. Dead. Carlos is gone and it hurts *every* day. But I'm still here. I will get married, I'll give you and Daddy grandbabies to spoil. We'll make new memories and—"

"I don't want new memories." Mama softened, and the tears flowed. "I want the old ones. The ones where my son was alive." She waved off any response, turning away. "Just get what you want from your things. There are other gowns." Mama turned to Ida Mae, her brown eyes soaked with tears. "Can you get Corina's passport from the safe? And show her where you put her gowns."

"Come on with me, baby." Sympathy laced Ida Mae's soft, low tone.

Corina could do nothing but obey. In silence. At the top of the stairs, Ida Mae paused. "She thinks I put your gowns in the garnet room. But I left them in your old closet. Didn't feel it was right to move them."

Corina kissed the old maid's cheek. "Thank you." At her bedroom door she asked, "Doesn't she even come in here?"

"She does."

"In a house of eighteen rooms, she makes over mine?"

"Go on in. You'll understand."

Turning the knob, Corina stepped into the room where she'd slept since she was two. Where she'd giggled with her girlfriends and dreamed her dreams. Where Tommy Barnes serenaded her the night before senior prom.

Gone were the shades of pink and purple. The walls were a burnt orange, and a thick brown carpet covered the ancient hardwood. Pillows populated the corners and wooden chairs replaced her furniture. Indoor palms and ficus gave the room a garden feel, and soft string music drifted from ceiling-mounted speakers.

Pictures of Carlos were tastefully dispersed about the room, and then Corina understood. "She doesn't want him forgotten."

"It's her biggest fear."

"His room is the same?"

"As the day he left." Ida Mae dusted her hand over a small wall table. "You live on, Corina. But Carlos will forever be a young, handsome, twenty-five-year-old with nothing to lose and everything to gain."

Corina crossed the hall and entered his room. It was untouched. Pristine. The curtains were drawn against the sunlight, but Corina could clearly see her brother's awards, trophies, posters, and pictures. All in the same places they'd been when he left for college, when he left for basic training, when he left this life.

"No one goes in except the cleaning lady once a week," Ida Mae said as she came in behind her.

Corina sank with sadness into the nearest chair. "Ida Mae, is it ever going to get better?"

"I don't know, darling, I don't know." Ida Mae's hands smoothed across Corina's shoulders. "Grief is a . . . well, not our friend."

"That doesn't give her the right to treat me as if I'm dead too."

"She loves you, Corina."

"She sure has a funny way of showing it." She glanced up at Ida Mae, who carried tears in her eyes. "This can't be an easy season for you either."

"Come now." Ida Mae wiped her eyes. "Let's find you a fancy gown for this here premier. Then I'll make us something scrumptious for dinner."

Corina took a final survey of Carlos's room. If she inhaled deep, she could catch a whiff of his hair gel. She smiled.

"Carlos, you use too much of that stuff."

"Shut up. It's my hair."

"I can tell you now, no girl is ever going to want to touch it. Here, let me help you."

"Fine, but don't say a word about this."

"It's our secret."

"I never thought this would happen to us, Ida Mae. We were going to have Sunday dinners once a month, spend our summers in Vermont, New Year's in Hawaii, creating a whole passel of new traditions with our families."

"Don't give up, shug. Like you said, you ain't dead yet."

Back in Corina's room, Ida Mae helped her choose a Versace, then carry her things downstairs. Then she paused in the safe room for Corina's passport.

"Ida, can you drive me back to the airport?"

"You know I can shug. I hate that you came all the way here for that gown . . . I should've told you . . . I knew I should've told you."

"It's okay. I wanted to see you and Mama anyway." And Daddy if he'd ever show his face.

Corina returned to the library as Ida Mae went for her purse and keys, ready to leave anytime Corina wanted. "Mama, Ida's going to drive me back down to Atlanta. My flight leaves this evening."

"Have a nice trip, Corina."

"The quiet room is lovely. Peaceful."

"Do you think he would've liked it?"

"Yes, I think *he* would." Corina inched toward her mother, bending to give her forehead a quick kiss. "I'm sorry about earlier."

"Never you mind." Mama lifted her face, her smile fixed, her eyes empty. "It's forgotten."

Corina knelt on the floor next to her, leaning against the chair, and for a few minutes, rested there, watching the midmorning sun move over the lake.

ELEVEN

ou must be joking." Corina leaned over the VIP reservation desk, iPhone in hand, her hotel reservation
displayed on the screen. "Here's my name, the date, and
confirmation number. Corina Del Rey. Look again."

After an eight-hour flight from Atlanta to Cathedral City,
she wanted nothing more than a hot, soaking bath, scrumptious
room service, and a nap. Not a cheeky hotel clerk who claimed
she had no reservation.

The clerk shook his head. "D-e-l-R-e-y?"

"Yes."

"Again, I apologize, but I do not see your name or reservation
number."

"How about under Beaumont Media? I listed them as my
company name."

The clerk brightened, his fingers moving quickly over the
keyboard. But his hope faded. "No Beaumont Media."

"But I *have* a confirmation number." She waved her phone
under his nose.

"I see that, but if I don't *have* it in the system I can't let you
have a room."

"Are you saying there are no rooms available? At all?" Corina loved this hotel. Walking across the white marble-and-stone lobby floor was like a stroll across a snowy street in heaven. The suites were luxurious. The food, divine.

The clerk winced. "I'm sorry, Miss Del Rey, but we're all booked. It's tourism season what with the art festivals, the summer internationals, the youth rugby tournament, and of course, the premier of *King Stephen I*. In fact, I'm surprised you were even able to make a reservation on such short notice."

"Apparently I did *not* make a reservation." Corina collected her wallet and phone, tucking them into her handbag.

"June is very busy in Cathedral City."

"Yes, I know . . ." She leaned over the desk and lowered her voice. "My father is Donald Del Rey." Never before in her life had she used her daddy's name. It wasn't how the Del Rey's rolled. But desperation drove her over her boundary lines. "Are you *sure* you don't have any rooms?"

"Oh, I see." The clerk leaned closer still, whispering. "Is he on The Wellington board?"

"No." She grimaced. So, The Wellington had forgotten the Del Reys. In five and a half short years. Corina looked to where a bell cap waited with her things, the morning light cascading through the glass ceiling and pooling at his feet. "Can you tell me where I might find a room?"

"We've a computer in the guest center, Miss Del Rey, and a phone book. But most hotels, if not all, will be booked."

"Let's hope somewhere in this big ole city there's a cancellation."

"I'm sure there is, but"—he leaned toward her—"not at an establishment up to your standards."

"Right now, any room with a bath and bed sounds perfect."

"Then I'm sure you'll find something. After all, your father is Donald Del Rey."

Oh fine, now he mocked her. Whatever happened to customer

service? Across the lobby, Corina met the bell cap and tipped him generously. Can you carry my things outside?"

"Certainly, ma'am."

The bell cap collected her suitcases and rolled them through the giant sliding doors, depositing them and Corina next to the bustling guest driveway, where two vans loaded with young rugby players had just arrived.

She watched them for a moment, envying their freedom and exuberance, their passion. She needed her passion back. Her exuberance for life.

Daisy's dream drifted across her thoughts from time to time, pieces of it starting to become Corina's own. The part where she was happy.

As for Prince Stephen? She wasn't strong enough to hope on him yet.

"May I help you, miss?" The bell captain approached, his starched white shirt already sweat stained.

"Yes, a taxi please." She'd cruise around the city until she found a decent hotel. She'd start with the Royal Astor and go from there.

"It will be a moment. We're quite busy."

Another van rounded into the hotel drive and deposited more rugby players. Corina watched as they hoisted their gear to their shoulders, laughing, full of camaraderie.

The air around them, in the city, was electric. Summer in Cathedral City. There wasn't anything like it.

Corina inhaled the scents and sounds. She should've done this a long time ago. But she allowed herself to be locked away. Allowed herself to feel rejected, scared, and frail.

Across the city, cathedral bells chimed the hour. Nine o'clock. Corina closed her eyes, listening to the clarion tones, grateful there was no one to stop it.

Three . . . four . . . five . . .

The gothic and Romanesque cathedrals with their heavenward bell towers were enchanting. The pride of the city. Of Brighton.

Seven cathedrals, built over a period of four hundred years, were a monument to the nation's Christian history. To faith in Christ. To prayer. For over two hundred years, the bells rang out at 6:00 a.m. and 6:00 p.m. in an orchestrated, syncopated, glorious sound. Corina never tired of hearing them.

The tradition began when one of the ancient archbishops wanted to remind the people of morning and evening prayers the year Brighton sided with the newly formed United States against the British during the War of 1812.

Tourists came from all over the world to experience the choreographed melody of the cathedral bells.

Meanwhile, Corina waited for a taxi. She checked with the bell captain, but he was busy with a limousine full of guests.

"I've not forgotten you, miss."

Corina tipped her head to the pale patch of blue peeking down between the buildings and listened to the last chime. The last beckoning to prayer.

Lord, thank you for getting me here. Thank you for a place to sleep.

She laughed, breaking the cobwebs from her tired soul. Just. Need. A. Bed. And. Bath.

Still waiting for her taxi, Corina dug her phone from her handbag and texted Gigi that she'd arrived safe and sound. Then she found the number of her friend Sharlene in her Contacts, wishing she'd arranged ahead of time to see her. When Sharlene's voice mail came on saying she was on holiday and would respond when she wasn't napping or on the beach, Corina hung up.

Between helping Mark step into his director role, and preparing for the premier and the interview with Clive, Corina had not organized the personal side of her trip very well. What friends did she want to see? If any at all? What memory lanes to stroll down? Most important, when and how did she contact Stephen? What would she say to him when she did?

Hey, dude, I came to love well. Whatever that means. You game?

She was about to check on her taxi when a woman approached, wearing a white overcoat with a fur collar and wool cap. In June? Corina stared a moment beyond polite.

"You're looking for a room," she said, making a statement, not asking a question.

Corina monitored the woman's movements. "And you are?"

"A friend." Her voice was thick and powerful, yet smooth and easy.

"My friend? Have we met before?" She didn't look or feel familiar.

"In a manner of speaking." She offered Corina a simple, cream-colored card. "There's a place for you right down the avenue. One block south."

"Excuse me? A place for me?" Corina hesitated but then took the card and read the simple lettering. "The Manor."

"Go to the corner of Market Avenue." The woman pointed toward the south curb. "Cross at the light and go down one block on Crescent. You can't miss it. A quaint little place in the shade of Gliden and Martings."

"Gliden and Martings? The department stores?" Corina checked to see if a bell cap was within shouting distance. "Look, I'm tired and not interested in whatever you're doing." Really? A huckster in the shadows of the great and grand Wellington?

"The Manor has a room for you. Please, go. With faith."

With faith. Corina's sense of eerie was balanced by a flood of peace.

Stepping back, the woman tipped her head toward the corner. "The traffic is stopped. You're clear to go."

With a gaze toward the avenue, then the hotel bell station, Corina sensed a sort of celestial pause, as if the world was waiting for her to move. The traffic in both directions was stopped at the light, mounting up, idling.

"Don't be afraid."

Corina stuck out the cream-colored card, willing the woman to take it back. "I–I don't think this is for me."

"You're in very safe hands. Remember why you came." She nodded toward the street, her hands buried in the deep, creamy pockets of her coat. She was ethereal, exuding a rapturous peace. "Best go or the opportunity will be lost. Lean into your faith. It's brought you this far."

"O–okay." Corina collected her luggage. While she had no intention of staying at the Manor, she was confident she wanted away from this woman in white wool and fur. In June!

Rolling luggage behind her, she crossed at the intersection, the woman watching. She'd go a block, then hail a cab and find a hotel. Never mind the weirdness of the world being in slow mo, even stopping for her while she made her way to the other side.

What was happening?

The city must be working on the lights. Yes, that must be it. Otherwise, traffic would not stop in all directions on a Friday morning.

Yet the moment Corina cleared the lane and stepped onto the sidewalk, the west-bound traffic light turned green. Cars zipped past. Pedestrians skipped along, their heels cracking against the concrete. The bell captain's whistle pierced the air.

And the woman in white? Gone. No sign of her on Market or Crescent. The *swirl*, like the one from last Sunday, a touch of the divine, coated Corina.

She paused, listening. Waiting and watching. But she was too weary to contemplate any further. Chalk the last few minutes up to jet lag. Or the way of summer in Brighton.

Of course, that was the answer. Weariness. And a bit of the wonder of this fine isle.

Adjusting her grip on her luggage, Corina made her way toward what should be the Manor, fully prepared to drop everything and run. If anything, *anyone,* jumped out at her, she'd be nothing but heels and elbows.

A few more tentative steps passed the end of Gliden and into the light of a Martings display window. See, there was nothing between those two . . .

Then she saw it. A small building nestled in the morning shadow of the retail giants. A rough and crudely carved sign hung above the door.

The Manor.

Corina stepped back to survey the establishment from the curb. But there wasn't much to see. Just the front of the inn, which was nothing more than a door and a large, single-paned window filled with a soft yellow light.

Adjusting her tired grip on her suitcases, Corina moved forward and tried the door, snatching back her hand when it yielded with a squeak. She pressed on inside, dragging her suitcases over the threshold. "Hello?"

The small lobby consisted of a sitting area, a stone fireplace, and a vacant reception desk. The wide board floor matched the dry wood of the fireplace mantel—dark and worn, without any gloss or sheen.

A piquant, cheerful woman with white hair floating above her heart-shaped face appeared behind the narrow registration desk. "Well, there you are. I was beginning to think you'd changed your mind."

"Changed my mind? I'm sorry, but I don't have a reservation. I'm—"

"Corina Del Rey. Yes, yes, we know. Come on in. Don't hover by the door." She came around the desk, hand extended for Corina's large suitcase. She wore a white peasant blouse and a black skirt with a laced tunic overlay.

"You know? Who knows what? And h–how do you know?"

The woman offered a sweet, bow smile, which weakened Corina's defenses. "We have your room all ready. Lovely it is too. On the fifth floor with a grand view of the city. Quite stunning, I says." She crossed her hands over her heart and sighed. "My favorite place on earth. I hope you don't mind the stairs. We've no lift. Or elevator, as you say in America."

"The clerk . . . at The Wellington . . . Did he called you?" How nice of him. And surprising, since he didn't seem all that eager to help. But what other explanation could there be?

"The Wellington? No, no one from The Wellington called." The woman snickered, covering her mouth with her delicate hand. "I really must walk round and see the city close up. I've not been here in quite a while. Now, shall I take you to your room?"

She was crazy. Certifiable. "Listen, I appreciate your cozy little establishment, but I think I'll try the Royal Astor." Or maybe a park bench. Surely there was one with Corina's name on it.

But the eccentric hostess paid no attention. She snapped her fingers and twisted her lips, pointing to a closed door beside the fireplace. "I always forget this part." She cupped her hands around her mouth. "Brill! Come for the luggage, eh, my good man? She's here."

No, nada, not doing this. The Manor was just too weird. Out there. Maybe Cathedral City's Hotel California. Corina stepped back once. But why did she feel peace? At home in the light and the space?

A drop of perspiration slithered down her temple. "Know what?" she said with a raspy croak. "I just realized I have a place to stay." She reached for the large suitcase, but the woman did not let go.

"My name's Adelaide." She offered her hand. "Please, don't go." Her tone canceled Corina's rising fear.

"All right . . ." Corina took the woman's hand in hers with a light shake. "I–is this place on Cathedral City's hotel register?" She didn't know what else to ask for proof of the hotel's validity other than to see their city license. Which felt slightly insulting. If the woman said yes, then she could exhale, relax. Enjoy this quaint, out of the way, back-in-time hovel.

"My dear lass, we were the first inn built in Cathedral City. By King Stephen I himself." Adelaide puffed out her chest. "Fifteen fifty-five."

"Fifteen fifty-five?" Four hundred and fifty years ago? Ah, realization dawned. This must be publicity for the movie. Surely. Which explained Adelaide's costume. And the lady in white. An actress trolling the streets looking for confused tourists to send here. Corina took a sly gaze about the room, hunting for hidden cameras.

"But never you worry. The place has been fixed up. Modernized, if you will. Save for the adding of a lift. But we got Brill. Ha. He's our lifter. Brill!"

"Here, here. Where's the girl?" A tall, big-boned man with a jocular face and thin, greying, curly tufts of hair squeezed through the side door, entering the lobby. "There she is. Well, how do you like that? Fit and pretty. None worse for the wear. How's the girl a-doing? What say you of this place?"

"F–fine." Corina's thoughts were on a crash course with her emotions, debating to the quick rhythm of her heart. Run-stay-run-stay. But this Brill? She liked him. Felt drawn to him as if she'd known him her whole life.

"Stop badgering her, Brill, and leave her be. She needs her rest."

"Then let's get her settled." Brill picked up the large suitcase and nodded toward the stairs. "Ladies first."

"Adelaide? Brill?" Strange how their names rolled off Corina's tongue so easily. Like she'd said them a thousand times. "How *did* you know I'd be coming?"

"It's our job to know." The twinkle in Adelaide's eyes bloomed as if God had created them from stars.

"Your job?"

"Come, love, we've plenty of time to chat after you've rested." Adelaide took hold of the smaller roller board, a thick gold chain with a gold medallion swinging out from under the pale purple tunic.

Corina hesitated. Follow or flee? Follow or flee!

Adelaide paused on the first step. "Are you coming?"

Follow. "Y–yes, yes I'm coming." *With faith.*

As they climbed the stairs, Adelaide ran a narrative. "Like I said, the Manor was built by King Stephen I, for his true love."

"Magdalena?" After brushing up on her history, Corina had high expectations for Hollywood's depiction of the larger-than-life King Stephen I and his queen.

"Oh yes. Weren't they the greatest of loves? Together they built the House of Stratton, established this kingdom. Oh, such was a trying time for the newly independent nation, but Stephen I and Magdalena loved well through—"

"Excuse me? What did you say? Loved well?"

"Yes, they knew how to love well. Magdalena was the woman who won the king's heart." Adelaide prattled on without answering, pausing on the third-story landing, breathing deeply. "She fought in King Stephen's army against Henry VIII. Their love was the foundation of the new kingdom. Such a gift, such love." Her blue eyes peered through Corina. "Don't you agree?"

"I–I suppose I do." Why did this woman speak as if she knew something?

Adelaide smiled down at her. "It's important to know history."

"Ladies, these burdens don't get any lighter standing here listening to you gab." Brill huffed and gruffed, but the tender old man would never blow down anyone's house.

"Hold your horses, Brill. We're going." Gathering her wind

and her skirt, Adelaide bounded up the steps, the gold medallion rocking from side to side, the keys in her pocket jangling.

Corina followed, rounding the narrow curved staircase to the next landing. "I'm looking forward to the film's portrayal of Magdalena." Come to think of it, the first queen would make a great sidebar to go along with her premier piece, and this woman seemed to be somewhat of an expert.

"Oh, they won't do her justice. You can't contain a woman like Magdalena on a movie screen. Such a beauty, she was, very much like you." Adelaide glanced back at Corina. "Dark hair, olive skin, eyes like amber stones. Independent. Brave, taking up her brother's sword when he was killed in the serf war." Adelaide paused on the fourth-floor landing for a deep breath, her eyes glossing over with a faraway gaze. "Oh how King Stephen loved her. Enough to defy his privy council. He wanted her at their table but his generals did not. She was too strong for those men. It was Stephen's first test at loving well."

Adelaide pressed on to the fifth-floor landing, the old wide board steps creaking.

"Test? What do you mean?"

"Could he be king and servant?" Adelaide raised her finger. "'Tis the number one rule in the kingdom."

"In Brighton?"

"In *the* kingdom. To rule one must serve."

Corina stuttered her next step. What was she talking about? *The* kingdom.

"Get along, lassie. Me arms are tired." Brill gently bumped her shoulder, and Corina stumbled along the dark passage under a low, exposed-beam ceiling.

"Hold yer horses, Brill. I'm a-telling her about the kingdom."

"Are we talking that already?" Brill adjusted the suitcases in his grip. "You said to let the girl rest."

"I see, today you decide to listen to me and quote meself back *to* meself." Adelaide led the way down a narrow corridor toward a wooden door while Brill grumbled in his chest and Corina snickered softly.

What a hoot, these two. How she got picked for this adventure she'd never know, but she made a mental note to keep an eye out for hidden mikes and cameras, and take notes for yet another story to go along with the movie review and premier story.

At the door, Adelaide worked a key into the lock and twisted the knob, exposing a grand, sprawling room that ran the length of the inn.

Corina hesitated, peering inside before going in. It was beautiful, inviting, and despite the icicles of trepidation about this place, the kindness of Adelaide and Brill stoked the furnace of peace growing in her spirit.

She hadn't known what to expect of a room here, given the condition of the Manor, but the space was exquisite, state of the art, with an open, vaulted ceiling, cream-colored, textured walls, and polished, gleaming hardwood floors.

A fragrance hovered and Corina breathed it in, filling her lungs.

As Corina passed into the room, Adelaide handed her the key. "You won't need it, but I pass it along as a sign."

Corina laughed though her skin tightened with chills. She gripped the key against her palm. "A sign? What kind of sign?"

"That it's yours, Corina. Just believe."

She froze, rooted where she stood. Did this woman know about Stephen? How? "Adelaide, what's going on here?"

"Quite loverly, isn't it?" Adelaide cradled her arms at her waist, smiling as she glanced around the room, quite pleased with it all.

"Quite." Corina crossed the room, taking it in. The outside wall was a large single-paned window, like the one in the lobby, that framed a breathtaking view of Cathedral City and the River Conour. "It's beautiful."

"Think you'd like to stay?" Adelaide's eyes twinkled.

Corina regarded the strange couple. "I'm not quite sure what to make of you two or this place. Is this some sort of movie stunt? What's going on here?"

"Movie stunt?" Adelaide patted her hand to her chest. "Mercy no, lass."

"Then what is all of this?"

"Ahem." The man of the place stood in the doorway, Corina's bags in hand. "Where do ye want these?"

"Brill, I'm so sorry. Just put them by the door. I'll arrange them later." She took the roller board from him and tucked it in next to a walnut cabinet.

"Yes," Adelaide beamed. "You will do nicely. You are the one."

"The one?"

Adelaide's eyes sparked with a glint that set Corina's spirit on fire. "Anyway, as you see, here's your bed." She patted the massive mattress covered with a cream-and-brown quilt. "It's made for dreaming, I say." She moved about the room. "Here's your sitting corner." She switched on what looked like an authentic Tiffany lamp. "And the loo is just down this jaunty little corridor."

Corina followed Adelaide around the bedroom wall into a bathroom haven. Tile and granite with a sunken whirlpool bath, a vanity, a shower with gold fixtures, all washed in the morning light sinking in through a large skylight.

"I don't know what to say." About any of it. The inn, Adelaide, her kingdom talk, and the friendship she felt with the odd couple. Corina inspected the porcelain sink, running her hand along the smooth, slate-colored granite.

"Say nothing but that you'll stay." Adelaide patted the cabinet's smooth drawers. "Here are your towels and linens. We'll leave you to get settled. If you need me, just tug on this here." She pointed to the thick damask pull next to her bed. "One Old World thing we hung on to. We thought you'd like it."

"Me?"

"Yes, you. Isn't everything to your liking? The colors, the furniture?"

Corina scanned the room. Very much so. All pieces she'd select. In fact, she'd debated purchasing a cabinet just like the one with the towels and linens. "Why won't you answer my questions about what's going on here?"

"My dear girl." Adelaide grabbed Corina's hands. "You have just flown all the way from Georgia. We have plenty of time to talk."

"See, that's what I mean. How do you know that?"

"My sweets, 'tis me job. Now, take your rest." She motioned for Brill to start down the stairs. "We'll bring up tea and cakes, leaving them outside the door. When you hear a knock, you'll know we was here."

"Wait! Hold on." Corina retrieved her purse from the bottom of the luggage pile, digging for her wallet. "Tip. I need to give you a tip." She offered two ten-pound notes to Adelaide. "One for you and one for Brill. Thank you so much. You're a life saver."

Adelaide shoved the money back at Corina. "Keep it. We've no use for it."

"No use for money?" Corina shoved the money at the crazy old woman. "Who on earth doesn't need money?"

"Folk who are not of this earth."

"Huh?" The word came as a dull reflex. A weak challenge from her soul to something Corina knew to be true in her spirit. This moment contained something from the Divine.

Adelaide's soft footsteps echoed down the stairwell as Corina sank through the light of the Tiffany lamp onto the chaise lounge, money still in hand. She was confused but oddly at peace.

While this place made no sense, Corina *knew* she was supposed to be here. Not by her intellect but by her heart. Otherwise, she'd be out of here in a Georgia Bull Dog minute.

After a few minutes, she collected herself and walked to the window, filling her lungs again with the peace that surpassed her understanding.

Cathedral City sprawled before her view. Breathtaking.

Ever since she came out of the fog of death in January, God seemed to be whispering to her. In small ways. Large ways. Through everyone from Gigi to Ida Mae to Melissa and Mama, Daddy, and Daisy. Stephen. And now perhaps this odd pair of Adelaide and Brill.

Unless they *were* actually actors posing as Old World inn-keepers to publicize the film. Corina glanced toward the door, listening, expecting to hear the sound of other guests arriving.

But her room remained quiet except for the timbre of her own heartbeat.

She just had to make sense of it all. She had to conquer her doubts about Stephen, be willing to risk her heart in God's hands. Would he come through?

God owed her nothing. In fact, he'd already given her a gift beyond measure when she neither deserved it or knew enough to ask for it.

But oh, this "love well" adventure was scary. Downright frightening.

What if this journey meant gaining nothing for herself but losing everything to God? To Stephen? What if the journey meant she returned home empty-handed yet all the more Christ-like. She shivered, the idea plucking at her sense of self-propriety and preservation.

She'd known all along this Brighton trip wasn't about movie premiers or celebrity interviews but about "loving well." About the motions of a prayer she'd prayed on a cold, hard chapel floor when she felt obliterated and empty.

TWELVE

riday afternoon Stephen waited backstage at the *Madeline & Hyacinth Live!* show for his cue, hot and sticky in his starched white shirt and dark blue Armani jacket.

The makeup artist hovered, patting the shine from his brow. "You'll cool off on the set. It's freezing out there."

A few feet from him, tucked in the folds of the stage curtain, Thomas scanned the crowd, talking to his team of three through the com tucked into his sleeve.

Stephen angled around the hulking bodyguard to see the bleachers. The audience of mostly women seemed harmless enough. He had insisted Thomas's security measures were over-kill, but the man stuck to protocol without wavering.

Stephen clapped him on the shoulder. Thomas glanced back with a nod. He should be grateful for the man's vigilance. It was Stephen's lack thereof that got men killed. His trust of another man with hidden vicious intentions.

He scanned the audience once again. But not for intruders, but for . . . who?

Corina? The look-alike Corina?

The encounter with the look-alike yesterday in The Wellington lobby tapped his feelings for her. The ones of love and affection he'd rucked to the bottom of his heart's playing field, piling on every excuse and emotional baggage he could find, never letting them up, never letting them free, never letting them score a try over the goal line of his being.

How did they dare push against him? He should've never gone to Florida.

"All secure, sir," Thomas said, low, in Stephen's ear. "Outside security is still sweeping the car park, but in-house we're all clear."

"Thank you. But I don't think the King's Office would've cleared this appearance if they weren't confident of security."

Thomas made a face. "You know my rule. Never underestimate dinosaur terrorism."

Stephen laughed. "Isn't that a 'blast from the past.' I've not heard you mention that term in a good while."

"I thought it time to remind you. Never relax your vigilance. An attack can happen anywhere, anytime, at any given moment, unearthed by the anger, passion, opportunity of mere men. Ignored by naive governments. We trick ourselves into believing it all might have gone the way of dinosaurs until it rears its ugly head. It's the tyrannosaurus rex of our day. Didn't you see *Jurassic Park*?"

"So what are you in this scenario? The velociraptor?"

"If you like." Thomas grinned. "I rather fancy that image."

Stephen shook his head, smirking, checking his watch. He was due on any second. However, Madeline and Hyacinth were cooking up a meal on stage with animated chef Connie Spangler.

The stage manager flashed "five minutes."

Still too warm, Stephen slipped off his jacket, draped it over the back of a stool, and took a seat.

Public appearances. He'd kept them limited since Afghanistan. Though lately he'd carried out his share of royal obligations.

However, a few years ago when the Brighton Eagles asked

Stephen to do a publicity junket—as their most renowned player—the Crown declined. Too risky. Too public.

Stephen spent most of his rugby years avoiding the spotlight, ducking into the locker room after a test to avoid the press. The recent Fan Day was one of his rare public appearances for the team.

The lads understood. Stephen told them his low profile was for security.

Every time he stepped on the pitch, however, he was aware of the risk. Someone might try to kill him. As time passed, Stephen handled more and more public appearances on behalf of the Crown. But security would always be maintained.

Madeline and Hyacinth had wanted him on the show for years. The King's Office reported they were "thrilled"!

The stage director approached with a bow. "Your Highness, you're on after the commercial."

"Thank you." Stephen hopped off the stool, adjusted his collar, and tucked his shirt into his jeans, then slipped on his jacket. He liked the casual prince-as-rugby-player attire. He exhaled. He was a wee bit nervous. But this should be fun.

The applause lights flashed and the camera's red light dimmed. Makeup artists scurried onto the stage like elves, patting and primping the show's stars, then backed away when the stage manager called, "Thirty seconds."

Thomas clapped Stephen on the shoulder. "Break a leg."

Stephen laughed. "Isn't one ankle enough?"

The show was back from commercial. "Ladies, hold on to your hats. We've a surprise for you today." Blond and fair-skinned, Madeline beamed at the audience, then at her cohost. "I'm beside myself, aren't you, Hy?"

"Don't you see the bags under my eyes, Maddie? I slept not one wink. Not one." Hyacinth, dark-haired and thin, with piercing blue eyes, slipped from her high hostess chair. "Ladies and gentlemen, please welcome to our show for the first time *ever*, His Royal Highness, Prince Stephen."

Stephen moved into a wall of cheers and applause, shoulders back, chin up, doing his best to minimize his awkward, booted-foot gait. He strafed the front row, shaking hands, waving at the audience. Then he embraced Madeline and Hyacinth, a break in royal protocol, and took his place between the presenters.

"Well, well, we're so excited," Hyacinth started, her comment fueling the audience.

A low chant began in the back. "Strat, Strat, Strat!" An abbreviation of his surname started by sports presenters when discussing the way Stephen maneuvered up and down the pitch.

"His sidestep is like, strat, strat, strat . . ."

Stephen acknowledged them with a wave, relaxed, smiling. He liked his identity as a rugby player. It made him an everyday man.

He felt quite sure he'd surrendered his essence as a prince when men died for him.

"Settle down or we'll never get to chat." Hyacinth walked past the cameras into the bleachers, patting the air down with her hands. "We've only five minutes with him and you've used one already."

The audience laughed but complied, yielding to Hyacinth's remarkable charm.

As Hyacinth returned to her chair, Madeline pressed her hand on Stephen's arm. "We are thrilled to have you. Tell us, what have you been up to, Your Highness?"

"Stephen, please, call me Stephen." He'd hear from Mum about omitting his title.

"Prince Stephen is your name. Who you are. His Royal Highness, Prince Stephen Marc Kenneth Leopold of Brighton Kingdom."

"Prince Stephen." Hyacinth had been around. She knew better. "How's your ankle? We're so missing you on the pitch for the summer games."

"It's coming on. Still a bit of physio yet to go, but I'll be back for the fall Premiership."

Cheers and whistles from the audience.

"Will you be coronated as Prince of Brighton in this downtime?" Madeline read the question from her cue cards. It felt odd, out of place, and perhaps strategized by the King's Office to get him to yield.

"We're still talking." A nonanswer always worked.

"So you'll be patron of the new War Memorial? We're so proud you served king and country along with the other chaps." Hyacinth applauded toward the crowd, stirring them to join in. "He's a hero on and off the rugby pitch."

Stephen went cold under the hot lights, shifting forward. He came here to talk about the movie premier. "No, no, the other lads are the true heroes. But it's all part of the dialogue." He shot Madeline a sly glance. *Move on. Change the subject.*

Madeline communicated to Hyacinth with her eyes and the pair moved on. Stephen's chill morphed into some sort of gummy perspiration, sticking to his skin. All the while the wide soundstage caged and moved in on him.

Daytime panic was not part of his struggle. Until moments like this—which were rare. Stephen breathed in, long, deep, staying off the very faint sound of a bomb exploding.

Then and only then was he desperate enough to whisper the only prayer he ever prayed these days. *God, help.*

He caught sight of Thomas in the audience, front and center, and focused on his friend and protection officer. Thomas nodded assurance, and Stephen's spiking panic abated.

These cryptic moments irritated him. He was a trained RAC airman, a seasoned rugby player. What right did the confines of a telly stage and mention of the War Memorial have to fill his veins with fear?

Because he knew if the world looked a little longer, a little closer, they would see right through him. At his core, he was a poser, a fraud. The exact opposite of a hero. In every sense of the word.

"Tell us what's going on this summer? We hear you have a busy diary." Hyacinth tapped his knee, catching on that Stephen had mentally stepped off for a moment.

"Quite right. Yes, busy." He gathered himself and all of his royal charm. "I'm attending the *King Stephen I* premier Monday, then I'm at the Children's Literacy Foundation Art Auction at the Galaxy on Tuesday. So yes, quite a bit going on."

"Speaking of the premier . . ." Madeline's expression sparked a different alarm in Stephen's chest. "We heard you've yet to select a date to the event."

Stephen worked up a laugh. "W–what?" Someone in the King's Office would pay for this.

"If you don't mind, Your Highness, we've been playing a little game lately with our audience and viewers." Hyacinth held up her iPhone. "You see, it has not escaped our notice that you have not been in the company of a beautiful woman in quite some time, Madeline and I the exceptions of course."

"Of course." He decided to relax and play along, a picture of Corina in his mind's eye. He'd just been in the presence of a beautiful, intelligent, loving, kind woman. She was one of the mold breakers.

"Ladies, since it seems impossible for any one of Brighton's fine lasses to catch this hunk of gorgeous prince"—Madeline laughed but her serious tone remained—"we want to hear more from you while Prince Stephen is here. For the rest of the show, tweet how you think a girl could catch the world's most eligible prince. Be sure to use our favorite hashtag, #howtocatchaprince."

"Or post on our Facebook page with the same hashtag," Hyacinth said. "You don't mind, do you Prince Stephen?"

He gave her a hardened expression. "Actually, Hyacinth—" There was the little matter of the rider. "I don't think anyone would be interested in tweeting about my boring ole love life."

Hyacinth tapped his knee, laughing. "We decided not to *talk* about your love life, you see." She arched her brow. "So we invented this fun game."

Ah, indeed, he did see. Next time he'd make the rider more specific. He should have expected them to pull some sort of stunt like this.

He gazed from Hyacinth to Madeline, then scanned the audience. Other than walking off, which sent the King's Office into a dither, he decided to relax and go with it, grateful the panic moment had faded as quickly as it came, and grateful the hostesses chose a game instead of intimate questions. Compared to Torkham, this was heaven. Might even cause a giggle or two.

"We'll ask Prince Stephen to pick the best one at the end of the show with the possibility of winning . . ." Madeline's next words packed a wallop. " . . . a chance to be his date to the premier."

The audience went raucous. The monitor displaying the tweets exploded with scrolling text.

What? No, no, no . . . Now that he *refused* to go along with. "Ladies, ladies." Stephen slipped from his chair, hands in the air. He'd fix this. "I am so flattered, but your intel is wrong. I *do* have a date to the premier."

"Oh my." Ignoring him, Madeline walked over to the monitor, laughing. "They're scrolling so fast I can't read them."

"Here's a good one . . . From CharonwithaC. 'Treat him like a regular bloke. He puts his trousers on one leg at a time like every other chap.'" Madeline glanced at Stephen. "Is that true? How does a prince put on his trousers?"

"We have a special royal prince trouser machine, you see . . ."

The audience laughed. Madeline slapped her thigh with a bit too much reverie. But Stephen was sweating again. Profusely. How'd the lasses like that about their royal prince?

He sweats. A lot.

"I like this one." Hyacinth joined her cohost at the monitor.

"From Everydaygirl. 'Be an honest girl with him. Listen to him but share your own soul.'"

Stephen nodded. No man liked to be held at arm's length. He fell for Corina because she loved him, put him in his place when necessary, and offered all of herself without restraint. He could trust her.

"Oh my, here's one . . . From LiddyWellborn. 'Ignore him.'" Madeline made a face with a visual check at Stephen.

He shook his head. "If she's ignoring him, he's not coming round to see her." Corina ignored him at first, but every time he saw her walking across the campus oval, her dark hair shining in the evening sun, his heart slipped a little bit further in love.

Then he managed a position behind her in the leadership course, and midsemester she finally spoke to him.

"Here's an interesting one." Madeline laughed, leaning toward the screen. "But I don't get it. From CorinaDelRey . . ." She looked puzzled. "Isn't she that American heiress?"

Stephen's heart yearned at the sound of her name. Corina? But surely not . . . Impossible. He left her in America. Surely someone was pulling a gag. He scanned the audience. Was she here?

"She tweets, 'Tell him American football rocks rugby.'" Hyacinth cackled, glancing back at him. "Now we know that's no way to win our Prince Stephen."

For the next few minutes, the hostesses read the tweets, making jocular comments, while Stephen's concentration faded toward the possibility of Corina being in the city.

No, surely she was catching the thread on Twitter. It would be 10:00 a.m. in Florida. She'd be at the start of her workday.

In the meantime, he kept smiling, nodding, laughing when appropriate.

"Here's my favorite. From DebShelton. Her tweet is all hashtags. '#fakeittilyoumakeit #pretendingtobeaprincess.'"

Hyacinth and Madeline continued reading tweets until the

amusement wore thin. Stephen downed a large glass of water, cooling his revving thoughts of Corina.

Madeline and Hyacinth returned to their chairs, going on about how fun it all was, gaining support from the audience, then challenged Stephen, rather boldly, to choose a winner.

"What do you think, Your Highness?" Hyacinth said. "I like LibbyWellborn. She seems like a sport."

"Deb Shelton stood out to me." Madeline gazed toward the board, watching the tweets roll through again.

They couldn't be serious. A blind date? To a royal movie premier?

"Wait, we have to share this one." Hyacinth spoke between rolling laughter. "From Tricia Gauss. 'Kiss a frog.'"

Laughter floated in the studio.

"Well, there's that . . ." Stephen said, doing a frog impression for the audience that earned him a round of applause.

"Here's another one . . . oh, it's quite different. From Agnes Rothery. 'Bird would be proud.'" Madeline tossed a look to Stephen. "Bird?"

The studio darkened as the light of merriment dimmed in Stephen eyes. Agnes. He'd not heard her name in many years. Bird had been one of his best mates. Before and during Afghanistan. Agnes was his girlfriend. When their tour ended, Bird planned to propose. But he didn't live to see her again.

Stephen tried to answer but lost control of his words, all the moisture evaporated from his mouth.

"Bird was his mate in Afghanistan." The answer came from the audience. Thomas. "He died in battle."

The reality of death punctured the show's atmosphere. Hyacinth ran her hand down Stephen's back as the audience rose to their feet with respectful applause.

"Can you tell us more about your tour in Afghanistan?" Madeline motioned for the stage manager to cut something. Probably the Twitter bit. "You've never talked about it."

"No, I can't. And I–I've a date, ladies, to the premier." The words came, weak, awkward, devoid of his princely charm.

He wanted to exit the set. Disappear. Oh that the floor would open up and make his way of escape.

Agnes? She'd tweeted in goodwill. But it did nothing but remind Stephen he'd failed her and Bird. Broken his promise. But he couldn't . . . couldn't go see her.

A subconscious account of what he owed these men ran through his soul daily. And he'd never have the means to repay them. So why see Agnes? Why see Carlos's sister? Worse, remain married to her, making love, creating a life and family together?

He comforted himself with the idea he'd instruct the King's Office to locate Agnes's address. It didn't mean he'd have to see her, but at least he'd know her whereabouts, make sure she didn't live in the city's impoverished east end. He could do that much.

Madeline was frowning at him. "Are you sure you can't take the winner as your date to the premier?"

"Quite. My date might not approve of my divided attention. My sincere apologies."

The hostess frowned and sighed. Next to her, Hyacinth quickly offered a *Madeline & Hyacinth Live!* show prize to the winner. "We're sorry it can't be a date with the prince to the premier, but—"

"How about tickets to the art auction? As my guest." Stephen had somewhat recovered and offered a safe alternative. He'd greet her then move on to his duties.

The audience applauded their approval. Hyacinth read Deb's responding tweet. "'Ahhhhhhhhhh blimey, yes!'"

"So Your Highness, who is your mystery date?" Madeline, without hesitation, barreled right into his inner sanctum. Meanwhile, the stage manager motioned sixty seconds to break.

"A *mystery*." Stephen put her off with his best grin. "You'll have to wait and see." He'd rope Mum into going with him. Her husband, Henry, wouldn't mind. Mum was a big fan of the cinema and Clive Boston.

Madeline turned to the camera. "We'll be right back with Prince Stephen. More on the premier of *King Stephen I* and his plans for rugby's biggest test, the fall Premiership."

The audience applauded and the lights went down. Stephen exhaled, expecting a break, but Madeline leaned into him.

"So, Corina Del Rey? You know her?"

"Some. Years ago."

"American heiress tweeting about how to catch a prince? Is she in the city?" Madeline gasped. "Is she your date?"

"Certainly not." *Steady, lad. Be a rock.*

"Then why did she tweet that American football is far superior to rugby?"

He reached for the cup of water offered him by a young woman wearing a headset. "Cheeky lass. You know how Americans can be. Tweet her back if you want to know." He'd done it now. Why would he say such a thing?

"Yes," Madeline said, sitting back, boring him with an intense gaze. "I believe I will."

She'd napped longer than she'd intended, waking up late in the afternoon when the sun had moved west, leaving her room in cozy shadows.

Pacing the room, shaking off sleep and jet lag, Corina washed up in that fantastic bathroom—she took pictures with the intent of remodeling her condo's ensuite bath—and let Adelaide in when she brought a bowl of steaming chicken, wild rice, and mushroom soup, and warm, buttery country bread.

The aroma awakened her inner growl. She was famished.

"Adelaide, this is amazing." *Slow down. Savor.* Corina dipped the edge of her bread into the soup. "But you don't have to bring me room service. Where do the other guests eat?" If there was a dining hall, like with a lot of Brighton rustic inns, most on the shore, she'd eat there.

"We've no dining hall. We will serve you in your room. 'Tis our privilege. We are servants."

"Do you serve all your guests in their room?"

She went to the door. "Rest. You've a long week ahead of you."

"Adelaide," Corina said, laughing softly. "Did you go through my things while I was napping? How do you know so much?"

"I keep telling you 'tis me job. I know why you came to Brighton."

"Oh? Why did I come?" Corina fished. What did the old woman know? Corina guessed her to be seventy-five. Eighty tops. Despite her smooth skin. She also had an unusual aura around her, like popping lights.

And Brill, he was a bear with a jelly heart, wasn't he? Kind, yet so . . . Corina searched for the word. Warrior-like. Was that it? As if he'd seen many battles. Though he bore no scars.

"You came to answer true love's call." Adelaide closed the door, and her gentle footsteps faded down the stairs.

Corina stared at the door. To answer true love's call. "Adelaide, how do you—"

Oh forget it. She'd only say, "It's me job."

True love's call. If only *he* would call. Corina supposed it was up to her to call him since the annulment rested with her. But for now the aroma of the soup beckoned her and she moved her tray to the bed and spied the TV remote.

In the corner, a flat screen powered up, shedding a bluish hue across the shadows. Spooning up her soup, Corina aimlessly surfed channels, stopping when she saw Madeline Stone from *Madeline & Hyacinth Live!*

She loved their show. They were just getting started when

Corina lived here. She took a break every afternoon to watch the show. Carlos was keen on Hyacinth, meeting her once at a party, but he didn't pursue her because he was deploying.

Dipping her bread into the soup—her taste buds were so happy—Corina was about to take a bite when Madeline announced the day's surprise guest, "Ladies and gentleman, Prince Stephen."

Corina choked on her bread, then burned her tongue with a gulp of hot tea.

Stephen. Her heart yearned. He looked . . . amazing. Tall, straight-backed, broad-shouldered, wearing a blue blazer and jeans. Not the baggy kind either. The kind that accented his muscled legs.

And his hair, so thick and wild, bouncing about his head, the free ends going their own way. Gelled or free, his hair made her want to bury her fingers in the dark strands.

Aiming the remote, she upped the volume, listening, laughing, furrowing at the tense look on his face when the hostesses mentioned the War Memorial.

Something bothered him about the war. Something about the event that sent him home surly and dark.

Now Madeline was introducing a Twitter game with the hashtag #howtocatchaprince.

On impulse, Corina scrambled for her phone, nearly toppling her dinner tray. She listened to them reading the tweets, laughing, shaking her head. These people had no idea.

She opened her Twitter app, hesitating. Should she? No, it was too risky. But something about being in this place made her want to break out, shine the light. Edge the tip of their secret into the light.

However, it might also tip off Madeline and Hyacinth. No one knew about their marriage. But that's because no one went looking. Their relationship had been whirlwind and private. The Military Ball had been the first time anyone had ever seen then in public together. And they made sure the media knew the prince and the heiress were nothing more than friends.

But if she tweeted, she'd tip him off. Why not? Let him know she was lurking about. At the very least, it might motivate him to contact her. Maybe deliver the news she demanded about her brother.

She inhaled, thinking. The tweets were rolling on the screen. Some of them were quite funny. What could she say that was both innocuous and telling? Sports. They were always debating the merits of American football versus rugby.

Their first kiss was after a debate on the rugby field. He was teaching her how to pitch the ball and she kept trying to pass like a Georgia Bulldog QB.

"Now you're just being obstinate." He swung her up in his arms.

"No, I'm trying to show you how to really get the ball down the field."

Their eyes met, and she slid down his body, her feet never touching the ground. He brushed one hand against her face, brushing back her hair, then lowered his lips toward hers.

Trembling so, she lost her hold on the rugby ball. It hit the ground with a thud.

"Are you going to kiss me?" Her heart churned in her chest, making her words wispy and barely audible.

"If you'd stop talking."

When his lips touched hers, time stopped, and she was lost in the heat of his passion and the power of his arms holding her. Then his hand slid down her back and rested on the curve of her hip. She drew him closer, letting go, telling him what words would not suffice.

I'm yours, Stephen Stratton. I'm yours.

Mercy . . . The memory stirred the dim and dull swaths of Corina's passions and her feelings for Stephen.

With a glance at the TV and a fortifying bite of Adelaide's heavenly soup, she decided to do it. Tweet. *"Tell him American football rocks rugby.*" Adding the hashtag #howtocatchaprince, she hit Send.

Sitting back, she waited, pleased with herself. She'd hidden in the shadows of secrets and death long enough.

THIRTEEN

*T*hat's the way, Leslie." Stephen skip-hopped around the Eagles' practice pitch with Leslie and a few of her teammates Saturday afternoon. Her Watham 2 Warriors team had won their test and advanced in the tournament. "Keep your legs moving."

He laughed, applauding her on, feeling the thrill of her run. She ran untouched across the try line, setting the ball on the ground, celebrating with her friends as they ran after her, bringing her down to the pitch and piling on.

After the Warriors' victory, Stephen joined their bench for a congratulations, creating quite a stir with their mums, and the lasses begged him to play.

"I can't, loves. My ankle. But how about some of my best tips for making a try?" They screamed—something boy rugby players never did—with hearty agreement. These girls were all courage.

The stadium crew brought round a cart and escorted Stephen with the girls to the practice field on the east side of the stadium.

In the glow of the lights and to the cheers of fans watching the next match, Stephen hobbled up and down the pitch with the girls, showing them a good side step and how to ruck out the ball.

Rugby was the best sport, and after thirty minutes with these girls, he was their fan. He'd speak to the King's Office and the Rugby Union about a campaign to strengthen girls' play. He'd be their patron and voice to the world.

Take that, Corina Del Rey. *You and your American football.* Can't suit up a girl in an American football kit.

Her tweet yesterday haunted him. Twisted about his chest all night. Where was she? Did she tweet from America? Did she fly to Brighton? If so, where was she? Did she bring the annulment papers? He was eager to have that part of his life signed, sealed, and boxed away.

He'd contemplated texting her, asking her if she'd tweeted on purpose. But he wanted time to think. He'd done nothing with her request for information on Carlos. There was nothing to do, really, except let her in on Brighton military classified information.

To be honest, he was grateful she'd not tweeted her request publicly.

Ask him for news on how my brother died. #howtocatchaprince

That would've had the defense minister ringing him.

Leslie ran across the field toward him, her friends trailing, and Stephen smiled, scooping her up with one arm. "I think you've got a future in the sport, Leslie."

She wrapped her arms about his neck, hugging him. "Thank you for coming to my game, Your Highness."

"My pleasure. I'm a rugby man, after all." Leslie's friends swirled around him, so he knelt down, careful of his ankle, and took down each of their names, promising to send them one of his special caps.

"I told you I was good, sir." No confidence lacking in Leslie of the Watham 2 Warriors.

"Be faithful in school and practice, be team players, and you'll all go far."

The girls' parents arrived, calling, "Time to get on." Stephen gave them high fives and watched them go, another twist in his chest.

He'd have liked to have had a family. Girls. Seven. And form a seven-side rugby team. Call themselves the Stratton Royals.

Thomas stood next to him. "A good bunch, eh?"

"A very good bunch."

"Are you thinking of Corina?"

How did he do that? Was Stephen so transparent? "No." Lie. "Just that . . . Well, it's of no matter. Ready?" He was hungry. And his ankle needed rest.

Stephen walked with Thomas to the car in silence, the summer afternoon full of the sun and wind, of shouts from the stadium, of victory and loss.

He was about to slide into the passenger seat when he heard her voice. "Stephen?" When he turned, Corina offered him a bold wave and a "Surprise!" shrug. He squinted through the light bouncing off the many windshields.

"Corina?"

"It's me." She took a step in his direction.

"How did you find me?" Stephen panned the sea of cars jamming the car park.

"I heard on the news you were here, so I caught a taxi. Then when I arrived, a man in blue coveralls told me you were at the practice field. I just started walking this way, and then"—she pointed toward the practice field—"you came walking out. Hi, Thomas."

"Afternoon, Corina." Thomas leaned on his door, smiling, shooting Stephen a look. One he preferred not to interpret.

"You caught a taxi from America?" Stephen said, trying to make merry, ease the tension between them. Well, the tension gripping his chest at least.

She pulled a face. "Very funny. I flew over yesterday. The

King's Office sent Gigi an invitation to the *King Stephen I* premier, and she felt I was the only one suitable to take her place."

"You flew all the way over for the premier?"

"And to interview Clive Boston."

"Clive?" The image of Corina sitting down with flirty, womanizing Clive sparked a green flame of jealousy. "I thought he avoided the press."

"Apparently he's agreed to an exclusive with the *Beaumont Post*. Shows how far he's fallen."

"Ha! More likely he heard you'd do the interview and he can't resist a beautiful face."

But did he blame Clive? Look at her, with those amber eyes and raven hair. She was stunning. And for the time being, his wife. Stephen fidgeted. This emotional trip was not one he should be taking. She was his wife on paper only and free to do what she wanted. "Congratulations on the interview."

"I'm half convinced he'll stand me up, but we'll see." She remained in the same spot, staring at him without wavering.

Stephen leaned against the car, arms folded, his left ankle propped on his right. "So it was you, wasn't it? The tweet?"

"I couldn't resist." Her smile faded. "But I see you were quick to deny me."

"No, I said you weren't my date. What did you expect? For me to reveal the full monty? 'Yes, Hyacinth, I know Corina *very* well.'" He arched his brow. "If you know what I mean."

"Har, har, but you could've said we were friends."

"To what end? It'd only put them onto us. Corina, we've annulment papers on the table. We can get through this with no scandal, no hounding paparazzi or media. With no disgrace to either one of us. Speaking of which, I think you should just go forward and sign them." There, that was rather princely, commanding. Getting the job done. Little Leslie had inspired him.

"Oh really?" She stepped closer, bringing her fragrances, her aura with her. "Well I think you should go forward and give me the details on Carlos that I want. So do you have any news?"

Stephen pushed away from the car, fired with frustration. "We cannot keep going round this mountain. You know what I know."

"Are you saying you know nothing? Because that's what I know."

"You keep beating this dead horse, love. There's nothing more to tell. He died a hero."

"I'll be here for about a week, in case you happen across anything more specific."

"I won't, but good to know." He folded his arms, staring at her, slapping bricks around his feeble, toppling heart.

"So, you really have a date for the premier?"

"Yes."

"No." This from Thomas. Traitor.

"Ah, I see." Corina adjusted the strap of her bag as well as her stance. "Thomas, are you free that evening?" she said. "I'm in need of an escort."

Stephen stiffened. What? She could not attend the premier with Thomas. They'd make a terrible couple.

"I'm honored, miss, but I'm the date of His Highness."

"So you don't have a date-date?" She leaned toward Stephen. "Just Thomas?"

"I've a date."

"Really?" This from Thomas again, who walked round the car to join Corina. "Who? Don't say your mum."

"Why not? She's a great patron of the cinema." He flipped his hand toward Corina, then leveled his gaze on her. "And a Clive Boston fan."

"Okay, Sir Blue Eyes," Corina said. "Don't get your knickers in a wad."

Sir Blue Eyes. The nickname slammed him like a defender and smacked his heart to the pitch, and he desired what he hadn't had in over five and a half years. Intimacy. Corina.

But with using the strength of every internal force, Stephen closed the cracking door of his inner soul. He could never be with her. A life of hiding the truth from the woman who had shared his bed crushed his sense of worth and reason. But if he told her, she'd never *want* a life with him. She'd hate him. And he'd deserve every negative emotion she could muster.

To him, there was no solution. There was only the canyon between them with no way across or around.

Distraction. He needed a distraction. Change the topic. "How did you say you found me again?"

She pointed to the southwest corner of the car park. "A man in blue work coveralls."

Stephen shot Thomas a visual query. "Does any of the crew wear blue? I thought all the uniforms were green."

"They are. I'll check into it." Thomas ducked into the car for his phone, dialing, walking off, leaving Stephen to face Corina alone.

Her yellow summer dress and pale orange clogs accented her olive-brown skin. She was lovely, and when the breeze laced a wisp of her dark hair across her eyes, he ached to touch her.

"You're here," he said from the depth of his soul, his voice low and intimate.

"I am." She didn't soften or step back. She held her ground with confidence. "Last time I was here at the stadium, you told me we were over. Why did Afghanistan mess you up so much, Stephen? Or was it me? Did you realize something you couldn't love about me?"

No, no. She was entirely lovable. "I was rather jacked up after Afghanistan. It wasn't you."

"Isn't that what they always say? 'It's not you, it's me.' Which is generally never true. It's always the *you* in that scenario."

"They? Who is they?"

"You know, they? People."

He patted his chest, laughing low. "Well not this people. Look, it was and is all about my last days in Torkham. Nothing to do with you." Well, not in the manner of finding her unlovely or undesirable.

Until his ankle injury and Nathaniel bringing round that silly marriage certificate, Stephen knew who he was and where he was going. Now his world felt inside out and upside down. Nothing made sense. He craved things he'd checked off on his life's list.

"Your flight? It went well?" He found casual conversation less painful.

"Yes, the new first-class seats are marvelous. Still, they couldn't prevent the man sitting behind me, with the worst breath, from leaning around and breathing on me."

"He was hitting on you." Lucky bloke.

"No, I think he—"

"Please, Corina, darling, have you looked in a mirror lately?"

"Yes, and I see the same face I've always seen. I see Carlos's eyes. We looked nothing alike of course except we had the same eyes." She exhaled, folding her arms. "I want him back, you know." She raised her gaze to his. "But he's not coming back. I miss him."

"I—I know you do." Because Stephen missed him too. Along with Bird and the rest of the lads who died that day. "Corina, I'll see what I can do."

"That's all I ask." She smiled, and it was worth the price of his promise. He'd talk to Nathaniel. See what tidbit the Defense Ministry would allow him to tell.

"You're at The Wellington then?"

"No, they lost my reservation."

"Did you demand a room anyway? You are Corina Del Rey."

"Ha, very funny. And yes, I actually tried that, but the clerk said they were all booked this weekend."

"Then where are you?"

"At this little inn. The Manor. Tucked in between Gliden and Martings."

"The Manor?"

"I'd never heard of it."

"At Market and Crescent?" Stephen stepped toward her, a blip of concern for her safety.

"Please tell me you've heard of it. The proprietors are sweet and kind but very odd. I wanted to hightail out of there in the worst way, but I don't know, I felt safe. Peaceful."

"Corina, there's nothing between Gliden and Martings. The Manor, at least the one I'm thinking of, was torn down centuries ago."

"Well, maybe this is a different Manor."

"Granted, I don't know every inn and hostel in the city, but I know that intersection well. Some of the boys and I used to play rugby Sunday afternoons in Maritime Park. Across the avenue. They barely squeezed an alley between Gliden and Martings, let alone an inn."

"Well, not today. I'm telling you, that's where I'm staying."

He didn't like this. Not one bit. "Corina, I'm going to have Thomas check this out. Something is amiss."

"Stephen, it's fine." She moved from her spot, closer to the car. "As odd as it seems."

From her bag, her phone rang. "Excuse me." Corina pulled her gaze away from his. "Hello?" She turned her back to Stephen.

He waited, watching, swimming through the cold waters of his soul. This was his chance. Persuade her to sign the annulment documents. Charm her. Be kind to her. Give her some detail about Carlos. Once she signed the papers, he'd be free. By fall he'd be back on the pitch. Life would return to a normal routine.

She hung up and spun round. "That was your brother."

"Nathaniel?" Stephen frowned. "What did he want?"

"To invite me to dinner tomorrow night. He's sending a car for me."

"Dinner?" *Nathaniel, you clod.* Inviting Corina to family dinner. As if she were his brother's . . . wife. "How did he know you were in the city?"

"Your sister-in-law saw my tweet on the *Madeline & Hyacinth Live!* show. She called my office."

"That Susanna, clever girl."

"I accepted the invitation."

"You do so at your own risk. You do realize Mum never held hope for me marrying. She might fall at your feet or something." Where was he going with this? Mum would fall at his feet once she met Corina properly and beg him to tear up the annulment papers. But Mum only knew snippets of the events in Afghanistan. That her son was wounded in a blast and men died. She didn't know Corina's brother had been one of them.

Stephen slapped another layer of bricks around his heart. He needed to close this open wound in his life and do whatever it took to get Corina to sign the annulment without intel on Carlos. To that end, he'd endure whatever came his way.

"I take it your family knows? Otherwise, Susanna wouldn't have paid attention to my tweet."

Stephen nodded. "They know." Nathaniel brought the whole mess to Mum when Stephen was in Florida. Then when Stephen returned home, she popped by to say her piece.

"I'd like to have been at your wedding."

"Mum, if I'd have told you there would've been no wedding."

"I'd have kept it a secret."

"And broken Brighton law? Sorry, Mum, it's not in you."

Thomas returned to the car, tucking away his phone. "No crew in blue coveralls. We think it was a parent or someone at the tournament."

"Who just happened to know where I was when Corina came

asking?" Stephen squinted into the sun. Something seemed odd about the scenario. "And wearing coveralls?"

"Half the stadium saw you ride off on the cart with the girls. I'd say there's a good chance. Anyway, I'm satisfied."

"Then how about this?" Stephen said. "Have you heard of the Manor? A small inn on Market and Crescent?"

He shook his head. "Not to my knowledge, but my specialty is security, not Cathedral City's hospitality."

"The proprietor said it was built by King Stephen I," Corina said. "The place is quaint, rustic. Trust me, I was as surprised as you. I spent a lot of my days here shopping Market Avenue and never saw anything like it between those giant stores."

Stephen paced, his senses buzzing. "Corina, someone is spoofing you. King Stephen's Manor was torn down." It made no sense. Wait a minute. He snapped his fingers. "It's a movie prop. Sure." He smiled at his clever solution.

"Then why am I in it? As far as I can tell, I'm the only guest. Besides, I already went there and—" She shook her head. "Adelaide and Brill are too genuine to be acting."

"The director, Jeremiah Gonda, is known for staging a scene from one of his movies in the premier city. I bet the proprietors are actors, Corina. And the inn just a set."

"If it's just a set, the director went all out. The place looks like it's four hundred years old, yet my room is twenty-first century with a flat screen, Internet, sunken tub, granite bathroom tiles."

"In King Stephen's day, this city was Blarestoney and its main commerce was on Market and Crescent. Most of the trade was from shipping and farming. Later King Stephen would discover the richness of the mountain mines. Anyway, the film was shot on the north side of the island, where they built a replica city. It'd be just like Gonda to put a piece of it in Cathedral City for a premier publicity stunt."

"And he picked me? Outside The Wellington? Sent some

strange woman in a white coat—yes, coat—to ask me if I needed a place to stay?"

Stephen laughed. "It's the perfect stunt. A beautiful woman, looking a bit tired and frayed, standing outside the city's most luxurious hotel. Sure, this is all part of the premier. He probably recognized you."

Corina visibly exhaled, her smile spreading wide. "You know, the more you talk, the more it makes sense. Why didn't I think of that? Daddy will have a laugh when I tell him. Mr. Gonda created a great setup. I slept like a baby last night, and the proprietors are a dream. The food, fantastic."

"Thomas? Can you check this out? See if Gonda registered the fake Manor with the city?" Stephen motioned to the car. "Corina, can we give you a lift to this mysterious Manor?"

She shook her head. "Thank you, no. I want to do some shopping."

"Then I guess I'll see you at dinner tomorrow night."

"Then I guess you will."

Stephen bristled as he dropped into the passenger seat, sensing he was in some sort of standoff or competition. What was she up to?

In the car, Thomas steered out of the car park. "You're being very gracious to her."

"She *is* my wife."

"So are you changing your mind?"

"No." It was starting to physically pain him to reject her. "But Nathaniel suggested I charm her to get the annulment documents signed, and since he so boldly invited her to the family dinner on Sunday, I might as well be a prince and win her signature."

"What if she's still in love with you?"

Stephen powered his window down, the wind clearing his head. "She's not. My only intention is to get her to see reason and sign the papers. Certainly I can achieve that without anyone being, or falling, in love."

Take note, chap. Take note.

Thomas headed east toward the palace, passing the stadium and the main gate. Stephen watched out the window, and there on the corner stood a round man in blue coveralls, waving. and smiling.

FOURTEEN

*I*t was Sunday evening, and the family waited in Nathaniel and Susanna's palace apartment for their guest.

Stephen paced in front of the cold fireplace, his skin warm and brown from spending the day at the stadium, watching the youth rugby tournament. Leslie's side failed today's test, but they'd given their all. He was proud of them.

The tournament kept him distracted from his ankle, from this evening's dinner with Corina as guest. The more he thought about it the more he wondered at her game.

She announced her invitation to dinner, and her acceptance, with boldness. As if throwing down the gauntlet. He knew her. She'd not stop until she got what she wanted.

"Stephen," Mum said, patting the couch cushion. "Sit. This pacing cannot be good for your ankle."

"I'm fine, Mum." Nevertheless, Stephen dropped into the wingback chair adjacent to his mother and Henry, whom Mum married a year after Dad died. They'd been university sweethearts until Grandfather, Mum's dad, decided he wanted a crown prince for his daughter.

Susanna entered, her blond hair flowing over her shoulder in wide curls. She wore jeans and a fitted blouse. "Corina is on her

158

way. The chauffeur rang up twice to say he could not find any building between Gliden and Martings. Just an alley. So I had Corina wait for the driver on the corner." She popped Stephen on the arm. "She seems really cool, dude."

"What do you expect? I do have standards."

Susanna perched on the arm of his chair. "I Googled her. She's gorgeous. Mum, have you ever met her?"

"No, but I'm looking forward to it." Mum gave Stephen the stink eye. The one she gave him when he was a boy and up to his short trousers in trouble.

"So, an heiress, a former Miss Georgia." Susanna leaned down to Stephen. "I've got to give you props for picking a Georgia girl."

Nathaniel entered on the tail end of the comment and chimed in. "Like brother, like brother. The Stratton men have good taste in women." He kissed Susanna and popped Stephen on the knee. "Be nice to Corina, please."

"I resent all of you. Treating me like a delinquent, an errant child."

"Then don't act like one, Stephen," Mum said. "You did marry this girl, then sent her away without a word to us. I can't quite understand it."

Stephen crossed gazes with his brother. Mum did not have the full intel. "Sorry, Mum, I just did what I thought best."

Henry folded up the paper he was reading and passed it to Stephen. "Says you're in the walking boot for another two weeks. Is that true?"

Stephen bent forward, tapping the contraption that was helping him heal. "More like six weeks."

"That long, son?"

"Sadly."

"They're attributing the Eagles' loss to Italy on Sunday to your absence. We need our best winger come the Premiership."

"Grady Hamstead's a fine winger, Henry." It pained Stephen

to admit it, but true was true. "He's faster than me in the clutch. They lost because they didn't manage the scrum."

Nathaniel's butler, Malcolm, entered. "Miss Corina Del Rey has arrived."

"She's here." Susanna jumped up, scurrying around the furniture to stand with Nathaniel by the living room door.

Henry and Mum stood, facing the doorway. Stephen positioned himself halfway between Mum and Henry, Nathaniel and Susanna.

For a moment, he resented her saying yes. Why couldn't she leave well enough alone? What was she hoping to accomplish by coming here?

He adjusted his shirt collar, squaring his scarlet-and-grey striped pullover on his shoulders. Sunday night dinners were country casual since Susanna took over the hosting. Jeans, a top, something she referred to as "deck shoes," were the standards.

Nathaniel and Stephen took to it right away. As did Henry. He'd been prime minister for years, but never a royal. Never caught up in staunch traditions.

Mum, however, found the change a challenge. Stephen glanced at her, giving her a smile. She was dressed in royal "casual." A skirt and blouse. Stephen was certain Mum didn't even own a pair of jeans.

He was proud of her, though, submitting to Susanna's changes, allowing her to be the king's wife, creating her own culture in the palace.

"She's given up so much," Mum told Stephen one evening. "Her country, her customs, her citizenship. I can give up Sunday night traditions. Learn to be casual."

And that was why Brighton loved their Queen Campbell.

Suddenly Corina was at the door, dressed in an elegant gold gown, clinging to her in precisely the right manner, and Stephen's thoughts on Mum fell off.

She'd pinned her hair in some sort of updo with soft curls lying on her neck, and Stephen swallowed as memories of the nights he lay with her, holding her, the ends of her hair brushing against him, filled every crevice of his being.

Their eyes met and she smiled. "I'm afraid I'm overdressed." She leaned toward Susanna. "I always thought Sunday night dinners were formal."

She moved into the room with classic confidence, curtsying to Nathaniel, then Mum, and all the scattered reasons why Stephen loved her came flying together.

"Corina," Susanna came round to her. "I'm so sorry. I didn't even think to tell you about the current dress code." The king's princess made a face. "I went Georgia-casual for family dinner night."

"It's quite all right." Corina smoothed her hand over her skirt. "My misunderstanding gave me an excuse to buy a new dress."

Mum caught Stephen's attention. *I like her.*

As he knew she would. Stephen stepped around to her. "Good to see you." He lightly kissed her cheek, and her fragrance pounded his heart. "I suppose I should formally introduce you." Though she'd already owned the room, conquering any and all awkwardness.

"This is my mum, Queen Campbell, and her husband, Sir Henry."

"How do you do?" Corina shook their hands and curtsyed again to Mum.

"My brother, King Nathaniel, and his wife, Princess Susanna."

"Your Majesties." Again, she curtsyed.

"Please, call us Nathaniel and Susanna," Susanna said. "I'm still working on the HRH part of my name." Then she tossed aside all protocol and snatched Corina in a "good ole girl" hug. "Another Georgia girl. I love it." When she released Corina, Susanna brushed her fingers under her own eyes. Nathaniel slipped his arm about her and kissed the top of her head. Stephen's green spark of jealousy flared. True love was the only thing he envied his king-brother. "I guess I'm a little homesick."

"I understand." Corina touched Susanna's arm in Georgia-girl solidarity. *In princess solidarity.* "My first semester in postgrad here was horrible. I was so homesick. Even with my twin brother here." The timbre in Corina's voice layered peace into the room. Into Stephen. "I couldn't wait for Christmas break." She laughed softly. "Then when it arrived I begged Daddy and Mama to fly over here for Christmas. Cathedral City is so magical that time of year."

"My first trip here was right after Christmas and I fell in love." Susanna had found a like heart in Corina. Stephen watched it unfold on her face.

Careful, Susanna love, she's not staying.

"I'm working on Nathaniel . . . talking him into a trip to Georgia next month."

"I'm having my staff clear my diary," Nathaniel said. "Corina, thank you for coming."

"Thank you for inviting me."

"And since we all know this business between Corina and Stephen, let's just get it out there, shall we?"

What? He was going to ring his brother's neck.

"Nathaniel." Stephen stepped toward his brother. "I don't think there's any need . . ."

"It's okay," Corina raised her hand. "Might as well deal with the elephant in the room. We're married. This may be my first and last dinner with the family."

Steam. Coming out of his ears. What sort of rotten game was she playing? *First and last dinner with the family.* Trying to gain their sympathies? Make him come off as an ogre, never bringing her round to the family. As of this moment, he no longer believed her humble, innocent, what-happened-to-my-brother routine. She was out for vengeance.

"I was starting to think my youngest would never find the right girl." Mum gave Stephen a teasing glance. "Seems he outfoxed us all. Save for this annulment business. Stephen I don't understand."

Yes, here it comes. He turned to Susanna. "Is dinner ready?"

"Malcolm will ring when it's ready." She gave him a look. *Behave.*

"I would like to say I'm sorry if all this marriage mess caused any of the family pain or embarrassment." Corina cradled the small clutch she carried to her chest and peered at Stephen. "I know we broke the law of the day, but it just seemed ... right."

Oh, she was good. Very good.

"It's quite all right, Corina," Nathaniel said. "All is forgiven."

"Except why are you two splitting apart?"

"Campbell, dear, that's not the elephant in the room, it's a whole herd of elephants." Henry smiled at his wife. "Let the children figure it out for themselves."

"I suppose you're right." But Mum gave Stephen the stink eye again and he knew he'd hear a good bit more before the week was out.

"Shall we address the other elephant in the room?" Susanna stepped forward, slipping her hands in her hip pockets. "It seems some of us are underdressed." She did a visual with Mum and Nathaniel. "Shall we change?"

"Please, don't change on my account," Corina said, but Susanna was already halfway out of the room, with Mum on her heels, cheering her on.

"Splendid idea." Mum turned back to Corina. "Begging your pardon, we shall return."

"I'll tell Malcolm to hold dinner fifteen minutes," Nathaniel said. "Does that give everyone enough time?"

"Plenty," Mum said. "Henry, are you coming?"

"Right behind you, love."

But Stephen remained planted. "If it's all the same to you, I'll wear what I have on."

Corina stepped toward him. "I had no idea it was casual night, so don't look at me like I one-upped you or something."

"You could've asked."

"You could've told me."

"What was with that business of your first and last time to have dinner with the family?"

She scoffed, shaking her head. "You're a piece of work. Nothing. Just a fact. Do you think I'll ever be back here once our marriage is . . . over?" She lost a bit of her bravado, her voice breaking.

"Susanna likes you well enough." He sighed, easing up on his suspicions and grinning at her. "Five minutes in the royal household, and you've turned us upside down."

"Well, I *am* a Del Rey."

Despite himself, he laughed. "For what it's worth, you look beautiful."

"I had fun shopping yesterday, visiting my favorite stores."

"Susanna said the driver couldn't find the inn."

"He couldn't. I had to walk out to the corner to meet him. There he was, waiting, squinting at the stores like nobody's business, shaking his head. He jumped when I said hello."

"I'll have to check it out. Come by this mysterious place."

She nodded, looking at him, then past him. "It's a free country."

"That it is." Stephen glanced down at his attire. He should ease up, change, be a sport. "Tell you what, I'll run to my apartment for my dinner clothes. I'm on the north side of the palace. I won't be long. Tell Susanna to start without me."

He dashed out, easy on his ankle, and slipped into the utility cart he used to cross the palace grounds, a little bit of a song, a little bit of a melody, skipping across his heart.

FIFTEEN

ere we are, miss." Malcolm, the butler, passed Corina a red-and-white china cup and saucer, golden-brown tea brimming against a gold rim. "This china set was designed specifically for Her Majesty, Princess Susanna."

"It's beautiful. Thank you." Corina perched on the edge of the couch. "May I ask, whose portrait is that over the fireplace?"

"Queen Anne-Marie as a young woman. She was a most beloved monarch."

"I remember her from history. She stood for women's right to vote in the mid-1800s."

"An original suffragette." Malcolm stood straight-backed beside the tea cart with his hands behind his back, gazing at the portrait. "The artist did her justice."

Corina sipped her tea. She was used to opulent mansions and ornate rooms with damask curtains, but this was a royal room. Beautiful with textured walls, high, arching windows, and polished wood.

Yet the stack of newspapers on the floor by a reading chair, the iPad tucked into a chair cushion, and the wide-screen TV above the fireplace told the story of real people. Of a family. Of a home.

"I hear you studied at Knoxton?" Malcolm said.

"Graduate courses. My twin brother was a part of the Joint International Coalition headed by Brighton's Royal Air Command. When he came to train, I came along to keep him company. He and Stephen—Prince Stephen—were friends."

Malcolm headed toward the door as voices resounded beyond the living room doors. Corina stood when Nathaniel and Susanna entered first, arm-in-arm, looking very regal. He in a dark, very fine tuxedo. She in a deep-red evening gown.

"How do we look?" Susanna spun around.

"Now I'm underdressed," Corina said. "You look fabulous. Susanna, is that a Melinda House gown?"

"Very good."

Corina motioned to her own dress. "Saw this in their shop window in the fashion district yesterday. Could not resist."

"She is really a genius. Melinda made Princess Regina of Hessenberg an icon overnight by just adapting her north Florida, cowboy-boots style."

"I've not followed her, but I'll have to do so." The news of Princess Regina, a Florida girl, discovering she was the long-lost heir to the Grand Duchy of Hessenberg's royal house came just as Corina determined to come out from under the fog.

"You should. She's wonderful." Susanna linked her arm with Corina's and leaned close. "She's one of us."

Corina laughed, warmed by the princess's camaraderie. "Then I'll read up on her right away."

"I'm sure I can arrange an introduction."

"Ahem, and what of me?" The king cleared his throat, pretending to straighten his tie.

"Most handsome, Your Majesty," Corina said.

Susanna walked over to her husband. "Babe, you look as handsome as ever."

The Queen Mum and her husband entered next, dressed in a black off-the-shoulder gown and a tuxedo.

"I think we should do this every now and then," the queen said, taking an appetizer from the tray Malcolm had begun circling around the room. "Either that or my husband needs to take me out to the symphony more often."

"Love, say the word . . ."

Corina had only observed the former prime minister for a few moments, but he was ardently in love with his wife. How lovely to find heart-palpitating romance a second time around.

Upon that thought, Stephen entered, resplendent in his black tuxedo, his white shirt giving a kind of light to the lean planes of his face. His strength and presence consumed the atmosphere. And he knocked the breath right out of Corina. She felt weak-kneed with love butterflies flitting through her belly.

He'd tamed his dark, thick hair, styling back the sides but leaving a saucy coil of bangs drooping over his high, smooth forehead.

Steady. Loving well doesn't mean falling back in love.

But had she ever fallen out of love? Corina set down her cup and saucer on the nearest table, hands trembling, looking over at Stephen to see if he was watching her, but instead seeing him moving toward her, filling the air with a clean, woodsy scent.

"You clean up rather nice," she said with a long inhale.

"Dinner is served." Malcolm opened the dining room doors.

Nathaniel offered his arm to Susanna. "Might as well go all out, then," he said, winking at his wife.

The queen took Henry's arm, leaving Stephen and Corina to follow.

He offered his arm, held her chair, then sat next to her.

As the salad was served, the conversation was of the Brighton summer, the art festival, and the theatre openings.

Of course, of rugby and the junior tournament going on at Cathedral City Stadium.

Then of the event of the summer, the premier of *King Stephen I*.

"The movie is being compared to *Braveheart*," Henry said.

"I'm looking forward to it." Corina sipped her water.

"Corina, Stephen said you're doing an interview with Clive Boston." The queen seemed delighted.

"That's the plan. I texted him yesterday and we're to meet at the premier, then get together the following day. But Clive is known to change his mind."

"Tell him Queen Campbell is looking forward to reading your piece."

Corina accepted the queen's warmth and friendship. "Thank you. That should give me some proper ammunition."

A footman cleared their salad plates and refilled the water goblets.

"Stephen," Susanna said, "you know if you don't show up at the premier with a date, Madeline and Hyacinth are going to have a field day with you."

"Let them do their worst."

"Corina," the queen said, reaching for her water, poised and elegant, "are you attending the premier with anyone?"

"Well, no—"

"Stephen," Campbell lowered her voice and leaned toward her son, eyeing the footman entering across the room with their main course, fried chicken and mashed potatoes. "Take your *wife* to the premier."

"Mum, I thought you'd be my date." Stephen flicked his hand at Corina. "She came to work."

"Won't it cause a stir if we show up together?" Corina said.

"Yes, thank you." Stephen huffed, popping his hand on the table. "She's right."

"In your own words, Stephen, let them do their worst." Campbell turned to the king. "Nathaniel, what do you think?"

"Mum, it doesn't matter what he thinks." Stephen pushed away from the table. "Corina and I are in the middle of an annulment." He glanced her way but kept his eyes above her head. "If I attend a premier with her on my arm, we will be a media spectacle. Every paper and blogger will have their say. We don't need anyone mucking up our past."

Corina's appetite faded as Stephen's tirade heated up.

"They could find out we were married."

"You are married," Nathaniel said, and Corina felt as if she were in the middle of a family fight. A family to which she did not belong. She wanted to escape to the comfort of the Manor.

"But all she has to do is sign the papers and then we are not. If word gets out we *are* married, the annulment will become a big hairy deal. What's the use in that? Nathaniel, you above all know what's at stake here—"

"See, there you go. Hinting of something more. Just what is at stake here, Stephen?" Corina tucked her folded napkin beside her plate and pushed away from the table.

"Corina, I don't think Stephen is implying any hidden motives." Campbell also rose from her chair.

"I disagree. Begging your pardon. But he's not telling me something. And until he does, his wagon is hitched to mine. I'd love to go to the premier with you. What time shall I expect you to pick me up?" Push. Shove. She'd get the truth from him one way or the other.

"Corina, Mum's right. There's nothing more going on."

"You said to your brother, 'You above all know what's at stake here.' I demand to know what that means." Her voice speared the room with tension, toppling the once peaceful dinner. Corina regretted her outburst, but there was nothing to do about it now. She blamed Stephen. He did this to her. Confused her. Made her crazy. Rewired her heart. Trembling, she turned to the princess. "I'm sorry. I've been rude. My mother would be humiliated. Susanna, thank you for dinner." She placed her napkin under her plate and turned for the door.

"Corina," Susanna said. "You don't have to go."

"Oh, but I do." Before she either freaked out, or . . . or . . . or crumbled into a weeping ball. She struggled, embarrassed, searching for the exit.

But the entry door was shut, blending into the carved walls. Corina whirled around until she spied a doorknob, and skirted toward it.

"Corina, wait." Stephen came after her, his hand grabbing her arm.

She broke away, charged into the living room, retrieved her clutch, and started for the foyer. "Stephen, I'm sorry. I shouldn't have come here tonight. You and I, we're like a ticking bomb. I don't get you. You don't get me. Shoot, I don't get me half the time." The love well message confused her, tripped her up. Why did God send a word but not understanding? She felt foolish and weak.

"Do *you* think we should go out in public together?"

"No." She sighed. "I don't know." She fumbled with the clasp of her clutch. "Don't you ever get tired of hiding? Living in the dark?"

He didn't answer, but the twist in his expression told her yes.

"You don't have to take me to the premier." She started for the door, hot, frustrated, not even thinking that her first and last night with Brighton's royal family ended in a fight. She was more Georgia redneck than southern belle at the moment.

"Corina—" Stephen blocked her passage with a swift sidestep.

"Not bad for a man with his foot in a boot."

"It's not my first go." He loosened his tie. "Let me drive you home."

"I'll take a cab."

He laughed. "There's not a cab stand outside the palace."

"Then I'll walk to one."

"You don't have to be so stubborn."

"Neither do you."

"Fair enough. What game are you playing?"

"Game? Please. I don't need to play games."

"Then why are you here?"

"For the premier."

"And?"

"The interview."

"I'm not buying it. Just like you don't buy there's not anything 'more at stake.'"

She stopped. "So there is something more." Her gaze landed on his, and the air between them was palatable. His cologne fragranced every part of her.

He started to answer, then withdrew his words and changed his expression. "No, no, there's nothing more."

"Then there's nothing more to why I'm here. Just a routine assignment from Gigi." To say she believed she had a divine call to try for their marriage seemed overwhelming to her. How would it sound to him? "And, the trip gave me an advantage to urge you along in finding out about Carlos."

"Then I have a condition of my own."

"Signing the annulment isn't enough?"

"Why *not* attend the premier with me? Like you said. Come a bit out of the shadows. Shock the world."

"What? Stephen, that's the exact opposite of wanting me to sign the annulment." She shook her head. "Besides, you told Madeline and Hyacinth I was not your date. Do you really want them digging into us?"

"What will they find? Nothing. No news stories, not even a photograph. The marriage certificate is in Nathaniel's safe hands. Other than the old and new archbishops and Thomas, who knows? Let's pull one on Madeline and Hyacinth. It should be good fun." His smile urged her yes further to the surface.

"I don't want my parents finding out in the press."

"They won't. Promise." Stephen tipped his head toward the

dining hall. "The chef made fried chicken for you tonight. His recipe is one of the best."

Corina glanced toward the dining hall. "No, I can't." She was too embarrassed. "Give them my apologies again. I'll send flowers tomorrow."

"Let me get the chauffeur to drive you home. I'll ride along, check out this mysterious Manor."

Corina exhaled, giving him a weak smile. "We never saw any of this coming, did we? That night we took the ferry to Hessenberg."

"I know I didn't see a lot of things coming."

"You know what I regret the most?" She walked through the foyer toward the front door. "You never gave us a chance. Never trusted our love."

These blips of honesty surprised her, freed her. She could see the impact had a reverse effect on Stephen.

The expression on his beautiful face hardened, and the tenderness in his gaze faded.

"Come," he said, ducking past her and hobbling down the portico steps. "I'll ring for the chauffeur."

SIXTEEN

*M*onday morning Stephen knelt on the edge of the pitch, removed his walking boot, and tied on his left trainer, the tip of his surgery scar peeking above his sock.

"Can I say again I'm not for this?" Darren, his physiotherapist, stood next to him, arms folded.

"You're free to leave, if you wish." Stephen stretched his legs, his ankles, going gingerly on his left one, then set his gaze down the length of the field.

"What? And be responsible for Brighton's prince and star winger permanently injured? My career will be toast."

"Then help me and stop protesting." Stephen bounced lightly, testing his ankle strength.

"Let me protest one more time. Your ankle is still weak. You've no side-to-side strength."

"Today's test is not about sidestepping a defender, just a light walk up and down the field."

"You can test it in the physio room."

"But I want to be out here." Because he needed to be in touch with some part of himself. Before the injury. Before the annulment papers. Before Corina arrived. Before her brutal honesty last night.

"You never gave us a chance. Never trusted our love."

He inched ever closer to blurting out the whole truth. Forget national and royal security. If she knew, she'd say more than "You never gave us a chance." She'd be the one walking away and never looking back.

Stephen had played out the scenario from all sides so many times it didn't matter what anyone said. If he told Corina her brother died saving his life, she'd despise him.

She was right. He didn't trust in their newlywed love. Not over her love for her brother.

"I just need to know my ankle is healing." Stephen started down the field, the fragrance of the earth rising with each step.

"We've X-rays, MRI's, and your physio sessions to tell us how you're healing. It's not as fast as we'd like. Remember, you've sprained this ankle four times."

How could he forget? Stephen had a vivid memory of each one. The first during a crucial university test. The second in the blast. Shot him out the back of the mess tent with Bird Mitchell landing on him as a human shield, protecting him from shrapnel and debris. His leg and ankle were wrenched sideways, trapped under their weight.

The third was his first year with the Eagles. During the Premiership when he found himself on the bottom of a ruck.

Then he took care with his ankle, training faithfully, taping up before each test, watching his steps on the field.

Then last March he went down again. Freakish, really. He'd played the move over in his mind, watched team film, and nothing looked or felt out of the ordinary.

Stephen made his way down the field, trying not to wince. Darren walked alongside. "If you're not careful, you'll set yourself back."

"But if I don't challenge myself, I'll miss the fall season."

Corina spoke right about one thing last evening. Stephen was tired of being careful. With his life. With his heart.

"You're limping," Darren said.

"Of course. I've been in the boot so long I don't remember how to walk straight."

"Straight I'm not worried about. It's that you can't put down your weight." Darren's entire aura prepped for a hearty "I told you so."

Stephen pressed on, walking the hundred meters to the try line, then back again.

"Steady on," Darren said when Stephen turned round to walk it again, picking up his pace, adjusting his gait and his weight, putting more and more pressure on his healing foot.

He was feeling good. In his right state of mind.

"I might forgo the walking boot for tonight's premier. Wear a real shoe."

"Then I'm taping your ankle before we leave the training room."

Stephen laughed and attempted a soft side step, popping Darren on the arm. The physio shook his head, grinning. "You're overestimating yourself, Stephen."

"Ha-ha. I'm merely revving up." The wind cruised over the field as the edge of sunlight peeked over the top of the stadium. Stephen broke into a small jog.

"Stephen, please—" Darren ran round in front of him. "If you want to stretch your mobility, let's go to the physio room."

"One minute." Stephen visualized each step, placing his foot squarely on the ground, breathing steady, willing away twinges and pain.

He added a bit of speed, landing solid on each foot, right, left, right... His left ankle gave way, dropping Stephen to the ground. He rolled with pain, moaning from his core.

"How bad is the pain?" Darren anchored his shoulder under

Stephen's and hoisted him up so he balanced on his good foot. "Let's get to the physio room."

"Don't say it."

"That I told you?"

"There, you said it anyway." So the sum of Stephen's fears was realized. He was not healing quickly enough, and at thirty-one, injury could sound the death toll for an athlete. If he didn't heal soon, his career would be overrun by a younger, more agile and athletic, healthy Number 14. And he'd be left with his haunting nightmares and a secret annulment.

"Off we go to an ice bath and a tight wrap. And let this be the last of such training sessions."

He was losing. On all sides. His career, his health, his purpose. Even his so-called marriage. If Stephen gave any consideration to the divine, such as an all-knowing, all-seeing God, he might bow a knee and ask for guidance.

But he'd seen God's answer to pleas for mercy that evening in Torkham, when his mates lay moaning in their own pool of blood. Then each one, to the man, died.

He didn't understand that God. Where was the God of love and goodness? And if he truly existed, how could Stephen expect *that* God give him any more than he had?

His very life and breath.

In the warm ambient lights of her room, ribbons of twilight floating past her window, Corina readied for the premier, wearing a second gown she'd purchased in the fashion district from the Melinda House shop.

The Versace from home remained in the wardrobe. She was starting over. Starting new.

The coral sheath gown flared at her knees into a small train.

The beaded bodice was designed with a scalloped neckline and off-the-shoulder sleeves.

A final check in the mirror and Corina was satisfied. Delighted, really. She felt internally quiet yet excited. Beautiful. Exactly how an elegant gown should make a girl feel.

The saleswoman had gasped when Corina walked into the showroom wearing the gown and stepped up on the pedestal. The recessed lighting cascaded over her, igniting the gold beads and white sequins embedded in the dress.

"It's even more stunning than we imagined," the woman had said, her hand at the base of her throat. "It seems as if it was made for you."

Made for you . . . Words she'd pledged to Stephen on their wedding night. *I was made for you. I know it.*

A flurry of jitters batted around her ribs. He'd be here soon. Stephen texted confirmation this morning that he'd arrive to pick her up at seven o'clock.

"Corina?" Adelaide's voice came through the door along with a gentle knock. "Be you needing some help?"

Corina answered the door, warmed by the sight of the petite proprietress. "Come in."

"My, my, don't you look beautiful. Absolutely glowing." She wagged her finger at Corina. "Such a force, true love."

"What do you see, Adelaide?" Corina returned to the floor mirror to finish pinning up her hair. She learned a lot of hairdo tricks during her brief stint with beauty pageants. "You seem to know more than you've been told."

"Here, let me help you, sweet one." Adelaide brought a chair over for Corina to sit, then took the pins from her. The woman's tender touch soothed Corina's battered emotions. Her exchange with Stephen last night remained with her all day, and she waged one-sided arguments with him. She nearly told him to forget their date when he texted to confirm, but relented.

How could she quit on this "love well" journey so easily? Patience might be required.

"Everything will be all right," Adelaide said, sweeping up Corina's hair.

Corina peered at Adelaide through the mirror. She'd broken down this afternoon and confided in Adelaide about her date with the prince. She had to tell someone. Bearing all of this alone burdened her. Stephen had Thomas. And his family. She had no one.

You know so much, Adelaide. And I know so little about you."

"I told you, I'm a servant."

"Who's servant."

"Yours. His."

"The king's? The producer of the movie? Stephen's? Of the inn? And is Brill your husband?"

Adelaide ducked behind Corina's head and gently pushed the last pin into her hair. "Brill is me fellow servant." She stepped around in front. "The prince won't be able to take his eyes from you." Adelaide brushed her hand gently over Corina's cheeks. "Tears? Love, what are these tears?"

Corina laughed low, holding the woman's hands in hers. "You're ... you're just so kind."

"Your lonely heart will brim with love very soon." Adelaide stooped to see her face. "Just believe."

"See, there you go again. How do you know my heart will brim with love?"

She tapped the corner of her eye. "I sees what I sees. And I know how lonely you've been. We all watched and waited as he prayed for you."

"He? Stephen?" Corina gripped Adelaide's wrists, willing a straight answer from her.

"Jesus, of course. He is the King of the kingdom."

"He prays for me. A–and you saw him?"

"But of course." Adelaide turned for the door. "Now, I've the perfect adornment for your hair."

Corina tried to protest, but the flames Adelaide kept igniting within her incinerated her words.

Tiptoeing over to the door, Corina leaned out, listening. The theory of the inn as a movie prop with Adelaide and Brill as character actors weakened with every interaction with them.

They were just too real. Too sincere. Too otherworldly. Dare she believe it?

Also, the inn was too weird. As if built for one. Why would a director go to all the expense of a "stunt inn" for one?

On her return from the art festival this afternoon, Corina noted there were no other floors. As she climbed five flights to her room, each landing only led her up the next set of stairs. No windows. No corridors. No closed-door rooms.

"Here we are." Adelaide bounded off the top step into the room, carrying a polished, dark wood box. "I just love this piece." She set it on the bed in front of the mirror. "Sit here and I'll fit it on."

Corina sat, squinting into the box. "What's in there?"

Adelaide lifted the lid with a *hmmm* of delight. Inside, lying on red velvet, was a delicate, single-tiered, diamond tiara.

Corina jumped up. "Adelaide, no. A tiara? I'm attending the premier with Prince Stephen. I cannot wear a tiara." No need to go into the whole "wife of a prince" confession. "Where did you get that?"

"Love, sit yerself down," Adelaide commanded, authority rising from her graceful frame. "How I came by it must remain my secret, but I will tell you it is a very special piece. Been in me care for, well, quite a time. Please, sit. It will look lovely atop your dark hair."

Shaking, Corina refused, hands clasped at her waist. "I can-*not* wear a tiara. I'm going to a movie premier with a *prince*. What will people think?"

"That you are a princess." Adelaide perched the tiara delicately on her fingertips.

Corina jumped to her feet, backing away from Adelaide. "I demand to know what you know."

"I know what you know." Adelaide gently grasped Corina's hand, drawing her back to the edge of the bed.

"About me and Stephen?"

Adelaide nodded. "'Tis me job."

"I don't know how or why you know, but if you do, all the more reason you cannot ask me to wear a tiara tonight. And if you know royal history, then you must know royal protocol. 'A woman in the company of the prince cannot wear a crown or tiara unless she has her own peerage, or has been given such by the House of Stratton.' Adelaide, I do not have *any* peerage." How she remembered this protocol, Corina would never know. The words just came rushing out as a valid and perfect argument.

Adelaide examined the tiara, then settled it on Corina's head. "Brighton Kingdom is not the only kingdom to hand out peerages. A princess should wear her crown."

"Someone in the King's Office told you, right? Or the archbishop?" Corina said, wincing as Adelaide settled the crown on her head. She'd worn diamond tiaras before—for her sixteenth birthday party, for her debut. But never in the company of a true prince. "Are you from the *Madeline & Hyacinth Live!* show?"

Adelaide sighed. "Will you stop? I'm neither with a movie nor television show. Mercy, you've stories as if from fairyland. Why not ask if I'm your guardian angel? There . . ." Adelaide stepped back, smiling, looking pleased. "This was fashioned for Queen Magdalena by King Stephen I."

Corina leaned to see in the mirror. "Adelaide, how did you get this? It belongs to the royal family. I cannot possibly wear it." All of the Del Rey wealth could not replace such a priceless heirloom.

"The crown belongs to the Manor."

"What? H–how is that possible?"

"Because I am the keeper of the Manor." Her eyes twinkled. "When you entered the land, so did we. Therefore, the tiara."

"We? Who's we?" Corina's spirit churned as if on fire.

"Well, Brill and me." Adelaide adjusted the tiara one last time with careful precision, her pink tongue tucked against the side of her mouth. "There now . . . Beautiful. A true princess crown. As beautiful as Magdalena, I say."

Corina's eyes met Adelaide's, the moment sublime but ever so real. "How many have worn this tiara?" The light beaming through the diamonds nearly mesmerized Corina. In this moment, she was a princess.

"One." Adelaide brushed her hand over Corina's skirt, then gazed into her eyes. "And now you. Do you have your pouch, or whatever you young women call it today?"

"Pouch?" Corina laughed, feeling free, rather regal under the tiara. "Do you mean clutch?" Corina held up the beaded purse.

"Clutch, yes." Adelaide pressed her hand to her forehead. "I can never remember." Leading the way down the stairs, the proprietress waved Corina out the door along with Brill, who stood stiff and formal, chin tucked to his chest, all the while smiling.

"Have a good time, miss."

"I will. Thank you for everything." Corina paused at the door and pointed at her crown. "Are you sure this tiara works?"

"Love, indeed. The tiara works."

Stephen stepped out of the limousine, gazing over the rough-hewn inn tucked between the iconic, legendary department stores.

The Manor.

Last night when he rode in the car with Corina back to the Manor, she'd been proven right.

There was an establishment tucked between the twin department stores. There was no missing it. Though the royal chauffeur drove right past, three times, claiming he saw nothing but an alleyway. Stephen recommended he see an eye physician at once.

But he had no more time to ponder. Corina came through the door into the evening light. Stephen drew up straight, gobsmacked by her beauty. A force he'd never deny she possessed.

All day he debated this outing. Even after he texted her. His intent was not to draw near to her but to end their relationship. Yet whenever she was around, she chipped away at his resolve. He became weak and double-minded.

Her power over him drove him to his knees that June evening on top of the Braithwaite. She was his kryptonite, and he feared spending more time than necessary with her would break him. It was enough that he survived the tropical storm evening in her flat.

Steady on. Remain focused. Stephen conjured up an image of her brother and Bird. Dead. *Live with that reality, mate.*

Once he'd sorted his perspective, put it back in order, he approached her, buttoning his tuxedo jacket. "Good evening."

She nodded with a slight curtsy. "Good evening. You look nice."

He swallowed. "As do you." His gaze rose to the sparkling diamond tiara. "Corina, what's on your head?"

"A tiara." She touched her hand to the jeweled circlet. "The woman who runs this place gave it to me."

"A tiara? Are you quite serious? You cannot wear *that* to a movie premier with me."

"Why not?" Corina shot him with a dagger of defiance. "I didn't ask for it. She gifted it to me. You can hardly see it with my updo."

"Hardly see it? Perhaps if one were blind. The diamonds are shooting prisms all the way to the park." He gestured with attitude toward Maritime Park. "I *must* ask you to remove it. Royal protocol prohibits non-peerage females to wear a tiara around princes or kings. I'm sorry, it's old fashioned but it is still in effect. The media will be lit up with wonder."

Her countenance flared. A look he knew well. *It's on now.* "Too late now. If I take it off my hair will be ruined."

"Then ruin it. What's a bit of muss? Isn't that the popular look today?" A push of panic and he stood before her. "Did you tell the proprietress? Does she know?"

"I didn't tell her."

At the curb, the limousine motor hummed, waiting. A sprinkle of an evening rain breezed over their heads. Then faded.

"The media will be all over us. They're going to want to know who you are and why you're wearing a tiara."

"Pardon me, Your Highness, but I don't need *you* for people to know who I am. I have my own reputation. The Del Rey name is not unknown in the world. If people ask, I can tell them it's from my ancestors who, if you go back far enough, were Castilian royalty." In the haloing streetlight, he could see her trembling. "If anything, the press might just want to know why a Del Rey is attending a movie premier with a rugby player."

He stared. She stared back. He broke first, laughing. "Get in."

"Are you sure?" She took a wide berth around him. "Can you risk being seen with me?"

"Fine. You've made your point. Just slip inside, Corina." He bowed, swinging his arm toward the opened limo door. "Please. The air-conditioning is getting away."

She hesitated, and Stephen realized he'd tapped her stubborn streak. If she didn't get in soon, he should expect she'd turn on her heel and start down the avenue.

"Are you going to walk?" he said after a moment.

"Yes, I didn't come all this way for you to insult me."

He leaned toward her. "Then just why did you come all this way?"

She walked toward the curb and raised her hand. "Taxi!"

Stephen stepped in front of her. "You came looking for me, didn't you?"

She sighed and her warm, sweet breath filled his chest. "See you at the premier. Taxi!" But the red city cab zipped on past.

Laughing, Stephen pressed his hand to the back of his neck. The woman drove him mad. But he deserved this. Fair and square. Yet how could he keep his heart at bay, remembering why he couldn't be with her, when she crawled under his skin and remained there.

"Corina, please, get in the limo."

"Go on, you'll be late. Taxi!" Another passing motor didn't even see her.

"Get in." He stepped up behind her.

She turned to him, reaching up for the tiara, tugging it. But the piece remained in place. She frowned, gave up, and tapped her finger against his chest.

"You want to know why I came here? Because I realized I was still married and I don't know, call me crazy, I wondered if maybe there was still something between us. That maybe God—"

"God? What does he have to do with our marriage? I have little business with the Lord."

"But he probably has business with you. You're the freaking Prince of Brighton. Or you're supposed to be. Have you had your coronation yet? No! I wish you'd get your head out of your rugby kit long enough to realize how much more there is for you to do on this earth." She pulled on the tiara again, but it still remained in place. "What is with this thing?"

"How did this turn into a lecture on my life? Playing rugby is my mission on earth." This was way out of her jurisdiction. "Have you been talking to my brother?"

"No, but I read, observe. That's why I know there are secrets beneath your bone and muscle." She stepped into the street, stumbling after another speeding cab, nearly getting run over.

"Corina."

"Stephen."

"For Pete's sake." He lowered his shoulder and, with ease, wrapped her in his arms and cradled her against him.

"Stephen, what are you doing?" She pushed her hand against his hard chest, kicking her legs.

"I'm taking you to a premier." He peered at her, their faces so close . . . He could steal a kiss if he wanted. And oh, he wanted.

"You're a brute." Her accusation melted into a laugh.

Thomas jumped out of the back. "Sir, what are you doing?"

"Step aside, mate. Wild lass coming through."

Bending carefully, Stephen settled Corina into the back of the limo and slipped in next to her.

"You're crazy," she said, moving to the center of the seat, smoothing her skirt and patting the side of her hair. "Did the tiara stay in place?" She snatched a small compact from her bag and inspected her hair. "Though I suppose you'd like for it to fall off."

"No, I wouldn't." Stephen collected himself, smoothing his tie and straightening his jacket. He tapped the driver's window. "Crack on." With a peek at Corina, he felt a smile stretching across his heart. "You said it was romantic the last time I picked you up."

She snapped the compact shut. "Good, the tiara is still in place. Not even a rambunctious prince can remove my crown."

Thomas spit a laugh. "If I didn't know better, I'd say you two were an old married couple."

"Never you mind, chap." Stephen shot him a warning glance. "Corina, did you hear me?"

"I heard you." She reached to tap Thomas on his knee. "You look nice."

"Thank you, Corina. As do you."

"Even with the tiara?"

"Yes, it's very . . . you. Beautiful."

"At least one man in this car thinks so." Corina flipped her hand at Stephen. "See how to be *nice*?"

"Fine, I apologize if I was not nice. But showing up at a premier with a prince wearing a tiara is not a good idea. Royal protocol and all that."

The conversation idled as the limo moved through the downtown traffic toward the theatre district. But Stephen felt himself swirling down, aching to sweep Corina into his arms again.

Seeing her tonight, regal and elegant in her gown, wearing the tiara as if she'd been born to do so, only awakened the reality that everything he'd whispered to his heart about the end of their marriage was nothing but his own deluding fears.

SEVENTEEN

avenous. The paparazzi hounds hovered around the limousine as the driver pulled up to the Royal Theatre's gold carpet.

Corina leaned to see through the window as red-vested attendants carved their way toward them. She clutched her bag to her adrenaline-pulsing heart.

While this wasn't her first movie premier, it was the first time she'd stepped out of a limousine with a prince. *Her* prince. Try as she might, her body throbbed with the reality that she was his wife.

"Ready?" Stephen glanced back at her, tugging on his shirtsleeves, adjusting his collar. "Let the fun commence."

"Oh, we haven't started having fun yet? I thought it began when you swooped me up in your arms."

He glanced back at her with his swoon-enticing smile. "That fun was for you. Now mine is about to start."

"Ha! Very funny. Such a witty boy."

"Are you sure you want to get out wearing that tiara?"

Corina touched the delicate piece. "And leave it in the limo?" She gave it a light tug. Holy smokes, it was like, glued, to her head.

"The driver and the car are in the palace's employ. The tiara will be fine in here."

She ran her finger along the headband, trying to lift the piece from her hair. "I'm a Del Rey. No one should be surprised if a multi-millionaire's daughter wears a tiara." The band didn't slip or lift from her head. "Stephen, I couldn't get it off even if I wanted."

"What?"

"It's stuck."

"How can it be stuck?" Stephen pinched the top with his finger and thumb, giving a light pull.

"Ouch." She shoved Stephen's hand away as his door opened. "Never mind."

Thomas got out first, addressing the security team already on site. "The prince will exit the motor first . . ."

"Thomas was right. It looks good on you." Stephen's blue eyes searched hers for a moment. Was he going to say something? Bring up the last time he carried her again? On the night they were married. "Remember, if anyone asks, we're *merely* old friends." He slid to the edge of the seat and stepped into the blaze of camera flashes and choir of voices.

"Naturally," she said to his back. "What did you think I would say?"

Corina followed him out, emerging into the electric excitement of the media and the fans, blinded by the camera flashes.

"Prince Stephen, over here."

"Your Royal Highness, what do you think of a movie about your ancestors?"

"Sir, will you be back on the pitch this fall?"

"You, miss, over here. How do you know the prince?"

Corina looked toward the sound of the voice and a flash exploded in her face.

"Are you Corina Del Rey?"

"Corina, come," Thomas said, shoving the crowd aside for Corina.

Once she cleared the initial stand of photographers, he cut ahead to be with Stephen, and the crowd wanting access to the prince swarmed and pushed her aside.

Darn it. She elbowed her way back in, charging forward to the white press line where Stephen had stopped to talk to reporters.

"I'm looking forward to the film. Jeremiah Gonda is one of my favorite directors. And who doesn't love an Aaron Heinly script?"

"Do you think the film will accurately portray King Stephen I?"

"It's a movie, lads. Let's not make too much of it." The remark sparked a hearty laugh. "But yes, I think it will capture the heart of our liberator, a warrior and king. Would Clive Boston play any other kind of character? He's always the swashbuckling hero."

Corina jammed her shoulder against a wide-bodied photographer and shot him her Miss Georgia pearly whites. "Pardon me."

Still, she couldn't make her way to Stephen. He was barricaded by three protection officers. Thomas roamed, checking the crowd. When he saw her, he smiled, giving her a slight nod.

"Prince Stephen, is that your date behind you? Corina Del Rey?" Deanna Robertson from the *Informant*. Corina knew her from her time at Knoxton. And Gigi knew her. She was probably one of her minions.

Stephen glanced back, and in that moment, his expression, the light in his eyes, deposited something in her. She was one with him. Neither time nor distance, nor the threat of annulment, could change the truth.

And he was part of her.

He held his arm out toward her. "This is Corina Del Rey, an old mate from university. She's reporting on the premier for the *Beaumont Post*, but most of you are familiar with the Del Rey family. American entrepreneurs and philanthropists."

Thomas moved her forward and into another blast of flashes and voices.

"Are you the one who tweeted on the *Madeline & Hyacinth Live!* show?" Deanna asked.

"Yes, I—"

"—was pulling a prank." Stephen answered for her, chucking his arm around her shoulder, giving her a buddy-ole-pal squeeze. "We like to quarrel over the merits of that crazy American football."

"Sounds like a lover's quarrel." Deanna was just digging for a bone to chew, wasn't she? Or did Gigi have her up to something?

"Deanna, quite funny. We're merely friends," Stephen said.

"And football is far superior to rugby, of course," Corina said with a slight curl to her lip.

Stephen laughed, shoving her slightly aside. "Your audacity is both foolish and brave. You speak such things on Brighton Eagles territory?"

"Speaking of rugby, Your Highness . . ."

Stephen fielded a few rugby questions, showing them his ankle without the walking boot, assuring them he'd be playing by the fall.

But Corina witnessed a fault in his confidence. And when he started for the theatre, she caught the slight hitch in his walk.

She hurried to catch up to him, but the protection detail closed in like a steel door and locked her out.

"Hey, wait for me." But her voice only blended with the shouts and cries already peppering the theatre.

"Here you are, miss." A tuxedoed attendant held the door for her. "Are you with the prince?"

"Technically."

The air inside the two-hundred-year-old theatre was cool and crisp, the atmosphere vibrant with music, voices, and clinking glasses.

The walls were propped with faux Greek columns from

which carved lion heads watched over them. Corina squeezed and wove her way to Stephen, keeping a keen eye out for Clive. She was to meet him here before the film started. But the scoundrel never responded to her text today.

When she found Stephen, he was surrounded by women. She nudged him with her elbow. "What's the big idea?"

"I don't know, what *is* the big idea?"

"You just left me back there."

"I thought you were with me."

"Pretty hard to be when the protection detail boxes me out." She fumed. Hurt. But not wanting to be. "Just tell them to look out for me, please."

"Sorry, I thought Thomas was on it." Stephen turned to his small gathering. "Corina, may I introduce the woman who plays lady-in-waiting, Gillian—"

"Laura Gonda. We know each other." Corina leaned toward Laura, the director's wife, and kissed her cheek.

"How are you? I was so sorry to hear about Carlos." Laura held on to Corina's hand. "He always made me laugh. Such a waste."

"We miss him every day." Beside her, Stephen stepped back, fixed on swirling the champagne in his glass but never drinking. It was this business with Carlos. Every time it came up, he changed ever so slightly.

"How do you know one another?" he said after a moment.

"Laura starred in a movie Daddy coproduced."

"A fantastic movie and experience," Laura said, sipping her champagne. "Love the tiara, Corina." The actress tiptoed up for a better look. "A family heirloom? I remember your mother speaking of crown jewels from Castile, right?"

Corina made a face at Stephen. *Ha!* "Yes, but this one is not one of ours. It's on loan from a friend."

"I'm so jealous. I wanted to wear one, but Jeremiah wouldn't let me. Something about royal protocol." She snorted a laugh.

"But really I think he's afraid I might start to act like I'm princess because of this movie."

"Why not?" Corina said. "My grandmother used to say every little girl should play princess now and then."

"What's going on over here?" Actress Martina Lord peered over Laura's shoulder.

"Martina." Laura looped her in a hug. "I was just telling the prince and Corina that Jer refused to let me wear a tiara tonight."

Martina's gaze flitted to Corina. "Well, at least Corina pulls it off well." She offered her hand. "Good to see you." Martina played Magdalena, warrior and first queen of Brighton Kingdom.

"You know Martina as well?" Stephen asked, sounding a bit put off.

"We met in Atlanta." Corina kissed the lean cheek of the southern-born-and-bred actress. "I can't wait to see your portrayal of Magdalena. What an exciting character to play."

"I hope I did her justice." Martina reached for a drink from the passing server. "She was quite a woman, strong in battle but fierce in love." She held up her glass, glancing around the group. "To the royal—Wait, Your Highness, Corina, you don't have a glass. Server, pardon me."

Corina smiled. Martina was so deliciously and boldly southern. In short order, she had champagne in Stephen's and Corina's hands.

"Now, my toast. To the royal family of Brighton, the House of Stratton. May you reign another four hundred and fifty years." She bowed to Stephen. "May you find a love as true as King Stephen I did."

Laura raised her glass. "And to Queen Magdalena for her love, beauty, strength, and perseverance."

Corina raised her glass with a side glance at Stephen. "To the House of Stratton," he said, sweet, low, a bit somber.

Martina waved her hand between the two of them. "We've

established how we know each other. How do you two know each other?"

"We met at uni." He smiled at Corina, breaking off whatever bothered him moments ago.

"Uni?" Martina made a face. "What's a uni?"

"University," Corina said. "I did some postgrad work at Knoxton. We were in the same course." She wanted to slip her arm through his, kiss his cheek, and tell him everything would be all right.

"I see. The same *course*." Martina gave the word a flirty tone, trying to make something naughty out of it.

"A leadership class."

"Prince Stephen, you cad." Clive Boston, larger than life, barged into the tête-à-tête with savoir-faire and a wild mop of blond hair.

"Clive." Stephen shook his hand. "I hear you gave a stellar portrayal of my ancestor."

"Of course I did. It was the role of a lifetime." His brown gaze skimmed past his costars and landed on Corina. "Corina! There you are. I hear you've been hunting me down."

"With a sawed-off, double barrel."

Clive laughed, too loud. Too much. "Clever girl. I like clever girls."

"Are we still on for tomorrow?"

"For you, gorgeous, anything. Is that tomorrow?" By his exhale, she could tell he'd been drinking. By his slur, she could tell he'd been drinking a lot. Clive squeezed past Stephen, roping his arm around her. "Why have we not been in touch more?"

"Her brother died, you cad," Laura said. "She's been mourning."

"Easy there, Laura, I'm just asking." Clive cut a dark glance at Corina. "Wasn't that some time ago? I remember hearing it on the news."

"Five and a half years." She shrank back from the actor's close encounter and created her own space.

"I'm terribly, terribly sorry, Corina. I'd love to talk about it."

"Oh my word." Martina rolled her eyes. "Clive, you're such a lousy flirt. And stop drinking like a fish. What are you, twenty?"

"Martina, don't be jealous." Clive chucked Corina under her chin. "True beauty moves me. I can't help it."

"Then move out of the way, chap." Stephen clapped his hand on Clive's shoulder, removing him from the inside of the circle. "Give the woman air to breathe."

"Your Highness, if I didn't know better, I'd accuse you of being jealous."

"Not at all, but you're drunk and rude." Stephen mimed tipping back a drink, implying Clive was sauced.

"Begging your pardon, I am not drunk. Well, maybe a wee bit." He held up his thumb and forefinger, giving Corina a sly smile. "I told you, true beauty moves me."

"Yeah, and it moved you all over the set with the extras," Laura said.

"What's this?" Clive pressed his hands to his chest, feigning hurt. "My friends ganging up on me, ruining my chances with this amazing woman?"

Corina raised her hands. "Clive, your reputation is safe with me. Now, where do you want to meet? I'm free all day."

"Two o'clock. The Strand Cafe. I've been dying for one of their sandwiches."

"Perfect. I'll see you then." The Strand was on the other side of Maritime Park, not far from the Manor. Just a quick taxi ride.

The theatre staff was making rounds, whispering to the cast in a low tone, gathering them to the other side of the lobby, and Corina found herself alone with Stephen.

First thing out of his mouth. "Be careful with Clive."

"I'm well aware of Clive's ways. The question is why do you care?"

Stephen set his untouched champagne on a passing tray. "Just because we're going our own ways doesn't mean I want you to end up with a bloke like Clive."

"I suppose it's none of your business, but thank you."

"We are friends, aren't we?"

"So you say." She passed her champagne flute to one of the servers. "We meant too much to one another to be otherwise."

A photographer passed by, snapping their picture before either could protest.

"Your Highness?" A man in a tuxedo cut through the crowd, bowing when he stopped in front of Stephen. "Welcome to the Royal Theatre. Your box is ready." He motioned for Stephen to go through, closing in behind him without the slightest glance at Corina.

Before she could maneuver in behind the prince, the protection wall cut her off again.

Corina exhaled. *Okay, just follow the usher inside.* Stephen's dark head rose well above the others, so she could follow him to his box.

But at that moment, the theatre lights flickered and the entire throng waiting in the lobby shoved toward the doors, filling the wide, carpeted stairs. She lost sight of Stephen and had no idea which set of stairs, behind which doors, led to the royal box.

Hanging back, Corina waited for the other guests, movie watchers, and her fellow media members to fill the theatre. Then she stood just inside the main doors, searching the balcony and the second tier and grand boxes for sight of her royal man.

"Miss, you must have a pass to get in." One of the ushers gently tugged on her arm. "The film is about to start. I need you to remove yourself."

"I'm here with the *Beaumont Post* to cover this premier." She opened her clutch. "I have the invitation right—" No, no, no, she'd left it in her room. The tiara business got her all flustered.

"Unless you can produce press credentials or an invitation, I'm afraid you'll have to leave."

"I can't leave. I came with the prince. I'm Corina Del Rey." One of those names had to pull some weight with this kid.

"The prince is seated with his party in the royal box. If you don't leave, I'll have to call security."

"I'm his party." She fumed at him and jerked her arm from his grasp. "Okay, I'll go, but if you'll just talk to the prince, he'll tell you—"

He laughed. "I am not to disturb the prince for every crazy who claims she's with him."

"Look," Corina said, pointing to her head, "I have a tiara."

Then he appeared. "Corina." Stephen leaned over the ornate, carved banister. "This way."

"What took you so long?" Corina freed herself from the usher and started up the stairs.

"Begging your pardon, Your Highness. I didn't know."

"I tried to tell you," Corina said over her shoulder and down the banister.

But the usher was gone, ducking through a set of double doors.

"I thought you were right behind me," Stephen said.

"I got shut out. Again. Can you please talk to Thomas?"

"When I arrived at the royal box, I had to stand for a reception line. He was watching the entrance."

"Never mind. We're here now."

When they were ensconced in their seats, she faced the screen, feeling ridiculous. Perhaps it was time to reckon with the raw truth. He wasn't going to change. He wasn't going to sweep her off her feet again, declaring his love. He didn't want their marriage restored. He wanted to move on. Without her.

She was never going to truly be the wife of Prince Stephen.

EIGHTEEN

He lost sight of her during the movie's after party. She was cool toward him when he caught up to her after the showing. But rightfully so. He'd left her behind, and for the life of him, he couldn't reckon with his rude actions.

After all, he did invite her to the premier. But suddenly she felt all too close, too real, and the memories of her soft skin beneath his and the flame of her kisses nearly distracted him from the opening scene where King Stephen I and his men rose from the southern bay like sea monsters, surprising King Henry VIII's army as they slept on the beach.

As the film credits rolled and the audience rose to their feet with abandoned applause, the theatre spotlight swung to his box and Corina stepped into the shadows.

He walked with her to the after party, but he was swarmed as they entered the room, and she was gone.

Stephen perused the food table, choosing a smoked salmon on toast point hors d'oeuvre.

Impulse. That was his superpower. What he did well. When he hesitated or overthought something, people got hurt. Joy became sorrow. Peace became war. Friends became enemies.

So tonight, when Corina suddenly appeared to be the perfect

wife for him—comfortable in his world, acquainted with the likes of Laura Gonda and Martina Lord, and charming the "wow" out of Clive the cad—he panicked. Moved away from her because his impulses stirred.

Marry me. Again.

So Stephen created distance between them. He didn't blame her for being upset. Finishing his hors d'oeuvre, Stephen moved through the crowd, greeting guests, who prattled on about how "it was such a fabulous film."

But he was ready to go. This wasn't his scene. Despite his rugged, rugby-man reputation, any and all exploits with wine, women, and song were merely unchallenged legend.

Why disappoint people with the truth? The Prince of Brighton was a homebody. A wounded, unworthy man.

He'd tried numbing his pain with drink after his tour but quickly discovered he had to choose. Be drunk or be disciplined.

Modern rugby demanded he stay fit and on top of his game, mentally and physically. Drinking made him the opposite. Rugby turned out to be his only true salvation.

Just over his shoulder, he saw Corina working through the crowd, the people responding to her. She looked divine under her sparkling tiara. Bravo for defying royal protocol.

"Sir?" Thomas tucked in next to him. "It's nearly midnight."

"I'm ready to go." After midnight, the music changed dramatically, and previously well-mannered citizens with a sense of decency lost their minds, and maybe a piece of their souls, with raucous music, strong drink, and backroom antics. "Let's collect Corina."

"She'd said she'd take a taxi." Thomas shouldered his way through the crowd, making room for Stephen, nodding to the protection officers waiting by the door.

"Not again." Stephen stepped faster. He'd just seen her, so she couldn't be too far.

"The limousine is coming round," Thomas said.

Through the doors and into the clear cool night, illumined with roaming spotlights, Stephen slammed into the wall of tenacious paparazzi.

"Prince Stephen, this way. What did you think of the film?"

He quickened his gait. "Quite splendid." *Where'd you get off to, Corina?* "For a moment, I almost called Clive Boston 'Granddad.'"

The laughter slipstreamed along the night air.

"Your Highness, where's your lady friend?" A photographer ducked under the media rope and ran alongside him. "Corina Del Rey, if I'm not mistaken. Are you two an item?"

"No, we're not." Clear enough? But the truth of the matter gnawed at him. They *were* an item. A couple. Man and wife. Why couldn't he just say it? Be free of it? *But we're getting an annulment.*

Because then the "why" questions would come.

Thomas intercepted the photographer, urging him to move on, just as Stephen spotted Corina at the taxi stand, her hand raised, hailing a cab.

Breaking away from the protection detail, his tightly wrapped ankle tired and burning, he limped toward her.

"Stephen, where are you going?" Thomas's voice barreled after him.

"For a stroll." Stephen linked his arm through Corina's and, without a word, moved her away from the curb and into the shadows of the giant spotlights. "You were going to leave without saying good-bye." At the curb, Stephen checked the motion of the traffic, then dashed across the thoroughfare as headlights from the oncoming lane sped toward them.

"Gee, Thelma, what's your hurry?" Corina pulled away from him but kept up with his stride.

"I'm in the mood for some puffs."

"Puffs? At this hour."

"Puffs are grand at any hour."

Thomas appeared off Stephen's right shoulder, relaying

commands through the com tucked into his jacket sleeve. "Bring the limo round. Heading east on Bakery Row."

"Home of the best bakery and eateries in all of Europe."

"Thomas, how could you box me out? I thought you of all people—"

"Sorry miss, my duty is to the prince. When we're in large crowds—"

"Blame me. Not Thomas." Stephen slowed as they stepped up onto the sidewalk, into a triangle streetlamp glow. "Is it too late to apologize?"

"For what?" She sighed, glancing away. But he caught the soft sheen in her eyes. "I'm starting to think you're right. We should've never happened."

"I'm sorry, Corina. I just don't want a lot of prying questions. What do you say? A box of Brighton's best pastry? A cup of hot sweet tea with thick cream?" He loosened his tie, unbuttoned his collar, pointing to the lights of the old Franklin Bakery. "We came here on our first date, remember? You had your first taste of puffs." They'd gone to dinner with friends. His mate Harry had leaned over during the first course and said in no small whisper, "Marry her. And I'm not kidding. Find a way."

She drew up, slowing her step. "They weren't my first puffs. I vacationed here as a kid. Please tell me you've forgotten the stories of—"

"Yes, your maid, Ida Mae, trying to converse with the locals."

Corina laughed low, a melody that lingered with him longer than the movie's dynamic score. At least in this moment. "She'd come in from the shops. 'I declare, Horatia, but I think I got yet another weddin' proposal.'"

"Because grocer colloquialism said, 'If ya make me a spry dish with what here I'm selling ya, I'll make ye my bride.'"

"Which meant, 'I'll give you the best house deal next time you come into the shop.'"

Their laughs blended with the sound of the night, the scuff of their heels. Corina stopped, leaned on his shoulder, and popped off her shoes. "Ah, finally. They were killing me."

"Thomas!" Stephen snapped with a flare. "Carry milady's shoes to the motor car."

"Oh good grief, I'm not going to ask the man to carry my shoes."

Thomas held up his hand. "I don't mind at all."

Corina dropped the spike-heeled shoes to his palm. "Then thank you very much."

With a light press of his hand on her back, Stephen urged her forward. "That night we dined at—"

"Ten Bluedon Street."

"Precisely. Then we went for puffs."

"Franklin's has the best in the city, so much so they never close," he said, leaning to see around her sheen of hair. *"Come on, I mean, you've spent the better part of the night with me."*

"Yes, and I'm starting to be concerned for my reputation."

He laughed. He liked who he was around her. Relaxed, himself, unaware of his princely stature. But yet, didn't she make him want to be all he could be as a royal?

"So, a walk to Franklin's for a box of puffs?"

"I don't know . . ." She chewed on her bottom lip in contemplation, and he thought he might just slip her into his arms and taste her lips.

"Tell you what . . ." He retrieved his mobile. "I'll ring your brother. Ask his permission." He dialed as she laughed. "Carlos, chap, this is Stephen. Yes . . . your sister . . . doing splendid. We're debating going for a box of puffs . . . at Franklin's . . ." He glanced at her in the ambient light of 10 Bluedon Street and his heart slipped a little over love's edge. "Might I have your blessing to coax her along? All right, sounds like a fair offer. A box of puffs, chocolate, for the brother."

"Carlos, you're a rotten big brother." She held up her finger and mouthed "by one minute."

"He says a man has to eat."

"I miss him," she said, chewing on her bottom lip, like that night so long ago.

Her soft confession speared his heart. Clearing his throat, he walked round her. "Puffs it is, then." What was he doing? *Let her go. Be done with it.* Did he think he could dance around the truth forever? That he'd not impulsively spill it all?

No matter how he sliced it, Corina Del Rey came attached to her brother, and alive or dead, he would always be a part of their relationship.

Around the corner, Stephen stopped in front of the bright window of a small bake shop. The sign above the door read Franklin Bakery. A Brighton landmark.

"Shall we?" He opened the door. Thomas entered first, then Corina, followed by Stephen. Along the curb, the limousine slowed then stopped.

Stephen approached the counter as the proprietor came round the corner, dusting flour from his hands. "Prince Stephen." The surprise in his voice displayed in his eyes. "Your Highness, welcome to Franklin's. Lovely to see you. A box of puffs?"

"You know me well, Mr. Franklin. And a couple of boxes for my friends out there." He tipped his head toward Thomas and the limo lads. "Add a round of teas."

"Coming right up. Cinnamon?"

"The best kind. But toss in a few chocolate." Stephen peeled several pound notes from his money clip and set them on the counter before turning to Corina. "Shall we choose a table?"

She chose one by the window, and when Thomas nodded his consent, Stephen led her over.

"What did you think of the film?" he said after a moment.

"Are you asking the woman or the amateur critic?"

"Whichever one wants to answer?"

"The critic thought it was well done. The cinematography

was stunning. The acting . . ." She waffled her hand in the air. "Martina as Magdalena and Laura as Gillian were excellent, but Clive as King Stephen . . . He was just too much like his super spy Scott Hunter character. Jason Bourne meets James Bond in 1552, you know? I felt like it was a Bond-Hunter-Bourne flick only with a serf army wielding bow and arrows instead of CIA spooks trained to take out their opposing asset with the back of a cell phone and wad of chewing gum."

Stephen chuckled. "Well said."

"However as a woman and premier reporter, I loved every minute of it. King Stephen was so noble and heroic. I thought Magdalena was beyond courageous."

She glanced up when Mr. Franklin—an heir much like Stephen, only to the bakery world, the son of sons of sons of the founder—who regularly worked the night shift, appeared with their puffs and tea. And Stephen's money.

"On the house tonight, Your Highness."

"Are you sure?" Stephen hesitated, then reached for the pound notes. "Thank you."

"In honor of the premier."

"For the premier." Stephen stood, shaking the man's hand.

Corina pulled one of the light pastries from the box and dipped it in her tea, just like he'd taught her the first time they shared puffs.

"It's the only way to eat a puff. Dipped in hot sweet tea."

"What about you?" she said. "Did you enjoy it? What was it like watching your ancestor come to life on a movie screen?"

"Eerie, inspiring. I thought the film was well done." He reached for his napkin, dusting the cinnamon from his fingers. "There were moments when I found it hard to believe that the blood of a brave chap like King Stephen I, even though Clive was a bit too Scott Hunter, runs in my veins."

"Why is that hard to believe? You fought for your country same as he did. Perhaps you're more like him than you realize."

"Or less." King Stephen I had loved Magdalena without reserve or fail. Even in the difficulties when his council stood against him. Stephen peered over his cup of tea. How could he love Corina faithfully when he bore her brother's blood?

She could never forgive him. Rightly so.

"I'd like to think I'd pick up my fallen brother's sword, if I could."

Stephen dipped his puff in his tea. This conversation edged on danger. *Just let it go.*

Dusting cinnamon from her fingers, Corina reached up to work the tiara from her hair. "I shouldn't have worn this out with you. I only dug in my heels because you demanded I take it off. I've probably further offended your family." But the crown would not budge. "That Adelaide . . ." Corina growled low. "Did she glue it on? She's going to have to cut this out of my hair or I may have to wear it all week."

Stephen stretched across the table, touching her hand. "Leave it be. It's becoming."

She settled back, swirling her finger through puff crumbs. "Do you realize this was our first public outing? At least officially."

"I suppose, yes. I never considered it."

She drew a long breath and dusted the cinnamon from her fingers. "No one ever knew."

"We hid our relationship well."

"And it was fun but . . ." She peered at him. "But when a girl gets married, she wants the whole world to know."

Stephen shifted in his seat and heard his heart kerplunk. From his proposal to the secret marriage, he'd robbed this woman of everything romantic. Everything a woman desires.

Maybe impulse was his nemesis, not his superpower.

Yet she did it all willingly. Gladly. Because she loved him.

A slow perspiration started across his forehead, heat sinking into his face and neck. And how did he repay her? With an abrupt end and cold silence.

"It's odd . . . this thing between us." In the quiet moments, his heart popped open on its own. A small thread unraveling in his carefully brocaded emotions. "Married but not married."

"Very odd." She leaned on her elbows and dipped her puff in her tea again.

"I'm sorry." His clipped confession floated out on a cloud of shallow emotion. He could offer a world of apologies, but would it still be the balm her wounded heart demanded?

She sighed. "Can we just enjoy this?" She offered up her half-eaten puff. "Why spoil the evening with the conversation we're *not* going to have?"

He smoothed his hand over his napkin. "All right. But tell me about the business of you tweeting during Madeline and Hyacinth's show."

She pinched her lips, but her laugh leaked through. "I don't know . . ." Her golden-brown eyes snapped. "I felt ornery."

"What were you trying to do? Alert the media?"

"No," she said with a defensive air. "I wanted to alert you, then watch you proclaim the glories of your boorish rugby."

His laugh rolled. "Boorish rugby." He slapped his hand over his heart as if truly speared, then regarded her, awash with humility. How did she offer him such patience and kindness? It disrupted him. Knocked at his soul.

"Yes, boorish. I mean, what's it all about? Running up and down the field in a line, tossing the ball behind you?"

"It's about being the most superior, toughest sport in the world."

She made a face, wrinkling her nose. "Yeah, I'm not getting that."

He snorted, pressing his fist to his lips. "Rugby is far superior to your American football, darling."

From across the room, Thomas spoke out. "Careful, Corina, you're talking to one of the world's best wingers."

"Thank you, Thomas," Stephen said, puffing up, anchoring his arm on the back of his chair. *Indeed, one of the best.* It felt good to have someone proclaim his excellence in front of his wife. Not that "wife" mattered in the long run. *Don't let loose too much, mate. She's going back to America.*

"Best winger in an inferior sport. Does that really even count?" Nonchalant, she shoved a puff in her mouth, chewed, and swallowed before going on. "Thomas, I thought of you more as an honest man, speaking the truth. Even to your prince."

"I am, ma'am."

Oh, now the lass was just begging for it. "Tell me how many countries play your brand of football?"

She shrugged. "Doesn't matter."

"Over a hundred and seventeen nations play in the Rugby Union. And your American football? A dozen, perhaps?"

"See, that's why it's superior. It takes time, talent, training, money to play. And since when did quantity equate with quality?"

Thomas laughed. "She has you there, sir."

"Hush, or you'll be on palace foot patrol."

Thomas winked at Corina and headed for the door. "I'll just join the lads and leave you to it, Corina."

"Stephen," she said, leaning toward him once Thomas had gone, holding her teacup in her long, slender hands. His lips buzzed with a desire to kiss her fingers. "Have you ever *played* American football?"

"You mean the game with the lads under a helmet, wearing all sorts of protective gear? No. A game for the ladies." He caught her mid-sip. She snorted and spewed a small shower of tea. "Ah, lovely. Spitting on your date." He brushed his tux with exaggeration.

"Not my date." She dabbed the table with her napkin. "No, you made that clear. Anyway, why do you think they wear the gear? Because—"

"They're weak," he said, letting the date comment slip past, choosing instead the soft ground of a sporting debate. "And I said I was sorry."

"Weak?" She jutted out her chin with a challenging gaze. "And oh no you did not."

"I think I just did. I'm sorry for any rudeness."

"Listen, American football is a full-on, run-at-each-other-like-freight-trains contact sport. In rugby, y'all just hug each other down to the ground, and apology accepted."

He jerked forward, eyes wide. "Oh no, *you* didn't. 'Hug each other to the ground?'"

"I think I just did."

"All right." He rubbed his hands together, well aware he was treading on familiar ground, venturing into fall-in-love space. "How about a little wager?" Beyond the window, the protection officers paced, passing around the box of puffs, sipping from paper cups. The hour had grown late and Stephen didn't want to make them wait too much longer to go home, but he wasn't quite ready to leave Corina's company.

"What kind of wager? And no sucker bets, like name the all-time leading scorer in rugby."

"Dan Carter, New Zealand. He's a hundred caps. I was aiming for half of that by now."

She glanced down at his bandaged ankle. "Will you be able to play soon?"

"The fall Premiership is my goal." He didn't mention how he pushed himself this morning on the pitch and ended up with his foot in an ice whirlpool for ten minutes, enduring a stern lecture from his physiotherapist.

"What's the bet?" With that, a lock of her black hair bounced between her hazel eyes, twisting to the tip of her lean nose.

"The first day we spoke ... where were we?"

"That's the bet?"

"That's the bet."

"Do you want to lose?"

"I aim to win."

"And if I win?"

"I will declare, in the city square—my city, mind you—that American football is the most superior sport in the world." He winced. Could his soul endure such a thing? Such a lie? Even for her? For true love? "Isn't that what you Americans really believe?"

"Absolutely. It's true."

"But if I win," he said, leaning toward her, propped on his elbows, inhaling the intoxicating scent of her skin, "you must stand in the square, declaring that rugby is the most superior sport in the world."

"You're kidding." But her smile told him she loved the wager. "You must not believe in your sport very much, Stephen."

"I believe wholeheartedly in my sport and this, shall we say, throw down."

"Deal." She stuck out her hand.

"Deal." He hesitated, then took her hand in his. As he feared, her touch blew passion over his dormant fires. He didn't want to let her go. How easy it would've been to pull her into him and reacquaint his lips with hers.

"Professor Reuben's class. When you sat behind me. That was the first time we spoke."

"As I suspected. Wrong." He slapped his hand on the table. Dates were not typically his specialty, but he'd never forget the first time he saw her, spoke to her. He could count every day he spotted her crossing the oval, her hair floating behind her. "Off with you now to the city square."

"Wrong? I remember expressly—"

"Do you remember the first day of fall semester? Outside the registrar's office? You came out the door so fast you ran into someone, dropping your books."

She gasped. "That was you?" She made a face, refusing to believe. "No, that man was . . . nice. He picked up my books, asked if I was all right. Apologized even though it was my fault."

"Did he say something like, 'Afternoon, miss. I'm so sorry. I seem to be in the wrong place at the wrong time these days'?"

She crossed her arms with a defiant chin raise. "What was I wearing?"

"Not fair. I'm a man, Corina. We don't notice outfits."

Her eyes twinkled as she leaned toward him with smug confidence. "What was I wearing?"

"A pink top. Jeans. Flip-flops."

She froze, eyes wide. "It was you."

Stephen popped another puff in his mouth, took a long, satisfying sip of his tea, and pushed away from the table. "Well, we'd best get on with it."

"You never said anything."

"Some memories are just mine to treasure."

"I can't believe you."

"Crack on. Enough stalling." He offered her his hand.

She rose slowly from the table, her eyes like blipping saucers. "You're serious? You want me to shout in Cathedral City Square that rugby is a superior sport? I'm a woman of society. An heiress. Never mind a journalist for the noted *Beaumont Post*."

"I'm the Prince of Brighton and a star winger. If the situation were reversed you'd show me no mercy. We'd best hurry." He glanced at his thick, jeweled watch. A gift from his paternal grandfather, King Kenneth III. "It's half past midnight. Timely for the late dinner crowd driving home past the square." He led her to the door, threading his arm through hers. "What do you say? The roundabout? It's a central place. Best start warming up your voice. I want this declaration loud and clear."

"You seriously want me to shout a lie in the middle of the city square. From the roundabout."

"No, I want you to shout the truth. It's only a lie to you because you refuse to believe it."

"Or ... because it's actually a *lie*. At least to me."

"Corina, really now, warm up your voice. Me-me-me-me-me."

"Oh, I'm warm." She crushed her clutch bag between her hands. "My declaration will be loud. And very clear." She snarled at him, stepping into the night. He muted his laugh. Muted the simmering stirrings of love.

"Don't be angry, love. To the square," he said into the night. Thomas and the security team shuffled along beside them.

"Where are we going, sir?" Thomas said. "Corina, your shoes, ma'am."

"Thank you, Thomas." She snatched them from him, pausing to slip them on, propping her hand against Stephen's shoulder for balance.

"We're off to the roundabout in the city square, Thomas," he said, walking on when Corina was ready.

"Now? The traffic will be substantial."

"Of which I'm most grateful." He glanced at Corina. She was silent. A bit too silent. He could almost hear the cogs of revenge cranking in that beautiful brain of hers.

Stepping off the curb, the five of them dodged the traffic of Bakery Row toward the thick roundabout thoroughfare.

"Again, what is this all about?" Thomas, the ole mutt with a bone.

"Corina is going to declare truth." He cut across a side street lined toward the park, ducking through the shadows of Victorian brownstones and ancient, thick-trunk trees burdened with leafy fat limbs.

"What sort of truth?" Thomas pressed his hand into Stephen and Corina's backs, urging them across another side street and finally onto the grassy roundabout in the center of the six-lane Broadway thoroughfare. A river of headlights flowed toward them.

"Just you wait, Thomas," Corina said. "You'll see."

Stephen halted midstride. Something was amiss. "What do you mean, 'Just you wait'? Not sixty seconds ago, you were protesting."

"You wanted a declaration of truth. A declaration of truth is what you'll get."

"Stephen, sir, please, we're in the middle of the lane." Thomas motioned for the other officers to get Corina to the roundabout.

Hurrying as quickly as he could, ignoring the twinge in his ankle—he'd pay for this tomorrow—Stephen landed on the grassy roundabout center, inhaling, deciphering the feelings flowing through him. Fun? Happiness? Joy? All of the above? He'd not felt such textures in so long. "Corina." He focused on her. "Repeat after me, 'Rugby is the most superior sport in the world.'"

"Rugby is the most superior sport in the world." Stiff, straight-laced, and staring into the wave of white headlights moving toward them.

"Very nice, but with more meaning."

"Rugby is the most superior sport in the world." Corina repeated the words in a flat, meaningless tone.

"Love, listen, I won the bet. Fair and square. Don't you agree?"

"I was set up."

"But you made the bet. Face it, you thought you were going to win. So, please, with a bit more vim and vigor. After all, you'd demand all that from me and more. Perhaps a dance or some such."

"Sir, is this really necessary?" Thomas positioned his team facing north and south on the circle, watching the roundabout, but he was nervous. Agitated.

"Yes, it is. Now . . ." Stephen flattened his palm against the carved marble base of the King Leopold II statue, leaning, taking the weight off of his sprained and complaining ankle. "Which way should she face?" He gazed north, then south, ignoring how the wind brushed her hair against his cheek. Nevertheless, the subtle encounter with her sent a wrecking ball against the wall of his heart.

Meanwhile, Thomas gave low commands to the limo driver

through the com in his sleeve. "Pull round to the west corner of the side street. We'll dash over when this business is done."

"South I think," Corina said, turning round, her hip grazing his arm. "More oncoming traffic."

Another touch like that one and he'd be engulfed. "Well then, give it your best go."

She inhaled and started to let go, but then glanced back at him. "You know this is ridiculous."

"I know nothing of the sort. Quite the contrary, this is most antiridiculous. So crack on. Let's hear it." He folded his arms, hobbling, balancing on one foot, his heart beating in two directions.

Did he want to merely laugh at what will be her weak declaration of rugby's superiority? Or take her in his arms and kiss her?

"This will make you feel better?" She asked, glancing at him through the threads of approaching headlights, her tiara sparkling.

"I think so, yes. But you see, it's the matter of the bet." He slapped his hand against the base of the statue. Like King Stephen I, King Leopold II rescued Brighton from a Russian conquest in the Great Northern War.

Stephen glanced up at the marble image of his great warrior ancestor. Another man like King Stephen I who fought for Brighton's freedom with might and courage.

"It's late. We best get on home. Come down from there. You don't have to do this."

"What? Why?" Corina snatched his arm, jerking him round among the shadows. "What about the bet?"

"What do you want me to say? Yelling some trite words about rugby will truly undo the damage that's been done between us? Why bother?"

"Because some things are worth fighting for. Stephen, since when did you give up so easily? If you want something to change about these last years," she gripped his arms, shaking him, "do something about it. Come back to me. Let's work this out."

"Impossible." He withdrew from her. "If you only knew." He stepped off the curb, watching the traffic, Thomas aligning on his right.

"Then tell me!" She lived in a world of subtle secrets between Adelaide and Stephen. It was starting to get on her nerves.

"Corina, to the limo." Thomas broached no room for protest.

A growl came from her, so low, so vicious, Thomas actually stopped in the middle of the thoroughfare. "I'm so sick of the secrets. So sick of the cloaked meanings and shaded answers. What in tarnation happened in Afghanistan?"

Stephen turned back toward the roundabout. "Please, let's go."

Arms stiff by her side, tucked against her shimmering skirt, Corina tipped back her head. "Go Georgia Bulldogs! Go Georgia Bulldogs! Go Georgia Bulldogs! G-E-O-R-G-I-A! Go Dawgs! Sic 'em! Woof, woof, woof!"

Thomas snorted, then breathed deep, swallowing his laugh.

"Corina," Stephen hobbled back up on the roundabout, "no, no, no!" He clapped his hands, gaining her attention. "That's what you were planning all along, weren't you? Not 'Rugby is the most superior sport in the world.'"

Still stiff, and slightly trembling, she belted again into the night. "American football is the most amazing sport in the world." A few of the motors slowed, honking their horns.

"You do not follow directions well at all, do you?" Stephen said, which, truly, he found was one of her most endearing qualities.

She leaned into him. "Go Dawgs. Sic 'em. Woof, woof, *woof*."

"Did you just *woof* at me?"

"Woof!"

"You're a welsher. That's what you are . . . a first-class welsher."

She exhaled, pushing against him. "Me? A welsher? Look who's talking. I think *you* made a promise to love, honor, and cherish—"

Impulse. The spark of his existence drove him to grip her to him, tightening his hand around her waist.

In the ghostly light of traffic, his lips captured hers, the familiar curves of her body beneath his hands. The heat of her skin soaked into every pore.

Her reaction was stiff and cold upon first touch, but after a long breath, she let the tension go and swooned against him, wrapping her hand about his neck, her lips softening, warming.

He was at once *home*. In the very intimate, enveloping world of her love. And he wondered if he'd be able to escape this time.

What are you doing?

He broke away, the tooting of car horns startling him into reality. Stepping back, he corralled his need to kiss her again with a big gulp of air. He felt buzzed, stunned, encountered by a true force.

"W–why did you do that?" Her breathless question came without guile.

"We best get on, Corina." He released her and started for the limo. That force? Of a loved woman? Was one he could not combat. He'd tasted it and even the nightmares of hell were not strong enough to resist it. "It's late."

But resist he must.

What right had he to enjoy life, make love to his wife, rear children, holiday on the shore, while the families of the men who died for him tottered on, trying to rebuild their lives? Sons and daughters being raised without their fathers. All because of him.

No, he was not worthy of the happiness of her kiss. And that was his burden to bear.

NINETEEN

The butterflies from his kiss lingered with Corina all night, fluttering down to her toes as she dreamed. His kiss was the kiss of a man who had feelings for her. Who perhaps still loved her.

Kicking back her covers with a good Tuesday morning stretch, Corina crawled out of bed and opened the curtains. Perching on the window seat, cradling a small velvet and fringe pillow, she watched a muted dawn gently wake up Cathedral City. Adelaide was right; this was one of the greatest cities on earth.

She exhaled a contented sigh, wrapping her arms around her raised knees. *His kiss* . . . She'd always have *that* kiss.

Their honeymoon month had been filled with such kisses and the passions of young lovers—mind, body, and soul.

Stephen was her one and only. Then and now. There would be no one else for her. He'd pledged the same love and devotion to her when they danced to their own symphony atop the Braithwaite. Did he really change, fall out of love with her those silent weeks toward the end of his tour? Did the explosion hurt him that much?

Corina tossed the pillow to the seat, a slow revelation dawning. But of course . . .

He came to Florida with the annulment papers when he could've just mailed them with a note. Perhaps adding a phone call for propriety's sake.

Wait, she had to think about this, process. She paced from the window to her bed and back again, her pale pink pajama bottoms sagging at her hips.

Why, *why*, did he refuse her? Deny his feelings? Hide the truth?

Carlos. His name seemed to be at the core of things. No matter what Stephen's intentions when he arrived in Florida, she had set the conditions. Once she threw down the gauntlet of wanting information, it gave Stephen a way out of the annulment.

He wasn't forthcoming about Carlos because if he gave her what she wanted, she'd sign the papers. She'd promised. So he'd withhold and they'd remain married. He *must* still love her. That's why he flew to Florida. To see her and test his feelings. To test hers.

But Corina's reasoning had weak spots. What if she'd signed right away? Then what would Stephen have done? Or what if she were remarried or engaged?

Okay, good questions. She shoved her hair away from her face. The tiara came off smoothly once she arrived at the Manor, and it waited in its box for Adelaide.

He probably already knew she wasn't married or in a relationship. "*You're not exactly hiding.*"

Corina pressed her hand over her heart, smiling. His words said annulment but his actions said, "I love you."

A laugh bubbled in her chest. Stephen didn't want those papers signed any more than she did.

However, proving that provided a set of complications.

For now, she'd have to trust her husband. And whatever intention the Lord of all had on his own heart when he told her to "love well."

Corina propped one knee on the window seat and leaned

against the sill. Brighton was her home away from home. Cathedral City, her city. The sapphire shores of Brighton Kingdom made a beautiful contrast to her Georgia red-clay roots.

For the rest of her time here, she'd help Stephen remember how good they were together. Their love was full of possibilities. Forget wars and disappointments, annulment papers and wounds of the heart. She had to hang on to her man, play the full four quarters, make her own goal line stance.

Corina set her hand on her hip where his rested, and she felt the heat of his touch. Though when he dropped her off last night, he was rather out of sorts and mentioned nothing of seeing her again.

Lord, are you praying for me? You have to show me the way.

Rain clouds darkened the dawn, and the first hint of a morning shower pattered against the pane as Corina loosened the corset strings of her heart and breathed in each tender emotion she held for her husband.

Her musings were interrupted by the hard ring of her phone. Gigi's ringtone.

"Well, how was it?"

"Wonderful." Corina lowered her phone and cleared her throat. There was too much emotion in her voice.

"Wonderful?" Gigi echoed, hard and concrete. "Are we talking about the movie premier or something else?"

Corina ran her hand through her hair. Wake up, wake up. Focus. "Of course the movie premier. It's late at home. Are you waiting for first editions of the European papers to be posted to the Internet?"

"You know I always do. So, you were just referencing the premier? For a moment it sounded like you were talking about a kiss."

"A kiss? Who kissed someone?" Corina sobered. No way could Gigi know about the roundabout. "I, however, was talking about the premier. It was wonderful." She put some of the *breath* back in her speech. "It was a night of movie stars, evening gowns, champagne. Clive Boston."

"And royal princes?"

"Yes, right, of course Prince Stephen was there for the family."

"Tell me, how'd you end up in his limousine? Wearing a tiara, no less?"

"Someone loaned it to me. You saw a picture? In which paper?"

She laughed. "All of them. Where did the tiara come from?"

"A friend of mine, from here, loaned it to me." Corina pressed the heel of her hand to her forehead. Amateur. She should've remembered the morning papers. She'd been away from the news game too long and become naive about the world's digital eye. Not to mention she'd been too distracted with Stephen to remember Gigi.

"The *Liberty Press* claims you were his date."

"Not exactly. We're old friends from uni." There, she'd clung to the party line.

"Is he the man who came to see you? That night in the parking lot?"

"Gigi, seriously, you're still on that parking lot thing? Almost two weeks ago and in the dark of night? Please, it was nothing. Listen, it's still early here. I just woke up. Can I call you—"

"You can run, but you can't hide, darling." Gigi's snide laugh pierced every one of Corina's love bubbles. "I know about your tweet to the *Madeline & Hyacinth Live!* show."

"Fine, I tweeted. He was a friend of my brother's. We used to argue rugby versus football."

"So he just happened to call, inviting you to the movie premier with him? Is that why you decided to go to Brighton?"

"No. He didn't invite me until after I arrived Really, Gigi, you're making way too much out of this."

"I'll be the judge of that, thank you."

Corina changed the subject. "You'll be glad to know my interview with Clive is at two today. He's *really* looking forward to it."

"He's looking forward to flirting with a beautiful woman who just happened to be the date of Prince Stephen."

"We're *just* friends."

"Fine, but tell me, is he as delicious as he looks?"

Positively. Corina cleared her voice of all romantic intonations. "He's okay."

"Well, then don't succumb to Clive's charms, Corina."

"Why not?" That'll get her off Corina's scent. "He *is* yummy, and he's rich—"

"So are you."

"Gorgeous. Charming."

"Is there a point? You cannot convince me you are remotely interested in a two-bit, blockbuster, thriller actor when you have Prince Stephen on the hook."

"Gigi, I do not, repeat, do not have Prince Stephen on the hook. He's an acquaintance. If you print anything about us—"

"Darling girl, you best pick up the morning papers in your part of the world, because 'us' has already been printed."

Hanging up, Corina tossed her phone into the mound of ruffled bedcovers and opened her laptop, hands shaking.

One by one, she brought up Brighton's papers. She and Stephen made the front banner of the *LibP*.

At Last a Princess for Our Prince?

Were they serious? One puny outing and they speculated marriage? She surfed over to the *Sun Tattler.*

She Comes with Her Own Tiara

"Who writes this stuff?"

The *Informant* posted the most salacious headline.

Finally! The Prince Has a Lover

"A lovely image of you, Corina."

Corina swung around to find Adelaide bent over her shoulder. "You scared me."

"Sorry, sweets, your door was unlocked. Yes, you and the prince make a loverly couple." She leaned closer to inspect Corina's Mac. "Aren't those newfangled computers something?"

"They're something, all right." But Adelaide's sweet voice comforted Corina's ruffled soul. "What was I thinking going to the premier with him? What was *he* thinking? I should've just gone on my own. And without that blasted tiara. Look, it just raised everyone's suspicions."

"'Tis not easy to love well, dear one." Adelaide's honeyed, granny gaze bloomed into a beacon, steady and strong. "You can play it safe if you choose, but it's the brave, those who face their fears, who tame the world, who win the day. Walk on waves." She started straightening the bed covers, shrinking back into sweet innocence.

"Where did you hear 'love well'?" Corina got up and tripped alongside her. "And where are the other guests? Am I the only one?"

Adelaide tugged on the damask bellpull. "Brill will bring your breakfast." She smoothed the quilt and plumped the pillows. "Yes, you are the only guest."

"This is the only room?"

"If there's only one guest, there is need for only one room."

"Adelaide, do you know the lady in white who sent me here?"

"She was to help you find your way. You are never alone. We are the keepers. The watchers." To the window, Adelaide shoved the curtains the full way open and straightened the window seat pillows.

"Keepers of..."

Brill, the old bear, appeared in the room with a tray of tea, eggs, bacon, and toasted muffins. It smelled divine.

"Set it there, Brill." Adelaide pointed to the table beside the chaise lounge. "She's a busy day ahead."

"Does she now?" The old man winked at Corina with a nod toward Adelaide. "Don't mind her. She can be a bit bossy."

"There's nothing wrong with me ears. I can hear you." Adelaide brushed her hand over the desk and lamp, then inspected her hand for the nonexistent dust. "Corina, if you spend time fretting over what was, you'll lose passion for what is meant to be, to see what God has written on your heart. You'll walk limp, like the prince, and never arrive at your position of authority. Hear me?"

How did she switch from demure to commanding in less than a breath? "I hear you."

"The path to life and love is pressing forward to what lies ahead. Not dwelling on what lies behind. That tiara is a sign to you. Accept it or deny it, but do not fret about it."

"Don't you see, the past is my future? If I don't reckon with it, how can I go forward?"

"He called you to walk the waves and you stepped out. Don't stare limpid-eyed at the shore, now." Steel. Each word, like a sword, trimming the fat of Corina's bravado.

"And if I fail?"

"You fight. You win the day. Just like King Stephen I and Queen Magdalena. And because of their love, they loved others. Well."

Corina laughed, sinking down to her bed. "But I'm not the only one involved here, Adelaide. What about Stephen?"

Adelaide stood by the door, one step from leaving. "This isn't about two but one. You. Your heart."

"But I can't love him if he doesn't love me."

"Think on it. Love is vast, rich, textured. If you limit yourself to only romantic love, you will never love well."

"You mean love as friends?" The notion settled disappointment on Corina. She wanted to be more than friends with Stephen. Truth was, she couldn't imagine life without him.

"This is your journey." Adelaide returned to the interior of the room, her eyes a portal of power and fire. "I'm only here to help you see." Then she was gone.

Corina brushed the chill from her arms as a light rain splattered against the window and her spirit churned.

She prayed for a long moment before settling down to her breakfast. Sipping her tea, she thought of Stephen. And her crazy journey.

What was he doing this cozy, rainy morning? Was he thinking of her? It rained every day the first week of their marriage, and they used the time well, cuddled up with the intentions of young lovers.

Corina finished her breakfast, thinking, praying. Then put aside her musings, gathered herself, wrote and filed her premier piece, then prepared for an afternoon with the incomparable Clive Boston.

The rain had stopped by the time she arrived at the café a few minutes before two and stepped out of a taxi, the wind catching up the full pleats and thick hem of her red-and-gold sundress.

Clive wolf-called from just under the café awning. "Gorgeous legs, darling," he said.

Corina grimaced, holding down her skirt, letting the ends of her ponytail flutter across her face as she adjusted the strap of her messenger bag. *Ignore him.*

"How does it feel?" she said, air kissing his cheek. "To be the star of another hit movie?"

His blue eyes traced the rim of her scoop neckline. "I'd rather talk about how a grown man wearing makeup and playing pretend gets to spend his afternoon with a beautiful American heiress." His plastic smile and Hollywood white teeth hid things Corina could not quite discern.

"For this afternoon, I'm a plain ole journalist." She scanned the tables under the awning, then moved to see inside the café. Moderate-sized crowd inside and out. "Do you want to go inside or sit out here?"

"I've a table all picked out." Clive tipped his head toward a cozy spot on the far side of the café, near the street but obscured by a lush array of foliage.

Corina followed him, weaving through the tables. The few guests sitting outside, with their heads bent together in conversation, seemed unaware of the star power among them.

Clive whistled at a waiter, motioning for him to come over. "What'll it be, love?" Clive said, leaning into her, holding out a wrought iron and mosaic tile chair, his breath too warm and too close.

She leaned away, her attention on the waiter. "Latte, skim milk."

He turned to the young man who'd answered his beckoning. "She'll have a latte with skim milk. I'll have English Breakfast tea with cream, thank you, my good chap." Clive, he flirted with everyone.

"Right away, sir. You're Clive Boston, aren't you?"

Clive sighed. "This again? No, dear lad, I'm his cousin. The more handsome cousin, but what am I to do?" He grimaced and sat in the chair opposite Corina. The waiter started to say something, then turned for the café door, shaking his head.

"You're bad," Corina said.

"Just having a bit of fun. Corina, you are more beautiful today than you were last night. That dress is amazing on you." Clive twisted sideways in his chair and draped his arm over the back, breaking out his big cinema charm.

He was too much. Really. *Ignore him.* Corina retrieved her iPad as well as a pen and paper. She'd record the interview but take notes on things that stood out to her—the atmosphere, key statements, Clive's outfit.

Dressed for the street, he looked more like a New England blue blood from Yale than a British-Italian actor who grew up in London's East End.

His khakis were crisp and pressed, his pale blue Polo, lightly starched. He wore loafers with no socks. And his rogue dark hair waved freely.

He was a commitment phobic, skittish about domestic life, trading out his women every few years, each one younger than the last.

Corina launched a recording app, then tapped the screen to open her questions. "I've been thinking all morning about how to approach this interview and—"

"What's the story between you and the prince?" Clive drew a cigarette from the crumpled packet he retrieved from his pants pocket and touched the end with a lighter flame. He squinted through a slither of smoke, invoking his trademark, smoldering expression.

"We're friends. The End."

"Very clever. Love, I know when a man is marking his territory, and if we'd been outdoors in the wild kingdom last night, the prince would have pummeled me."

"We're just friends." She smiled. *Okay? Are you done?* "I read some of the reviews of the film this morning while writing my own, and I loved what the *Liberty Press* said." She read from the iPad screen. "'Boston transcended his pop-icon image to become one of Europe's most—"

"'Heroic heroes.' Yes, love, I read the papers too. What are they teaching film critics today? Heroic heroes? What sort of drivel is that? Can a hero be unheroic?" He arched his brow, anticipating her response.

"I suppose. If the hero is merely the protagonist. He can want to be heroic but end up failing. King Stephen I faced his fears and the insurmountable odds to defeat Henry VIII and win Brighton. He never backed down." Corina propped her arm on the table, feeling the breeze of her words. She had to be as brave as the old king to love well. "His mission was so clear to him and nothing else seemed to matter. Not even his own life."

"Did I portray all of that in the film?"

Clive appeared surprised at his own question.

Corina smiled. "I think so, yes."

"Bravo me. I should get an Oscar nod. To be honest, I thought I was a bit too Scott Hunter." Clive took a long draw from his cigarette.

"Maybe." She laughed. "A little."

Clive tapped the ashes from his cigarette. "I read up about you too, Corina Del Rey. I'm sorry about your brother. Is that the dark rainbow I see in your eyes?"

The waiter arrived with Corina's latte and Clive's tea.

"Yes, my brother had the courage of King Stephen I, I think," Corina said, staring briefly through the leaves toward the busy side street. "But he died doing what he believed in. Fighting for freedom."

"Were you close?" Clive anchored his cigarette on an ashtray stand next to his chair and dropped a dollop of cream from a small silver pitcher into his tea.

She peeled the lid from her latte, letting the hot liquid cool. "Of course. Very. We were twins."

"So the rumors are true. The incredibly wealthy, aristocratic Del Reys are a true, close-knit family."

Were. Not true any longer. "How is it," she said, tapping a bit of sweetener into her latte, "that you keep taking over this interview, asking all the questions?"

"Because you are interesting. I'm a bore."

"Not to your fans. Clive, you've been 'radio-silent' for a decade. Come on, let's talk about you, this film, and why you are finally sitting for an interview."

"You know what I find interesting? You say you were friends

with Prince Stephen at uni, yet I've never seen you with him. How did you two manage to avoid the press? You're too tempting, love. Too gorgeous to leave alone." Clive drummed his fingers on the table, the thin tendrils of cigarette smoke twisting upward. "Then some years pass and, *wham-o*, you're on his arm for a very public, very *royal*, movie premier."

Corina tossed down her pen. "So? It happens. Friends reconnect."

"It's just curious. Stephen is rather close to the chest when it comes to women."

"Can I quote you?" The air under the awning was warm but pleasant and the sounds of city life—engines, horns, and voices—gave the place and Clive a casual feel. "Clive Boston keeps track of Prince Stephen's love life."

The actor scoffed, watching her over the edge of his teacup. "Quote whatever you like. My questions have a single purpose. I don't want him angry with me if I ask *his girlfriend* to dinner." He set down his cup, reached for his cigarette, and blew a stream of smoke upward, scenting the dew with menthol.

"Tell you what . . .", she said. "Let me conduct this interview and we'll see about dinner."

Clive grinned. "You have yourself a deal."

Technically, she couldn't call dinner with Clive a date. She was *married*. And last night her husband had kissed her. But dinner with Clive might be enjoyable—*if* she stressed they were only going as friends. When Clive let loose and forgot himself, he was funny and genuine good company.

"The film . . ." Corina sipped her latte as she scanned her notes. "You told the *Times* of London that you'd never do another period film. 'Too exhausting,' you said."

"Excuse me," a young woman said as she moved in and hovered over their table. "I'm so sorry to interrupt, but . . . Clive Boston." She exhaled all over them. "I've seen every one of your movies."

"Thank you, love." He smiled as if she might be his one and only. "Where are you from?"

"Ohio. Can I please take your picture?" She batted her lashes and cooed. Yeah, *cooed*. Corina paused the recording and crossed her arms, waiting, puttying her impatience with grace. She'd never interrupt a conversation for a picture with a celebrity. But then she had grown up with the Clive Bostons of the world dining at her father's table.

"Picture? But of course. What's your name?" He set down his tea. "How about a selfie? Corina, love, come round. Get in the shot."

"I think she'd prefer just you, Clive."

The girl, who said her name was Brooke, hovered next to Clive and held up her phone to snap the selfie. Then he signed a wadded-up receipt she dug out of her bag and offered her several flattering compliments. She blushed, thanked him, then hurried off with a dance and a squeal.

He narrowed his gaze at Corina, taking up his tea. "Got to keep them happy."

"You're a softy." She started the recording again.

"Shh...don't tell."

"So why did you do this period movie?"

"I liked King Stephen I. Brave chap."

"That's it? You liked the guy so you changed your policy?"

"I read Aaron's script. It spoke to me. And of course, I never miss a chance to work with Jeremiah Gonda. Guess you could say all of the pieces were there."

"How'd you prepare for the role? King Stephen I lived five hundred years ago. How does one go from jetting around the world watching movies on devices that fit in the palm of your hand to being a warrior with only a sword and a gaggle of determined men?"

Clive sipped his tea, then took a long, crackling drag from his cigarette. "You're in love with him, aren't you? I had that sense from the photo where the two of you were walking off together. Toward restaurant alley."

Corina stopped the recording and reached down for her messenger bag. "If you don't want to do the interview—"

"Corina, love, don't be this way. What's the fun of a one-sided interview?"

"Our deal was dinner if you let me interview you. Not you interviewing me."

"Sorry, darling, I thought you'd ask more interesting questions. 'How did you prepare for the role?' The idiots from the *LibP* ask those sorts of things."

"What sort of questions do you want to answer?" She folded her arms, waiting, mentally composing her opening sentence. *Clive Boston is a scoundrel.*

"Like why a man with an IQ of one fifty and a degree in astrophysics craved the stage? The limelight?"

He had an IQ of one fifty? "Why *does* a man with a high IQ crave the stage?"

"Because he wants to be loved. Approved. Applauded."

"Doesn't everyone? At some level? So why acting? Why not the world of science?"

Clive raised his tea for a drink but set it back down before taking a sip. "Because it's fun to pretend. To be someone else." He stared at her. "Don't you think?"

"Why does my relationship with Stephen interest you so much?"

"He's the Prince of Brighton. Love is hard to come by for princes. King Stephen I certainly worked to win his queen. Built that manor for her. Defied his council over her."

"Love is hard to come by for most people. True love, anyway. So is that why you're an actor? To find true love?"

He laughed. "Good grief, no. If anything, the stage, along with the acclaim, is an actor's only true love. Besides, what one lacks in love one can make up in riches. The pay is fabulous."

She scribbled a note. *Research Clive's academic life.* "So money is better than true love?"

"No, but it's a nice consolation prize."

"We have money. Lots of it. But not one red cent of the Del Rey fortune can bring back my brother." Nor purchase her true love's heart. "I can't even buy the details of his death."

"I'm sorry, Corina. I must sound like an insensitive clod."

"Don't apologize. You were just being honest. I'm the one snapping." Their eyes met for a moment on the level plane of understanding. "So, you have an IQ of one fifty?"

"According to the test. If you can believe those things." The tone of his voice drifted, sounding more like an everyday man than an arrogant actor.

"And a degree in astrophysics?"

"Says the diploma in the bottom of my bureau drawer." Clive jerked when his phone buzzed from his coat pocket. "Pardon me, Corina." Walking toward the street, he talked in a low tone.

Alone, Corina hunted for the image Clive mentioned on her iPad, starting with the *Liberty Press.* She searched the inside pages, but instead of finding the photo, she found an update. A press release from the King's Office.

Tuesday, 15 June
12:00 p.m.

    The King's Office responded to our request for information on the Prince of Brighton's date from last night.
    The Prince of Brighton is not romantically involved with the woman who attended the King Stephen I premier with him. Corina

Del Rey, an American heiress and an entertainment reporter with the Beaumont Post, is merely an acquaintance.

The prince is focused on his ankle rehabilitation, eager to return to rugby for the Premiership. "Romance is not important to me right now," the prince said.

The Prince of Brighton will be in attendance for the Children's Literacy Foundation Art Auction tonight at the Galaxy.

Corina shivered despite the respite in rain and the sun peeking under the awning. Acquaintance. She'd been demoted from lover to friend to acquaintance.

Dismissing her at the premier was one thing. But issuing a statement?

Clive returned and sat down, his eyes on her. "Everything all right, love? Why so serious?"

Corina popped a smile, exchanging the *LibP* page for her recording app. "Peachy. And you? Hope the call was good news."

"Just a friend," Clive said. "Wanting a favor. Asking if I'd attend the Children's Literacy Foundation Art Auction this evening. I said, 'Why not?' Guess we can do dinner another night. Say, Corina,"—Clive covered her hand with his—"are you sure you're all right?"

"Yes." She exhaled. "As my granny used to say, 'I'm right as rain.'"

TWENTY

*F*oot elevated on the stool, his skin blue from drowning his ankle in a bucket of ice, Stephen scrolled through his mental diary, making note of the days ahead, a swath of sun blanketing his office windows.

The light thawed his cold bones though a hardened lacquer baked around his heart. He'd spent the ice session numbing his feelings for Corina.

Last night's kiss left him jammed up, and tossing and turning through the night. Just as he'd drift away, he'd hear her voice—*"Babe..."*—and feel her touch. Then he'd pop wide awake, wanting her.

At 3:00 a.m., he remanded himself to the media room and watched the film of the summer internationals sent over by Coach Stuart.

Around 5:00 a.m., he fell asleep and dreamt of nothing. Just the way he liked it.

"Sir?" Robert popped into the room. "Teatime."

"Good man." Stephen lowered his foot and massaged the blood back into his toes. His ankle always felt strong after the ice. But when his blood warmed, the weaknesses surfaced and his limp returned.

Robert trolleyed in the tea cart, setting up by the chairs. "You're all arranged for the art auction tonight, sir. The limousine will pull round at seven forty-five. Shall you dress at seven fifteen?"

"That's fine." Stephen popped a chocolate biscuit in his mouth. He expected the butler-valet-aide to exit, but when he turned, the man stood by the door. "What is it?"

"Your brother is on his way."

"Now? Did he say why?"

"No, only asked if you were on the premises." Robert backed out of the room.

Wonder what he wants? He couldn't be upset at the morning photos. He was on board with Stephen attending the premier with Corina. Which, when Stephen thought on it, was rather odd.

"Get her to sign the annulment papers," he'd said. Whilst his actions said, "Be with her."

Stephen was glad the kiss happened after midnight, in the shadows, without the probing eye of the press. Impulse could indeed be his very good friend. He'd not kissed a woman in a very long time. Five and a half years to be exact. When Corina kissed him good-bye.

"I'll go." Tears streamed down her face. "But I don't understand."

Silence. If he opened his mouth, he'd break. Tell her the truth. He had to remove her from his life.

"Tell me, do you not love me?"

"Corina . . ." He propped against the wall as she stood by the open door. Otherwise, he'd sink to the floor in a huddled mess.

"Then can you at least kiss me?" She brushed her hand over his chest, moving into him. Passion fired through him.

When her lips touched his, he remained stiff and unyielding. Cold.

Stephen pinched the memory and sipped his tea, searching for the telly remote. Wonder what Madeline and Hyacinth have to say this afternoon? The telly was already tuned to their station.

"Madeline," Hyacinth said, aiming the front page of the *LibP* at the camera, "this was all the scuttlebutt this morning, the prince with this gorgeous American, Corina Del Rey."

"Who tweeted our show Friday afternoon, yet he sat right here, denying anything between them."

"Hold on, Mads. That's the beauty of broadcasting live." Hyacinth held up a blue piece of paper. "The King's Office released a statement this afternoon, confirming Prince Stephen is not romantically linked with Corina Del Rey." She sat back with a face and posture that said she didn't believe a word of it.

"Oh, ladies, please, move on. What about your bloke Clive Boston?" Stephen talked to the TV. Talked to his heart. "Last week you couldn't get enough of him."

"Hy, you don't believe it?" Madeline reached for the paper. "I mean it's official, from the King's Office."

"I think they're just trying to get us off their scent."

"Ooh, you think there's a scent?" Madeline leaned toward Hy, releasing the paper to float through the air. The audience applauded, agreeing.

"There's a scent all right. And it's wearing American perfume."

Hyacinth and Madeline launched into a debate about their prince, the most eligible bachelor in Brighton, probably the world, and, ladies, they were losing him to an American.

They already had one American princess in the palace.

Stephen steamed, rising to his feet, talking to the telly. "It's none of your business."

Then they lit up the Twitter universe. "What do you think, ladies? Should the Prince of Brighton marry a Brightonian girl?"

Stephen shoved out of his chair. He needed to pace. Never mind his swelling ankle.

"Here's a good idea . . . a tweet from Rebekah911," Madeline said. "'Bring him back on the show and ask him.'"

The audience gave a rousing cheer.

Stephen popped the air with his fist. "Never, Maddie, never."

On that note, the study door opened and Nathaniel entered, dressed in black tie. "Talking to the telly again?"

"Madeline and Hyacinth are deciding my love life on national television. What's this about the King's Office issuing a statement?"

"We were flooded with inquiries this morning." Nathaniel smoothed his hand down the silk front of his tuxedo.

"Ignore them."

"You know that only goes so far."

Stephen sat down hard into the chaise chair.

"I loathe this." He motioned to the tea cart. Did Nathaniel want a cup? "Every time she turns around she's getting rejected."

"I didn't know you cared."

"Good grief, Nathaniel, of course I care."

"I see. I was confused by the five and a half years of silence."

Stephen shot his brother a dark visual dagger. "Is this why you dragged yourself over here? In a tuxedo? To talk about my failings?" He motioned to his brother's formal attire. "Where are you off to?"

"Bluffwood." On the north tip of the island, an hour's flight away, the stone-and-beam palace was used largely for state functions, celebrations, hosting parties and charities. "The Foundation for Education honoring Mum with a ball is tonight. We're wheels up in an hour. Anyway, I came to see how it went last night. From the photographs it looked as if you were getting on with Corina." Nathaniel moved to the tea cart and poured himself a cup.

"We got on well enough." The passion of the kiss boomeranged on him, buzzing over Stephen's lips

"The film is getting rave reviews. Did you like it? Susanna and I have a private screening this weekend."

"It was grand. On a blockbuster scale."

"How did you leave things with Cor—"

"I kissed her."

Nathaniel glanced at Stephen, his cup and saucer cradled in his palm. "And why did you do that?"

"I don't know rightly, but nothing's changed. I still want the annulment." Stephen reached for a low stool and elevated his foot. "I don't understand you, Nathaniel. You force me to fly to America to see her, demand I get annulment papers signed, then act as if you're cheering me on to win her over."

"I admit, I was angry with you at first. You acted in a foolish and irresponsible manner marrying her that way. I wanted this mess resolved."

"Why do I sense a 'but now' in your tone?"

"I've softened 'tis all. Talked this over with Susanna. Then I remembered my brother who manipulated my coronation guest list to include the woman you thought I loved but was too cowardly to admit it."

"Cowardly? No, I'd never assign those words to you Nathaniel. If anything you were too willing to fall on your kingly sword for the sake of the kingdom and perish the love in your foolish heart."

"Nevertheless, you were right. I did love her. Here you are, doing the same thing, not admitting you love Corina. Must be something in our brotherly blood. I think you should give your marriage—"

"Don't." Stephen waved off the rest of the conversation. "It's not going to happen."

"Did you like kissing her?"

"Not going to happen, Nathaniel."

"Do you still have feelings for her?"

"Not going to happen, Nathaniel." He'd stay stuck on this mantra until it got through his brother's thick skull.

"Do you need to book another session with Mark Pyle? Talk about what happened in Afghanistan? Because it seems to be holding you back from true love."

"What I need is for you to leave me alone, my ankle to heal, and to get back on the pitch. I can talk until I'm blue, Nathaniel, but nothing will bring back Carlos, Bird, and the others."

"So that's it then. Carlos is dead, so Corina cannot be your wife."

"The long and short of it, yes." The summation felt odd in his chest. For years he'd reasoned this all out in his head, but speaking it aloud removed all doubt.

"You can't assign motive to Corina, Stephen. Or decide for her."

"But I can't tell her the whole truth now, can I? About Asif. About my meddling. It's a matter of national and royal security."

"I hardly consider a recommendation as meddling," Nathaniel said. "Neither does the Defense Ministry."

"Perhaps, but it doesn't change the fact that my wife's brother died saving my life."

Nathaniel pursed his lips. "Are you sure you can never move past it?"

"Could you? Besides, I'm not sure whether *it* will let me go."

"Does it seem so insurmountable? Do you regret marrying her?"

"I try not to think about it. No looking back, just forward. Regret serves no purpose, does it? Which is why I carry on with rugby."

"You know you can't avoid being a member of the royal family forever. You are Prince of Brighton, coronation or not. Which is a matter to discuss later." Nathaniel sipped his tea, still standing.

Stephen laughed low. "Touché. You know I love the family. It's just when I'm on the pitch I feel I'm doing something for the country, for the lads in the military, for the youth."

"I think I've said this before, but it's worth repeating. You're not responsible for those men's death. Asif acted alone."

"But I recommended him. And Carlos Del Rey was in Peshawar, safe and sound, until I put in his name for our flight unit. As for the others, I suppose they knew the risk when they volunteered to serve with me. But who'd have ever imagined . . ."

"Stephen, somehow you have to fix this within yourself. This burden is too much for one man to carry the rest of his life."

"Perhaps it is my lot." Stephen made his way to the window and lifted the pane, letting in summer's breeze. Two stories below were the green hills of the palace grounds. An oasis amid the concrete city. "I was getting on fine until my injury—until you came round with that marriage certificate. I can't explain it, Nathaniel. But I was over her until I saw her. Then she showed up here and I'm less over her every day."

Because at the end of it all, Corina Del Rey was the love of his life.

"Has she signed the annulment?"

"Not yet."

"All right, well, try on this idea. Susanna suggested a mid-week retreat to Parrsons House, Wednesday through Friday morning. We'd go on the weekend but we're booked."

"What's that got to do with me?"

"We thought we'd make it a family event. Mum and Henry are packing in with us. Perhaps you … and Corina … could come along?"

Stephen laughed. "Invite Corina on a family getaway? After the debacle at dinner?"

"Susanna thought she deserved another chance. As do I. Mum's crazy about her. Consider yourself duly warned."

"Invite her out to what end? This is the exact opposite of fil-ing for annulment. Is this you getting back at me for meddling in your affairs with Susanna?"

"Certainly not, and if anything, I'm in your debt for your trickery. I suppose I see two options with bringing Corina out to Parrsons. One, you'll realize, as you've already indicated, that you're not over her and—"

"It doesn't matter if I'm over her or not, Nathaniel. Why can't you see that?"

"Or she'll sign the papers quickly and you'll be done with it."

"Not going to happen, Nathaniel."

Nathaniel moved toward the door with his usual air of authority. "Think on it. We're leaving in the morning."

When he was alone, Stephen stared at the muted telly screen—Madeline and Hyacinth were rather comical without sound—the predicament of his heart rolling out before him.

Being with Corina awakened the dormant part of his life, the part that yearned for more. Rugby only exercised one emotional muscle. But what of the rest? Surely he must be a bit lopsided in his strength.

Nevertheless, he could manage. Carry on. Stephen pictured Corina, lovely Corina, handing him a set of signed annulment papers. The idea plunged his soul, and instead of feeling relief and freedom, he felt alone, lost, and aching to shed the bonds of his invisible shackles.

The six o'clock cathedral bells pealed through the city, electrifying the misty evening with an ancient song.

Corina glanced up, an image of Stephen breaking through her thoughts, loose strands of her hair blowing across her face. "Is it six o'clock already?" Her interview with Clive had gone much better than expected. For four hours, he sat with her in the back corner table, watching the rain, chain smoking, and sharing about his life

"I love the bells. Makes me want to do something profound. Charge a hill or kiss a beautiful woman." Clive gazed at her as the choreographed bells resounded against the concrete and glass of downtown.

"The bells make me want to kneel in prayer."

Clive laughed. "Well, if that didn't douse my passion flames."

Corina dusted her fingers together. "My work here is done."

Clive grinned, dashing out his latest cigarette. After maneuvering the rough patches of Clive's personality, Corina and the star-actor-philanthropist hit a friendly stride that had them talking about everything from his career to babies to politics.

He was a much richer, deeper, kinder man than he let the public see. He shared about his impoverished childhood. His middle-grade teachers who recognized his brilliance. The patron who sponsored his Oxford education. His first love, who introduced him to the theatre. *"I never looked back."*

The sixth chime rang out, the song of the bells vibrating in the rain-soaked air.

"I think I'll never tire of the syncopated bells."

"If we think this is beautiful, imagine what heaven must be like." Corina collected her things, reaching for her messenger bag.

"Heaven? Huh, never consider it much," Clive said. "But what an incredible force. Seven cathedral bells ringing in unison." He tapped another cigarette from the crumpled pack until he saw the overflowing ashtray. He raised his eyes to Corina. "We've been here awhile."

"Four hours." The interview couldn't have gone better. She had enough material for a biography. She'd text Gigi that they should run the interview as a Sunday feature, both print and online, the month *King Stephen I* opened in the States. "I can't thank you enough, Clive. You are quite an amazing man."

"What do you think they're singing?" he said. "The bells?"

She peered into his deep brown eyes. "I'm not sure, but in my head I hear, 'Glory to God in the highest. Peace on earth, goodwill to men.'"

Clive inclined his ear. Was there a soft mist in his eyes? "'Glory to God ... peace on earth ... goodwill to men.'"

"Such a beautiful, powerful sound." One that reminded her she had a secret.

"I know it's late, love. As I said, I've this *thing* tonight, Children's Literacy Foundation Art Auction at Royal Galaxy Hall. Would you care to go? You do owe me a dinner." Clive splashed Corina with his smarmy Hollywood smile.

"I don't know." She patted her messenger bag. "I should get these notes organized." Besides, Stephen would be there. According to the *LibP.*

"*Pfffft.*" He waved her off. "Let them simmer. I find things are more clear when I leave them be." He stood, reaching for her arm. "Come, I need a date tonight or I'll be mobbed. A beautiful lass is the best deterrent. Besides, you can dispel the rumors. Tomorrow the headlines will be 'Is She the Prince's Girl or Clive Boston's?'"

"Very droll, but I'm not interested in any more headlines."

"Do you protest because your prince is the foundation's patron?" Clive folded his arms and leaned against the ornate iron pole holding up the awning.

"Clive," Corina said with a punctuated sigh, "I think you have a thing for the prince yourself."

His hearty laugh garnered the attention of those around them. The whispers started. *Clive Boston.* "It's just I know what I see." He tapped the corner of his eye. "I see love."

"You see nothing," Corina said, standing, slipping her iPad into the messenger bag.

"There are none so blind as those who will not see."

"Whatever, Clive." Blind or not, he'd managed to circle the conversation back around to the beginning. Speculation about Stephen. The truth? She wanted to see him. Save for the annulment papers, last night's hasty good-bye in the amber lights of the Manor might have been their last.

"Come, I'll drive you home." Clive roped his arm around her, steering her away from the café toward a private car park. "I promise to be a perfect gentleman."

"In the car or at the auction?"

He squeezed her shoulder. "Then you'll go?" He clapped his hand over his heart. "Be still. I may never recover."

"As a friend." *I am a married woman.*

"But of course."

Clive drove a Lamborghini, which had more horsepower than the Cathedral City streets could contain. Corina gripped the door handle as the actor gunned the gas, then eased off, then gunned it again to the rhythm of a blaring Steven Tyler song.

"Which hotel, love?" he said. "The Wellington or Royal Astor?"

"Neither. I'm at this quaint inn called the Manor between Gliden and Martings."

"The Manor? Why aren't you at The Wellington? Or the Astor?"

"The Wellington was booked. I never made it to the Astor."

His expression said he didn't believe her, but he zipped on through traffic, jerking the wheel of the Lamborghini as he changed lanes, belting out "Walk This Way" an octave higher than Steven Tyler.

When he turned down Market Avenue, he cut across two lanes to a flurry of car and lorry horns, careened around the corner to Crescent, and crashed-stopped on the curb by Gliden. He leaned to see out her window. "Where did you say you were staying?"

"There." She rapped her window, pointing out the small, thick-beam structure. "The Manor."

Clive turned down the music, squinting. "Corina, sweetheart, I see nothing between Gliden and Martings but a narrow, old alley."

"Where are you looking? It's right there." She powered down her window and pointed. "It's small but you can't miss it. See the light in the window?"

He jerked back into his seat, revving the engine. "If you don't want me to know where you're staying, lass, just say so. But making up a place? Tsk, tsk, I thought more of you. After all we meant to each other this afternoon."

"Clive, I'm not making it up." She brushed her hand over the chills skirting down her arm. "Watch, I'll get out and go inside."

"You're going to go inside? Of what?" He motioned with his palm up. "An alley between two department stores? Love, if you need a place to stay, I've a spare room." He surrendered both hands as if warding off her protest. "Strictly platonic. At least for the first night." He winked. "The guest rooms are on the other side of the house."

Corina glanced toward the Manor's front window where she could see Brill sweeping the lobby. "You really don't see it?"

"Lamb, I do not and I'm a bit concerned if you do."

Corina popped her door open and slipped the strap of her bag over her shoulder. "See you tonight? I'll hire a cab. Meet you there?"

"Corina, darling, I can't leave you by a curb. What will the prince say if anything happens to you?"

"Thanks for the ride, Clive." She slammed the car door and turned for the Manor as he sped off. If she'd not spent the last four hours with him, she'd believe he was pulling her leg with this no-Manor manner. But he'd been somber and sincere all afternoon once he'd settled down, letting his heart open, becoming her friend.

So, if he didn't see the inn, then how did Stephen? What about Thomas? A shiver descended on her thoughts.

What's going on?

Adelaide's piquant face appeared at the door. "You coming in? Supper's on soon."

"Y–yeah, sure." Corina glanced back at Clive's car, the red taillights disappearing, and crossed the threshold of the Manor.

TWENTY-ONE

The curved steel of Royal Galaxy Hall, designed to look like a spacecraft, embraced Corina as she walked through the doors.

The futuristic structure cast a cold blue glow over the five-hundred-year-old streets, over the ancient thatched roofs that still existed in the historical district of Cathedral City.

Corina snapped pictures with her phone, musing about the significance of architecture. How it represented where a people had been while speaking of where they are going.

Circulating through the showroom, the music thumping and bumping, she searched the guests for Clive. He'd texted, asking her to meet him by the children's finger painting display. But she was fine with viewing the gallery on her own for a few minutes. She might even buy a piece. The Children's Literacy Foundation was a worthy cause and she'd always wanted to collect art.

Cathedral City had been home to some of the world's most beloved renaissance artists. History credited them with moving Brighton out of the Dark Ages toward enlightenment.

At the children's display, Corina loved the finger paintings.

Such creativity. Especially the one of Jesus with a giant S on his chest. Maybe that one was coming home with her.

Around the wall to a display of acrylic by thirteen- to fifteen-year-olds, Corina ran into a group of men in tuxedos. Clive?

But he was not among them.

That's when she saw the Pissarro, one of the Impressionist paintings up for auction. Oh my, it was the "Rue du Roi—Avenue of the Kings."

Her heart filled with memories as she moved closer to inspect the piece. *God, what am I to do with this?*

The historical scene of the Avenue of the Kings from the top of the Braithwaite Tower, with the horses and carriages standing in the gaslights after a cleansing rain, was magical. Glorious. The view Stephen and Corina experienced the night he proposed. And it was to be auctioned.

"Extraordinary piece, isn't it? Eighteen ninety-eight." A woman wearing a Children's Literacy Foundation badge joined Corina. "We are blessed to have it. The piece was lost for the last five and a half years."

"Lost?"

"Construction workers found it in an old warehouse on the north side of the city. No one knows how it got there. We believe it belonged to a private collector, but we can't find the records. Can you imagine? The workmen brought it to us, suggesting we auction it tonight on behalf of the foundation. We will find a permanent home for this beautiful piece."

"This is my favorite view in the whole city," Corina said.

"Mine as well. My husband proposed to me on the Braithwaite." The woman sighed. "Do be sure to register if you haven't already. The auction starts in thirty minutes."

"Thank you." Corina watched the woman until the crowd folded in behind her, then turned back to the painting.

The woman's husband proposed to her on the Braithwaite? The painting was lost for five and a half years? It was too much. Too much. Was she to consider these signs or mere coincidence? Everything around her pointed to Stephen.

But he's not looking, God.

Flushed and trembling, awash with sentiment, she missed him. Missed Carlos. Even that crazy Diamatia that became her wedding gown.

"This is my favorite place in the whole world," she said as he slipped his arms around her waist.

"Will you miss me?" He set his finger under her chin and raised her face to his, bending for a kiss. He looked resplendent in his dress uniform, a gold royal braid across his chest.

"With every fiber of my being."

Holding her, he leaned against the twisted wrought iron railing that hemmed in the Braithwaite terrace, and they gazed into the glittering Rue du Roi.

"So beautiful."

"This is Cathedral City."

The bells chimed. Nine times. She rested her head against his chest, listening to his heart beat in time with the bells. How could she be so very happy yet so very sad?

"The Pissarro." Stephen's voice floated over her shoulder. "One of my favorites."

Corina turned to find him standing several feet behind her, surrounded by somber-faced auction types—a woman in a long white gown that washed out her pale complexion and a set of tuxedoed men.

Their eyes met, but for such a brief moment she wasn't sure he saw her. She started to address him, but the group moved, Stephen with them, without a word or glance toward Corina.

Thomas trailed behind, giving her a sweet nod hello.

She smiled, but barely, inhaling the truth. Stephen would *never* truly acknowledge her in public. Why should he? They were over.

"Don't give up, love." Clive leaned against the display wall, his face lit up with a cheeky grin.

"There you are. Where have you been?"

"Seriously, Corina, back alley drunks are more aware of what's going on than you."

"Don't start with this Prince Stephen business again."

He laughed and joined her, facing the painting. "We'd make a good couple, you and me. A power duo."

Corina regarded him for a moment, assessing his vulnerability. He'd confessed during their interview that he'd given up on love after an intense Oxford-years heartbreak.

"Clive, you rapscallion." Corina manufactured a solid, jovial laugh. "You're just dying to add me to your string of broken-hearted babes, aren't you?"

He collected himself, the light changing in his eyes. "You found me out, sly lass. But it was worth a try. I've no American heiress in my stable." He kissed her cheek, whispering in her ear. "But if you change your mind . . ."

Corina squeezed his hand. "You'll be the first to know."

"If you'll pardon me, I'll see what other beauties are about. Shall we catch up later, have an appetizer or two and call it dinner. You are supposed to be my date."

"Say nine o'clock?"

"Perfect."

Oh Clive. No wonder he hid from the press. He was hiding from himself.

"How did it go? With Clive?" This time when she turned, Corina found Stephen standing alone, his arms clasped behind his back. "Did he ask you to marry him? He's known for spontaneous proposals that don't go anywhere."

"At least he's honest about it."

Stephen scoped the area with a sly glance, then leaned toward her. "Nathaniel and Susanna are taking a few days at Parrsons House. You're invited. If you care to come."

"I'm invited. By the family I rudely walked out on Sunday night?"

"Don't make us out to be insensitive clods." Agitated, he shifted his stance, taking the weight from his booted ankle. "Do you want to come or not? Nathaniel and Susanna want to leave tomorrow."

"Do you *want* me to come?" Their eyes met, but only for a moment.

"I—it might be pleasant."

"Your confidence is killing me."

"Hey, do you want to go or not? Never mind, I'll come for you at eleven sharp." He walked off into a gathering of well-dressed men and women, waiting in audience for him, cameras flashing.

Corina bit back her grin. She was spending time in the country with her husband and his family. How lovely.

Now, to register for the auction and see about acquiring a treasured Pissarro.

TWENTY-TWO

Gigi

*H*er nose for news itched like a flea-bitten hound. Gigi pushed away from her desk and walked toward the window, hands on her hips, watching the river lap against the embankment.

The front page of the *Informant* ran a grainy image of Prince Stephen at a fund-raiser last night, and don't you just know, Corina Del Rey stood in the background.

Something was up, yet something also lurked beneath the surface.

Not to mention her boots-on-the-ground minions were failing her left and right. Not one had any intel on Corina or the prince.

Reaching for her phone, Gigi fired off a text to Corina.

ART AUCTION? W/ PRINCE. DO TELL.

NOTHING TO TELL.

Gigi paced to the window. Twin sailboats glided down the river toward the arched causeway, cutting through shards of sunlight.

She was just going to have to be persistent. Back at her desk, she fired off an e-mail.

> To: Madeline Stone
> Subject: Love this recipe
> Any intel on Prince Stephen and Corina Del Rey will be well worth your while.
>
> GB

Wednesday evening, as the sun set over the country estate, Stephen bent over the makeshift boules court.

A bit of Joplin ragtime played from under the lawn tent, where Mum and Henry reclined, holding hands in the space between their chairs, listening to music and watching the game.

A breeze chugged up from the surrounding valley, cool and sweet, fragrant with the dewy, dark earth of Brighton. Caught in the current, Corina's long, free hair billowed behind her back as she looked on, waiting for Nathaniel and Stephen to set up the court.

The drive to Parrsons from the city this morning had been pleasant, as if they'd determined without words to just *be*, forgetting the difficulty between them.

But being around Corina reminded him of why he adored her. She challenged his carefully carved spaces. She made him laugh. She made him want to be more, to test his boundaries, to be the man he was meant to be.

"Okay, we're ready," Nathaniel said with one last inspection of the court.

Susanna stepped foward, tossing the metal boule ball in her hand. "I say girls against boys."

"Susanna," Corina protested with a wave of her hands, "I'm horrible at this game. I couldn't hit that little red jack-thing if I was standing over it with a hammer."

"I'll take my chances." Susanna's expression made Stephen laugh. She was so utterly American. *I'll take those odds and win anyway.*

"Susanna, really, I'm horrible."

"Sounds fair to me." Nathaniel kicked four balls toward Stephen. "Winners earn bragging rights. Without one word of complaint from the losers."

"You're on, Mr. Big Stuff." Susanna shook on the deal, giving Nathaniel's hand a hard squeeze. "Georgia Girls verses Brighton Boys."

"Wasn't there a song about that?" Stephen said, snapping his fingers, humming, laughing.

"Not yet," Susanna tossed him a wink. "Now, move aside men. Corina and I are going to practice. Corina, sugar, all you have to do is roll the ball to the red jack there in the middle. Feel free to knock the guys' balls to kingdom come."

"Susanna, really." Corina ran her palms down the side of her shorts, nervous. "I'm horrible."

"Corina, you're not supposed to smack talk yourself. Come on."

Stephen strained forward with each of Corina's boule rolls, willing the ball toward the jack. But she was right. She wasn't very good.

"All right," Susanna said, popping her hands together, her voice every bit like Coach Stuart's. "You'll get it. Let's practice again."

"Enough practice. Let's play." Nathaniel moved to the top of the playing lane.

Stephen watched his prim and proper brother, the disciplined

King Nathaniel, grinning. The man was every bit as competitive as his wife. And twice as competitive as his brother. No way did he want to lose this little lawn tourney. He bowed toward his wife. "Ladies first."

"We'll take it."

Stephen captured Corina's hand as he walked past and whispered, "You can do this."

"If you say so." Her response was soft against his soul, her warm gaze peaceful. "But I'm not proud. I'm willing to let Susanna carry me."

He laughed, releasing her hand, and joined his brother. Another time, in a life undisturbed by war, this game would be Brighton princes against their princesses.

She was his wife but not his princess. An honor he'd robbed from her.

"It's ladies against the gents, I see." Mum walked out from under the lawn tent and joined the women. At fifty-eight, she was graceful and elegant in her linen slacks, cashmere sweater, and pearls. The Queen of Brighton, having lived with Dad for over thirty years, first as he was the crown prince, then king. After his death, Stephen wasn't sure she'd ever laugh again. But she'd found a new joy in Henry's love.

"We'll play one round for bragging rights. The rest for fun," Nathaniel said. "Mum and Henry will be discrepancy judges. Henry, remember I'm your king and this close to approving your new young businessmen project."

"Oh my word ... blackmail?" Susanna huffed, roping an arm of solidarity around Corina. "Never mind. We'll win anyway."

"Susanna, please." Corina verged on begging. "You overestimate me."

But the game was under way and Corina was to bowl first. Stephen crouched along the side of the court. "Get as close as you can to the jack. Give it a little hook when you—"

She paused with a sigh, glancing over at him. "Will you shut up? You're making me nervous."

Nathaniel muffled his laugh, pressing his fist to his lip.

Stephen rocked back on his haunches. "Fine, then, show us what you got, Del Rey."

Her roll barely made it halfway, but Susanna more than made up for it, bowling within centimeters of the jack. She would be tough to beat.

Corina cheered and slapped her partner a high five.

But Nathaniel's roll knocked Susanna out of play. "Oh, Stratton, you are going to pay for that one."

"Bring it, Stratton." Nathaniel snatched Susanna for a kiss and Stephen glanced away, hiding his envy.

Stephen hadn't easily warmed to Susanna's American flavor— she reminded him too much of Corina and what he'd lost—but now he couldn't imagine the family without her. He glanced round to Corina, catching her eye, smiling.

"Stephen, you're up, little brother. Show them how it's done."

The competition rocked between Nathaniel, Stephen, and Susanna—who was single-handedly defeating the men. With ten balls played, two remaining, Corina crouched for her final turn, spinning the ball in her palm.

"Just like walking the runway . . . it's a beauty pageant . . . a beauty pageant. Going to sing a song . . . easy-peasy." She released the ball, gently, and with a slight spin.

The metal piece rolled down the lane at the perfect speed, curved around Nathaniel's ball, and lightly kissed the jack. Then stopped.

"I did it!" Corina jumped, screaming, gaping at Susanna, who wrapped her in a celebratory hug.

"The beauty pageant queen brought her A game."

"Love, you did it." Stephen said, wishing he were free to sweep her up in his arms and kiss her. "I knew you could."

She tipped her head back, arms wide. "I love boules."

"Stephen, come on, mate. You're up." Nathaniel slapped his back. "We're still in this. For all the bragging rights."

"R–right." But he didn't want bragging rights. He wanted to see the expression on Corina's face when the girls won.

As he bent to roll his ball, a comfort he'd not felt in five and a half years coursed through him. He was coming home. The rest of the way around the bend.

Corina knelt on the ground, singing. "Miss it, miss it, now you have to kiss it."

Susanna laughed. "Oh my gosh, I've not heard that in years."

"It's the only talent I can bring to this game."

Stephen peeked at her. Oh, he'd kiss *it* all right.

Mum stood with Susanna near midcourt, watching, while Henry came alongside Nathaniel, cheering. "Come on, lad. For the gents."

"Don't you dare go easy on her," Nathaniel said.

"Never you fear." Balancing on his good foot, Stephen aimed and rolled his ball with gentle perfection. If he calculated right, his roll should bump Corina's and stop just shy of the jack.

"Come on, come on." Nathaniel paced alongside the court with the ball. "For all the bragging rights."

Stephen watched Corina, yelling at the ball, tussling with Nathaniel, laughing, singing at the ball, "Miss it, miss it."

She had to win. Stephen sent his own wishes toward the boule. *Come on, stop!*

The air over the lawn dropped to a whisper. Motions slowed. Sounds were muted. Colors bleached.

Then it happened. Stephen's boule stopped just shy of Corina's. He exhaled, falling off his heels onto his back, stretching out on the grass.

Susanna and Corina erupted with shrills and shouts, launching into some sort of wild winning ritual dance—must be an

American thing—that had the Queen of Brighton bumping hips with her daughter-in-law. No, her *daughters*-in-law.

Nathaniel stood over Stephen, offering his hand. "We gave it our best, say, little brother?"

"Absolutely, our very best." Stephen stood, his gaze, his heart, every sense in his body fixed on Corina. He had to tell her. Everything. He was sick of hiding, fearing, living for her in his own head. If she hated him, then she hated him.

At least they'd both know the reason why.

TWENTY-THREE

One moment she'd been celebrating. The next, trailing off with Stephen, his hand gripping hers.

"Where are we going?"

"Just come." Stephen strode ahead of her toward one of the motor carts. When she slipped in next to him, he started down the lawn, away from the family, leaving behind comfort and driving toward the unknown.

Corina peered at him. An end-of-day beard shadowed his jaw, and from under his dark lashes his blue eyes glowed with a reflection she did not recognize.

A dozen questions fired through her mind as Stephen steered the cart over the grounds, creating a path in the thick grass, but she kept them to herself. He'd talk when he was ready.

For now, it was enough to be with him, to hear the song of the night birds on the breeze.

Up a slight incline, Stephen urged the cart to the top of a knoll, through a stand of trees, and popped into a small clearing where a cultivated, low stone garden sat under six royal oaks.

He parked next to the wall and cut the motor, resting his hand on the steering wheel. "Besides me, the gardener is the only person who ever comes to this place."

"Stephen, it's beautiful." Corina stepped out her side of the cart. Heather and a deep pink foxglove grew near the wall, along with purple and yellow blooms she did not know. Between two of the trees, toward the back, sat an iron-and-wood-slat bench.

"I come here on Remembrance Day." Stephen stood beside her. "And December twentieth."

"W–what is this place? A memorial?" She glanced at him, hand to her heart, noticing the granite stones under each tree.

"Mine. Yes." Stephen reached into the cart for a torch and motioned for her to walk through the gate. "One year the team was playing in Australia, and I flew home to lay a wreath at these markers for Remembrance Day. I'm off the pitch that day. Don't care what's at stake."

Corina started down the path between a row of hedges. "You built this?"

"I needed a place to go, to remember what the lads did without the world watching." He aimed the torch beam over one grave marker, then another. "The bodies aren't here, but . . ." His voice faded as a slight shudder moved over his shoulders. "Their spirits are. At least to me. When I come here, the voices, the explosions, the turmoil stops. Peace. This place, along with rugby, keeps me going."

"A peace you couldn't find with me?" Why couldn't he just say it? He didn't love her enough to find peace with her.

He aimed the flashlight on her face. "It's not as straightforward as all that, Corina." Then he moved on, the torch shining on a brass plate attached to the bench. "*Memento semper.* Always remember." His voice was husky and deep. "Here lie my brothers. The six men on my crew."

She looked at him with an eye of revelation. "They died saving you, didn't they?"

"Yes." He took her by the arm and led her to the first granite stone on the right-hand side of the bench. "Here's what lies between us, Corina."

She bent to read a very familiar name.

LIEUTENANT CARLOS DEL REY
JOINT COALITION, INTELLIGENCE SECURITY
SON, BROTHER, FRIEND

"Carlos." She dropped to her knees, flattening her palm over her brother's cold name. "W–why is he here? I don't understand."

"The garden is a monument to the lads who died because someone else wanted me dead." Stephen walked to the next stone. "Carlos and Bird actually saved my life."

She jumped up, weary of this game. "These drips and drabs are killing me. Carlos saved your life?"

Stephen lowered the flashlight until it created a spot at his feet. Overhead, the blue edge of twilight covered them.

"The joint security forces faced some intense fighting in Torkham a few months after we were deployed. We lost our tactical specialist, so I recommended Carlos. He was one of the best. That's how he ended up in Torkham."

"We never heard."

"His transfer was still being processed when he was killed. He'd only been on base two days, Corina."

"He wasn't killed in a firefight was he?" Corina's heart drew pictures with Stephen's words, filling in the dark, sketchy shadows of her brother's death, of Stephen's radical change, and the end of it all.

Stephen sat down on the edge of the bench. "Things were quiet right after Carlos transferred in. We were planning a Deliberate Op, but there was some downtime from the chaos. Carlos was Carlos, making fast friends with the crew, offering insight from his time in Peshawar. I'd planned to tell him about you and me on his second night, figured I'd start letting the news out slowly."

With a sense of the surreal, Corina sat with her back to the gravestone, listening.

"The first mission started at zero hundred the next day and the camp was quiet, everyone trying for some shut-eye. But we were too keyed up to sleep. Carlos had just challenged several of us to a game of Nintendo when Asif entered."

"Asif?"

"Our interpreter. A Pakistani chap raised on Brighton's northern shore, a friend from uni, actually. He joined our unit after I recommended him to the joint council." Stephen carried a detached tone in his voice as he told the story. "I got up for something . . . I can't even remember what." It haunted him. "I told Asif to pull up, join us, but something was wrong. He looked sick. Stoned."

"Oh my gosh . . . Stephen." He drew her toward truth, unfurling his story. "He was suiciding."

"Yes." He fired up from the bench, agitated.

"How did Brighton military allow such a man to be on base? Don't you run intel on enlistees or civilian employees?"

"He checked out, Corina. There was no reason for suspicion. Nothing popped on his background. He'd gone to graduate school in Pakistan, then returned to Brighton, took a job, and lived a life like every other Brightonian."

"Apparently not."

"He'd been influenced by an underground radical sect of insurgents. No one knew. It took us four months to find them and root them out after the suicide. Asif returned to Brighton with a vow to kill members of the royal family for war crimes against his people. All he needed was opportunity."

"And you gave it to him." She shivered as the long-awaited details took form on a grassy knoll under the coming of night.

"Asif came to kill me." The words hit like stones and sank into her. "I knew it the moment I saw him . . . when I realized he was stoned. But I hesitated. I should've moved, told the men to get out. Carlos and Lt. Mitchell Bird, noticed something amiss the moment I did." Stephen ran his hand over his face. "Asif shouted that I had to die and opened his shirt to show he was loaded with explosives. He could barely stand, he was so canned. Whilst I hesitated, Carlos and Bird did not." He sank slowly to the ground in the middle of the garden. "I don't know why I hesitated. Why I froze."

Corina remained where she sat, staring at the last drape of daylight.

"Carlos tackled him while the words were still in his mouth. Bird ran for me, covering me with his big body as Asif detonated himself. We were blown out the back of the mess, hit the concrete, and next thing I remember is waking up in a field hospital. The other four lads were seriously injured and died hours later. I was swept away in secret, and until Command knew what happened, the entire squadron went on communication silence."

"It's taken you five and a half years to tell me this?"

"You do realize I'm breaking national security here?"

"Why? Why is it of national security? Why couldn't Daddy find out anything? Something?"

Stephen shot the flashlight beam at the trees. "Once we sorted out the event, Brighton Special Forces went into action. Eliminated Asif's little insurgent group. At that point, the biggest concern was copycats. Others of like mind making bold approaches to the palace, the King's Office, or our homes. The Defense Ministry and the Joint Coalition purposefully held the information, not releasing any details, not even to the families of the deceased, because we couldn't risk leaks or slips. They sealed the event under Top Secret National Security, with extreme security measures. Just a hint that it was possible to get close enough to a prince to blow him up, we'd all be in danger. I'll be in grave trouble if anyone finds out I told you."

"The last five and a half years finally make some sense to me."

"The security measure taken made it possible for me to play for the Eagles." He shoved up from the ground and walked among the markers, dragging his fingers over the smooth stones. "I'm glad it makes some sense to you, Corina, because it still doesn't to me. Men gave their lives for me, and how could I, a mere man, be worth another's life?"

"What do you think war is about, Stephen? Men laying down their lives for another."

"For the weak and oppressed, not for the wealthy and privileged. Not for a prince. One, whom when the war was over, would return to opulence and abundance, living a life of splendor, even pursuing his rugby dreams."

"So the likes of you and I don't deserve to have our freedoms preserved? We are not worth dying for?" She met him on the edge of the garden, the only light between them from the torch.

"We can buy our freedoms, Corina." His disdain surprised and tainted her.

"Not always. Nearly every royal house of Europe fell after the First World War. The czar and his family were summarily rounded up and murdered. Freedom is for everyone, not just the weak and oppressed. Carlos, one of the wealthy and privileged, by the way, gave his life to save yours. What does that say about you? About him?"

"Carlos was . . ." He glanced over at her, a small smile cresting his lips. "A very special chap. Never knew a more selfless bloke."

Tears burned in the corners of her eyes. "Why didn't you tell me he was moved to your unit?"

"I'd planned to . . . It all happened so fast. His transfer papers hadn't even finished processing."

She wiped her face with the back of her hand and joined him on the bench. "So, you just lied to me? Pushed me away when you came home and I flew back here to be with you?"

"I was in a bad way when I returned to Brighton. I wanted nothing to do with anyone, not even my own family. The moment I saw you, I was in that tent again, the detonation exploding in my ears, in my chest, in my mind. Your brother . . ."

"You didn't kill him, Stephen."

"Not directly, no, but when I see you, I see him. I can't be with you, Corina."

"Don't I get a say in our relationship? You married me because I said 'Yes.' How is it you get to leave without my 'Yes'"?

"I brought you here so you would understand. When you see me, you'll know I live because your brother died."

"You cannot decide my feelings for me. What I see, how I'll respond."

"Nor can you decide for me. When I see you, I see him." He gazed down at her, brushing her hair away from her face. She nearly melted into him. "I can't forget if I'm married to a reminder. I'm right and you know it."

"But I don't know it, Stephen. You say one thing but behave completely different when we're alone. Monday night, when you kissed me . . . are you saying it meant nothing?" She must remind him of who he was before the war. Kind, funny, sincere, whole-hearted, wonderfully romantic.

"What does it matter? At the end of it all, when life takes hold and the romance of it all is gone, you will wake up every day next to a man stained with your brother's blood. Please don't make me say it again."

"I'm not making you say anything. You're choosing to say it."

From his pocket, Stephen's mobile rang. "It's Nathaniel." When he answered, she walked off, collecting her thoughts, sorting a blend of relief and revived sorrow. She felt as if he wanted her to be angry at him. Hate him.

"He wondered if we wanted to be back for late tea and a movie."

"I don't know. I suppose." Corina returned to the bench,

scanning the other graves. "What of these others? Do their families know?"

"No one knows outside the Joint Coalition leadership except Nathaniel and top personnel in the Defense Ministry. Now you."

"I think the other families would like to come here."

"Nathaniel wants to proceed with my coronation as Prince of Brighton, and in doing so I'll be patron of the War Memorial, but . . ." He shook his head. "I don't want to wear the uniform."

"Think of what you could do for these men's families."

"I don't have to be patron of a War Memorial to do something for them."

"Have you done anything for them?"

"Not yet." He stood, but she remained seated. "Shall we go in?"

"I'm not sure I can watch a movie right now. I think I'll just sit out here."

He exhaled and joined her again on the bench, tucked his phone in his pocket, and turned off the flashlight.

From the trees, an owl hooted and the wind rustled a response. In the dark, Corina let her tears fall without restraint. She caught the drops slipping from her chin with the back of her hand.

Next to her, Stephen stared off toward the surrounding woods, his right leg gently swaying side to side, his left stretched long, resting his ankle. In what remained of the light, Corina found his hand and slipped hers beneath his warm palm. He flinched at first, then relaxed and entwined his fingers with hers.

They sat there for a long time saying nothing. Saying everything.

TWENTY-FOUR

*B*ack at the Manor Friday morning, Corina sat at the small curved desk tucked under the dormer walls and pulled out the annulment papers.

Unfolding the pages, she skimmed the small print, a sick feeling forming in the pit of her stomach when she read the definition of what she and Stephen were about to do.

"An annulment means no valid marriage ever existed."

But that was a lie. They had a valid marriage. At least in her heart.

A few lines down, Stephen had checked the "Mistake" box.

Was that how he truly saw things? She smoothed her hand over the pages, pressing them flat against the hard desk. Could she add her own box? Check "Coward"?

She pushed back and went to the window. She'd never forgive him for this, calling the marriage a mistake, ending it on his assumptions, abandoning the relationship when they needed each other most.

However, Stephen had delivered his part of the bargain. He told her what happened to Carlos. And Corina felt obligated to sign.

A fresh cascade of tears spilled down her cheeks. She was tired of crying. After her evening on the memorial bench with

Stephen, they returned to the house at Parrsons and Corina hid in her suite and spent a good part of Thursday there, weeping, remembering, praying.

This morning early, Stephen drove her back to the city with little conversation and dropped her off at the Manor. "The annulment?"

"I'll sign it."

But how could she? Corina sat on the window seat and gazed out over the city, her love for Cathedral City summer mornings nothing but a faint memory.

She glanced back at the annulment documents. Just sign and be done with it.

When her phone rang, she snatched it up, hoping for Stephen's number on her screen. But no.

"Miss Del Rey?"

"Yes?"

"This is Clem from the Children's Literacy Foundation. On your auction form you listed your local address as the Manor, but we can't find such a place anywhere in the city listings or on the map. Where would you like us to deliver your purchase?"

"Right, the Pissarro." She'd dueled for the piece with a stodgy couple who seemed to have no monetary boundaries. Well, neither did she. She'd not touched her trust from Grandmother Del Rey and the power of compound interest daily kept the one account very healthy. She could buy the Pissarro three times over.

She finally won the bid at ten million. The place exploded with applause. The Children's Literacy Foundation would have a grand year.

"Where shall we deliver it?"

"To Prince Stephen in care of the King's Office."

"Pardon?"

"The King's Office. Prince Stephen." She picked up the annulment papers again. She'd purchased the painting for Stephen, because, well, she thought he would enjoy it. Call it a "We're annulled!" gift.

"I'll need a special form to deliver to the King's Office."

"Fine. Do you need me for that form?"

"I just have to call the King's Office."

"Then call them."

"If there's a delay, I will ring you. Otherwise the painting will be delivered tomorrow."

Perfect. She flew home on Sunday. "With the note I wrote? Please include the note."

"I'll see to it."

Hanging up, Corina returned to the window. The streets below were quiet for a Friday. The wind had room to move and expand, dragging its train through the trees along the avenue.

Street vendors worked the sidewalk, preparing for the lunch crowd. Taxicabs lined the curb, the drivers huddled together, talking, flicking ashes from their cigarettes.

Love well.

Corina picked up the annulment papers. Was signing them loving well?

A light knock had her calling, "Come in."

Adelaide came around the door carrying a tray of tea and biscuits. "Top of the morning. How was your time away?"

"Enlightening." Corina tossed the documents back to the desk. By tonight she'd decide. If she flew home without signing, she'd have to be willing to face the consequences.

"You sound troubled."

"I bargained for something, got what I wanted, and am not sure I can keep up my end."

"Then you've a dilemma." Adelaide poured Corina a cup of tea and placed a thin, wafer-like cookie on the saucer as she passed it over.

"My head versus my heart." Corina pulled the desk chair

around, a small fire flickering in her belly from her private confrontation with the annulment.

"Tea time will make you feel better." Filling the cups with steaming, rich brown liquid, Adelaide handed one to Corina, then took one for herself. "This porcelain tea service is quite special." Adelaide sat primly on the chaise, holding up the cup and saucer.

"Really?" Corina inspected her cup. "This one has a small chip." She tapped the slight nick on the bottom.

"It's been well used. King Stephen I heard of the great porcelain cups made in China. He sent for a set, and it took nearly ten years then to arrive. One of the first sets ever to arrive in the West."

Corina lowered her cup and saucer. The air in the room changed again as Adelaide spoke and Corina felt bound by the electricity. "You're serving me tea in a four-hundred-and-fifty-year-old cup?"

"Kings and queens, the sick and poor, women and men, children have drunk from these cups."

"Where did you get them?" Again, why are they not with the royal estate?

"It lives with the Manor. Along with the tiara."

"Adelaide, you've quite the mission. Hidden tiaras, special tea sets."

The woman reclined against the cushy back of the chaise. "You've asked what Brill and I are about. Well, we're here to help you see what you are about." She raised her cup to Corina. "To wear the tiara, one must drink from the cup."

Corina considered her cup. "You mean to be a true royal one must drink from the cup of love and service."

"There, now, that wasn't so hard was it? Ruling by serving. It's how the Great Kingdom is structured. It's the love that moves heaven and earth."

The tracing of chills over Corina's arms multiplied.

"And that's how King Stephen I and Queen Magdalena loved?" She was catching on to Adelaide's wisdom.

"Yes. You and your prince have been given the same call."

"But he wants out, Adelaide. An annulment."

"That is your journey, love. All I can give you is heaven's vision." Adelaide turned over her saucer. "King Stephen I had his artisans design a cipher for their royal house. Do you see?"

Corina checked her saucer. On the bottom she found a crown crossed with a sword that matched Adelaide's. Underneath were the letters H of S. "House of Stratton."

"He used to serve his guests, rich or poor, noblemen or common men, with a whole set. Only these two remain."

"And I'm to do the same?"

"If you want to wear the tiara, then you must be willing to drink from the cup."

"If I want to wear the tiara, then how can I sign the papers?" Corina said, setting down her tea and snatching up the annulment.

"That I cannot tell you. What's in your heart?"

"That I love him. I came over here thinking I could win him back, you know? Love well. But maybe too much time has passed. We're not the same people we were six years ago."

"Just because he's not changed his mind doesn't mean you've not loved well. You've not failed." Adelaide finished her tea with an "ahh," and set it on the tray. "Now I must be off."

Adelaide collected the tea set and left Corina alone in her room with so many questions. Crossing to the desk, Corina fished her pen from her purse and hovered over the papers.

Love well. If she had her way, she'd tear up the papers, but she'd made a deal with Stephen. What if the first step of loving well was letting go? Of wearing the tiara of faith and drinking from the cup of esteeming another higher than herself?

"Lord, what do I do?"

Closing her eyes, breathing in, she peered at the documents.

And signed. She'd messenger them to the King's Office this afternoon.

By the time she returned to the *Beaumont Post*, her journey would be complete. She would be a single woman, having loved well, in word and deed, and through every shifting shadow.

TWENTY-FIVE

*T*his just arrived for you." Robert crossed the room with an envelope on a silver tray.

"Is this all?" Stephen tossed the envelope to his desk, sure it was the annulment papers. After he dropped her off at the Manor Friday morning, what more could be said or done than to formalize the end?

She'd promised to sign the annulment if he told her the truth. So he did. Ignoring the code of silence that went with classified.

The last two nights he woke in the darkest hours of night with the twinge of regret. Once she signed the annulment, she'd be out of his life forever.

What a very sad thing. No man should ever lose a woman like Corina Del Rey.

"Will there be anything else, sir?" Robert said. "Are you ready for luncheon?"

"Not yet, thank you." Stephen had gone straight to physio after he dropped Corina at the Manor. But feeling no strength in his ankle, he cut the session short. At the moment, the pain level nearly matched the hours right after surgery.

His vision of returning to the pitch for the Premiership blurred and faded.

Stephen sat, shoving away from the desk, taking a long, narrow view of the envelope. *Come on, chap, you flew all the way to America for this. Don't lose your courage now.*

A childhood catechism slipped across his mind. *Love is patient, love is kind . . .*

Stephen lunged forward, snatched up the envelope, and emptied the contents. However, instead of finding the thick annulment agreement, he found a single slip of paper with an address.

Agnes Rothery,
10 Mulchbury Lane,
Dunwudy Glenn, Brighton Kingdom 12R49-H

Bird's girlfriend. He'd be jiggered. The King's Office had located her. At his request after the *Madeline & Hyacinth Live!* show last week. Bravo, King's Office.

Stephen tapped the address into his iPhone. Dunwudy Glenn was a lovely, quaint village north of the city, two hours' drive. The map routed him straight to Agnes Rothery's home.

He considered his next move. Agnes knew nothing of how her man died. Just that he died a hero. She asked no more questions. Letting Bird and the past rest in peace.

But, by George, Stephen was tired of hiding from life because one rogue insurgent came gunning for him. While he'd not divulge national secrets to Agnes, he would at last keep his promise to Bird.

"If anything happens to me, see to Agnes, will you?"

"You have my word."

To carry on anew, he must deal with all the Torkham fallout. Mend his broken promises. Then perhaps, maybe, he'd feel somewhat worthy of the air he breathed.

Gathering the paper and his phone, Stephen went to his room, showered, and pulled on jeans and a button-down. He found Robert in the dining hall.

"Ring Thomas, please. Tell him he has the rest of the day off."

"Yes, sir." Robert frowned, the light in his eyes dimmed. "Might I ask where you are going? You know the King's Office doesn't like for you to—"

"Here's the address." He passed over the single sheet of paper. "I'll drive myself. But I'm going to pick up Miss Del Rey."

"Sir?"

"Taking her with me if she'll go."

"You'll have your mobile?" Robert knew little to nothing of the events in Afghanistan, only that he was to keep vigilant regarding the prince's safety.

"I have my mobile." Stephen offered up his phone as he headed down the long corridor to the garage. "I'll return late." Stephen paused before turning the corner. "Take the rest of the day for yourself, Robert. Go to the park. Enjoy the festivals and the city in the sunshine."

As Stephen zipped through traffic, the tension in his chest eased, the weight on his shoulders lifted. The wind cutting through his open window tousled his hair as warm sunbeams tanned his arm, resting on the door.

He beat the caution light at Market Avenue, taking a wide turn onto Crescent, then taking a cut through to the northbound lane to park by the Manor.

Was this ridiculous to call on her unannounced to ask her to ride along? He didn't care. Thirty minutes ago he anticipated her signed annulment. Now he was at her door, inviting her on a journey.

Besides, it would be good for her to meet Agnes. They shared something no one else shared. The men they loved dying in a terrorist blast intended for the Prince of Brighton. Perhaps they would form a fast friendship and heal together.

He also considered how much he might need Corina's courage and strength as he told Agnes he was five and a half years overdue on his promise.

About to enter the Manor, he saw Corina round the corner with a box of puffs under her arm.

"Hey." She slowed her step. "W—what are you doing here?" Her dark hair framed her face, flowing over her shoulders, and her amber-colored eyes were wide and clear.

"I've come for a favor." He bowed toward her. "You're free to answer no."

"What's the favor?"

In short order, he explained Agnes and Bird, how he promised Bird he'd see to her if anything happened to him and how he had failed on his promise. Time to make amends.

"I don't want to go alone, you see. Can't face all my demons alone. I thought perhaps you might enjoy meeting her. Bird and Carlos were the real heroes that day in Torkham."

"Are you going to tell her everything you told me?"

"No. But I want to see to her. Make sure she's all right."

"It's been five and a half years. Agnes has probably moved on, Stephen."

"But I must see. If she has, then so be it. That doesn't negate my promise to Bird. She loved him and I'd like her to know he died with honor." Something tender flickered across her expression. Something he'd not seen before he deployed. A piece of her heart. "Only if you want."

She glanced toward his Audi. "Where's Thomas?"

"This trip is just you and me, love."

"Stephen, I don't understand. I thought we were over. You told me the dark secret of it all, so why are we taking a journey together? Why do you need me to help you face your demons?"

He sighed. "Then I'll be getting on by myself."

"Oh for crying out loud." Corina shoved the box of puffs at

him. "They're fresh from a Franklin Bakery vending cart. Give me a minute to get my phone."

"Is this a pity response?" He followed her inside the Manor.

"Yes," Corina said, running upstairs while he waited in the small, quaint lobby, the thick, raw beams only inches above his head.

A small woman with a big smile approached. "Lovely to see you, Your Highness."

"Thank you. You've a nice place here."

The woman offered him tea, but he declined, unnerved by the intensity of her gaze and the sensation of heat it created in him.

But he felt drawn to her. Almost changed in her presence.

"Corina speaks highly of you," he said. "Seems you came to her rescue when she arrived in town with no reservation at The Wellington."

The woman's eyes sparked. "Indeed. No reservation at The Wellington. Well, we think highly of her. And you."

Stephen exhaled when Corina bound into the lobby, wearing a pair of jeans and a top, her hair back in a thick, sleek ponytail. Beautiful. Perfect for him. Princess on Monday night, soldier's wife on Friday afternoon.

Too late. Too late.

They were quiet in the initial moments as Stephen made his way out of town toward His Majesty's Bridge and the northern highway toward Dunwudy Glenn.

He had the radio on low for a soft serenade of music.

When he hit the open road and settled back, Corina opened the conversation. "How did you play rugby? Wouldn't you be a danger to the players and the fans?"

"Keeping everything classified helped. But I almost left the team the first week of training, realizing the risk I placed on everyone, my teammates, the players, and fans worldwide. It was too much to bear. Though I was half crazy with desire to play. Rugby became my therapy. My way to forget. I needed to run, compete, make a try. For *them*. The six who died."

"I get that, I do. I stayed home. Wasted five years thinking I could bring Daddy and Mama, especially Mama, out of her grief."

He pressed his hand on her arm, ruing any implications of a tender touch. Telling her the truth bonded them. As friends anyway.

"Dad saw my dilemma, stepped in and organized meetings, spurring a great deal of discussion behind closed doors with Rugby Union, Brighton Eagles, and the defense minister. With a promise from the Rugby Union to heighten their own security, as well as ours, it was agreed I could and should play. When Brighton Special Forces knocked out the cell Asif had been a part of, we felt more confident my life was safe, and thus the rugby world."

A bit more music in the silence, but he didn't mind. It was peaceful.

"Hey, remember the dress I wore to the Military Ball and to our wedding?" She held no reserve about speaking of their past. Stephen peered over at her. She was different. Changed from just yesterday.

"The white one with the feathery skirt? Designed by some recluse designer?"

"But he took so long I never got to wear it for its intended purpose."

"I remember you looked beautiful and, might I add, sexy." His teasing laugh followed. She popped him lightly on the arm.

"Exactly. Thank you, and it was made for me. There's none like it in the world. I went home for it before coming here." She slowed her confession, thinking. "Mama donated it and it was sold at a charity auction. I'd only been gone from the house a few months."

"Brutal. Did she give you a reason?"

"She made up something about me not needing it, but Stephen, it's like Carlos died and she tried to bury me with him. She turned my bedroom into a quiet room. Mine. I'm the one still coming home. Not to mention the house has thirty rooms. But she turns mine into an indoor garden shrine to Carlos."

"Much like my memorial?"

She regarded him for a second. "You two would get along then."

"Though I agree she should not have taken over your room."

"My room was across from Carlos's, and we had this adjoining second-floor veranda that wrapped around our rooms. The windows opened right onto the porch, so we used to climb out at night with sleeping bags when we were supposed to be in bed and stare at the stars, dreaming. He wanted to help people as young as ten. In high school, he was always rescuing people, coming to the aid of the defenseless."

Stephen swallowed, his skin hot with her confession. He powered down his window for a gulp of fresh air. He was the defenseless Carlos died for when he should have been the defender. He should've charged Asif and taken him down.

"You're quiet. What's wrong?"

"Thinking."

"Of that day?"

"Of what a sacrifice you and your family paid."

"Maybe now that the truth is out, at least with me, and you're making good with Agnes, you can move on."

"That's what the rugby pitch is for, love."

"What happens when your game ends? When you can no longer play?"

"I cannot imagine. I cannot."

The conversation went to gentler things, safe things—the art auction, philosophy, and puppies. She loved all things furry.

The shadows above the highway were long and lean by the

time Stephen turned down a tree-lined Dunwudy lane with seventeenth-century cottages on postage-stamp-sized lawns.

From the passenger seat, Corina counted the house numbers. "Five, six, seven . . . ten. There . . ." She tapped her window when the car cruised past a brightly painted cottage with a golden thatched roof.

Stephen slowed and eased down the narrow driveway. The reality of what he was about to do pricked at his nerves. When he called Agnes to say he was coming, she sounded dubious.

"The Prince of Brighton is coming here?"

Cutting the engine, he rattled the keys against his palm, staring at the house nestled between giant royal sycamores.

"It's going to be fine," Corina said.

"I guess so."

Out of the car with Corina by his side, Stephen made his way up the walk, carrying the weight of his delayed promise.

At the front stoop, he rang the bell. The door eased open and a boy, about five years old, naked from the waist up, glared up at them with big green eyes. "Mum, it's a man and a lady." His shorts were dirt stained, and his muddy socks were sinking into his shoes. A shock of his blond hair curled away from his freckled forehead in a classic cowlick. Stephen liked him instantly.

"Baby Bird, step back." A woman came from down a narrow, dark corridor. *Baby Bird? Bird had a son?*

"Your Highness, please come in. I can hardly believe it. The Prince of Brighton in me own home." Agnes pulled the boy aside, smoothing her hand over his hair, making way for Stephen and Corina to enter, offering a weak curtsy. "Sorry about the boy. He just came from his gram's, playing in the mud by the looks of him." Agnes waved her hand at her son, shooing him down the hall.

"Not to worry. We're sorry to barge in. I appreciate you letting me come." Stephen ducked under the small doorway, thinking he should be bowing to her. Honoring her sacrifice. "This is Corina Del Rey."

"Of course. I see'd you in the papers. Loverly to meet you."

Corina extended her hand. "It's my honor."

Agnes and Baby Bird's home was small and warm, clean and tidy, fragrant with tomato sauce. But the afternoon air floating through the opened kitchen window was no match for the heat.

"Sorry about the heat. We've no central air in these old homes." Agnes turned a floor fan toward the sofa, motioning for Stephen and Corina to sit. Her voice quavered as she hugged Baby Bird to her, sitting in an adjacent chair, her eyes glistening. "I can't believe you're here. Bird used to write me all the time about you. Stephen this, Stephen that." Her laugh refreshed the room. "'Hardly believe he's a prince,' he'd say. But Bird always said if something happened to him, you'd come." She leveled a pure, tender gaze at him. "I was a-wondering if he'd just made it up."

Stephen brushed his hands down his jeans, nervous, captured again in the reality of pain his life caused. "I'm sorry, Agnes. I just couldn't—" His confession exposed his weakness. His shame. "Losing Bird and the others hit me hard. I couldn't make sense of it all."

"You being the only one to live, I get it, sir. Survivor's guilt." She pointed to a stack of books in the corner. "I read all about it. It helped me, you know, to understand why he died and how I was to go on. We was going to get married before he deployed, but we couldn't afford the license, so we waited, planning to use his hazard pay." She laughed again, popping her leg. "Imagine, using hazard pay for a marriage license. Ain't that some kind of irony?"

Then she fell silent and Baby Bird reappeared with clean clothes but mud still covering a good portion of his body. He buried his face against his mum, peeking at Stephen under his golden bangs.

"Agnes, I should've come sooner. Especially because I am a prince. Please . . . forgive me. I'm sorry."

"Nothing to forgive, Your Highness. 'Twas a dark time for us all." She twisted her fingers together. "You are a prince, after all. With duties to tend. And a star winger. Baby Bird here loves rugby. Oh, where are me manners? I've tea and biscuits." She shoved the boy aside, heading for the kitchen.

But she stopped cold as a sob rolled through her.

"Agnes." Stephen rose and gently held her shoulders. She turned and fell into his chest. With a glance at Corina, whose eyes brimmed, Stephen cradled Agnes, letting her weep.

This disturbed Baby Bird, and he tugged on his mum's skirt, wanting to know why she was crying. Corina slipped from the couch.

"Your mama is just happy to see the prince. I hear you like rugby. Do you have a ball?"

He curled his lip at her. "You talk funny."

"Baby Bird!" Agnes peeled away from Stephen, wiping her eyes with her hand. "I'm so sorry."

"That's all right." Corina tweaked the boy's nose. "I'm from America and I think you talk funny too. Now, where's that ball?"

He ran off without another word.

"He's full of it. Keeps me hopping." Agnes pulled a handkerchief from her handbag by the front door.

"He's Bird's?"

She nodded and blew her nose.

"Did he know?"

She pressed the wadded up handkerchief into her palm and shook her head. "I wanted to surprise him. I found out a month before he was due home, so I thought to make it a late Christmas present. One month to go. That was all. One lousy month." The boy bounded into the room with his rugby ball. It was half the size of him yet. Agnes patted his head. "Mitchell O'Connell the Third. Bird's boy."

Her eyes glistened and her lean shoulders seemed too delicate to bear her burden alone. "Bird and me was two of a kind. Joined at the hip like we was made to be together. My only family, and I never figured a life without him, then there I was, alone and pregnant. Not legally his wife yet. We did things backwards."

"He's beautiful." Corina knelt in front of Baby Bird. "Do you want to go outside? I can teach you some of the basics of the world's best sport, American football."

"What?" Stephen balked, laughing. "Pay her no mind, Baby Bird."

But he was halfway out the back door, cheering.

Corina gave Stephen a smug look and walked round him. "Coming, Baby Bird."

"She's lovely."

"Yes, she is." Stephen perched on the arm of the chair and took Agnes's hand in his. "I promised Bird I'd look out for you."

"But I'm not his proper wife. You don't owe me anything, though I sure would like something for Baby Bird." Her cheeks flushed red as she glanced down at the chair, picking at a loose thread. "I know Bird would want more for his son than I can give him." She wiped her tears with the back of her hand. "I'm not ashamed to ask if you're offering."

"How are you getting on? You've a job?"

"Bird's parents mind Baby Bird for me while I work at the school. Teaching assistant. It doesn't pay much but keeps this roof over our head and food on the table. Thank goodness, or I've no idea where we'd be. I just want the world to know Bird has a son, Your Highness."

"Please, call me Stephen."

"I don't want to be a charity case. If the military would just recognize Bird's paternity, I'll have the orphan's benefits."

"Let me see to it. And, as a favor to me, for my mate Bird O'Connell, I'd like to pay for his education."

She cracked with a hard sob, hand to her mouth, pressing her forehead to Stephen's shoulder. "Everything Bird said about you is true. Absolutely true."

Stephen fumbled with an awkward pat on the woman's shoulder, then settled his hand on her back and shared her sorrow.

Through the kitchen window, he could see Baby Bird in the yard with a couple of boys, trying to toss the thick rugby ball like an American football, sloshing through the mud. Oh the way of little boys. He'd figure a way to make sure Agnes had a grand washing machine and dryer.

"Agnes." Corina had returned, silently moving into the conversation. "My twin brother, Carlos, died the same day." Agnes raised her head, drying her cheeks with her hand. "He served in the Joint Coalition with your Bird. With Stephen. I still miss him. My parents . . . I don't think they'll ever be the same."

"Love, I'm so sorry." Agnes flowed from Stephen's shoulder to Corina's, and for a long time, the women wept and embraced. Healed.

The back door slammed, Baby Bird returning, his little footsteps thudding against the old hardwood. "Did you know my Da?" He tugged on Stephen's hand.

"I sure did. He was a good mate." Stephen swung Bird's son up into his arms, burying his face against his small, little-boy shoulders. Which at the moment seemed broader and more manly than Stephen's own.

"I can't breathe. Let me go." Baby Bird squirmed, kicking to be free. "I'm not your doll."

"Baby Bird," Agnes said, releasing Corina and lightly flicking the boy's head. "You're speaking to the Prince of Brighton. Show respect."

"It's okay," Stephen said and slid the boy to the ground. "He's Bird's son all right."

Baby Bird puffed out his chest, anchoring his fists on his waist. "I'm going to be a pilot, like him. He was the best."

"Pilot?" Stephen peeked at Agnes. Bird was a mechanic.

She shrugged, a thin pink hue sweeping across her cheeks. "It's what he wanted his Da to be. So I said, why not?"

"Indeed, why not?"

Something bubbled over in the kitchen and Agnes hurried off, Baby Bird running after her. "I'll be right round with a spot of tea and cakes."

When they were alone, Corina soothed her hand down Stephen's back. "You all right?"

He inhaled, steeling the rise of his own cordoned off memories and emotions. "I'm glad we came." Raising his hand to her face, he stroked her jaw, not caring about the past, the future, only this moment with her. "I'm glad you're here." And he realized . . . Corina had always been his rock. "Even though I'm going to have to uncorrupt Baby Bird about this football business." His heart palpitated with a yearning to pull her into him and kiss her. He slipped his hand around the back of her neck and stepped toward her. "Corina, I—"

"I was standing at the stove when I realized . . ." Agnes had returned. "Oh, begging your pardon."

Stephen stepped back, embarrassed, agitated. Relieved. He had no business kissing Corina. He cut her a glance. She had no business allowing him. "Not at all, not at all."

"It's just that I realize the Prince of Brighton is in me house." She set the service on the center table and curtsyed again, this time, low and proper. "This is my granny's tea set. She bought it in France on her honeymoon."

"It's lovely," Corina said, taking a seat as Agnes poured, avoiding Stephen's gaze.

The conversation moved to life after Afghanistan, how Agnes

came by the cottage and her job, her supportive family, all peppered with Baby Bird's observations about life and his mum.

"She's bossy."

"I wouldn't be if you'd mind me now, would I? Hmm?" Agnes arched her brow at her son.

Baby Bird grimaced at Stephen in such a way he laughed and, mercy a-mighty, he saw a piece of himself in the lad.

Once the tea was served, Agnes raised her cup. "To Bird, the best man I've ever known. May he rest in peace."

Stephen raised his cup. "To Bird."

"To Bird and Carlos," Corina said.

"To Carlos."

"To Carlos."

"Who's Carlos?" And Baby Bird set them all to laughing.

The afternoon faded into evening in Agnes's living room, sharing, laughing, remembering Bird, Carlos, the bond of family forged by trial.

Stephen did a spell on the back lawn with Baby Bird. Teaching him the superiority of rugby, taking care with his ankle, while Corina accepted Agnes's request for ideas on making over a small room in the back of the house.

And that night, Stephen's family grew by two.

On the drive home, Corina relaxed against her seat, her eyes in a sleepy daze. "Thank you."

"For what?"

"You invited me to go with you for you, but in the end you gave a great gift to me. I didn't feel so alone anymore. While my parents never want to talk about Carlos, Agnes talked so freely about missing Bird, about their son. I got to reminisce about Carlos."

"None of this would've happened without you."

"Why do you say that?"

"Because you could have signed the annulment in Florida,

but instead you demanded something of me. And it challenged me."

"I think I stumbled upon that request by accident, driven by my own need for closure."

She fell silent and he let it be, sensing there was something more. In the glow of the dashboard lights, he found her hand and gave it a gentle squeeze.

"I love you, Stephen." She wrapped her hand around his, not letting go. "I tell myself I shouldn't, that our marriage is over, but I love you. Not just as a friend but as my husband"

The confession engulfed him. Consumed him. How could she love him? If he had no response before, he was drowning now just trying to understand.

But she didn't seem in need of an answer. He peered sideways at her as the Audi moved down the straightaway, their hands still locked together, her eyes closing as she drifted sweetly off to sleep.

Gigi

In the world of journalism, no news was bad news. Gigi scanned her e-mail one last time before going home. Nothing. Even Madeline Stone came up empty. Though Gigi suspected the Brighton TV presenter didn't try very hard. Of course, she'd keep the best bits for her own show with that gaudy Hyacinth.

Gigi clicked out of e-mail, thinking, mulling. She should be able to just get the skinny from Corina, her very own employee. She needed a new strategy. The old one wasn't working.

At her office window, she gazed at the stretch of river between the Eau Gallie and Melbourne causeways. Maybe, at fifty-six, she'd lost her mojo. For the first time in her life, she considered the impossible. Quitting. The very idea made her shudder.

A foreign feeling, a strange word never before allowed in her vocabulary.

She was Gigi-*freaking*-Beaumont. The woman who started this company from scratch when the worldwide web consisted of nothing more than AOL, tech geeks, and cyber perverts.

She was ambitious, competitive, with instinct and ingenuity, and a callous soul. Whatever it took to get ahead, she did it. And she harbored no regrets.

She'd married her third husband just to gain access to his wealth, mastering a stellar prenup giving her half of his assets at their divorce.

But today a weariness settled in her bones. Her conscience woke from a long sleep and knocked on her heart's battered door. *Leave her be . . .*

Bested by a tenderhearted, broken beauty from Georgia.

Gigi returned to her work, opening her presentation for the four thirty online meeting with the division directors. Maybe they would have some ideas how to revamp the *Beaumont Post* brand. Find a new life in their fading, albeit fearless leader.

About to head through the bull pen to see if anyone happened upon a salacious tip—after all, she'd imported the best scouts, sources, and news diggers in the world to her seaside domain—when a new e-mail from a strange address dropped into her inbox.

801laurellane@bmail.com

The sounds from the bull pen faded. Gigi's warm blood chilled and her hand, resting on her mouse, trembled.

801 Laurel Lane? Her flat on the north side of Cathedral City when she worked for Brighton Broadcast Company.

Robert? Dear, sweet Robert. With an exhale, she opened the e-mail. Tuesday at eight. What could *he* possibly want?

Thirty-five years ago he'd wanted to marry her but had nothing to offer but his heart and devotion.

She was just starting out, wildly ambitious, full of herself and her dreams. She refused to tie herself down to a man with no means, no name. A servant in the palace.

When she left him for the last time, she made her intentions clear. "I'm bound for greatness, and I need a partner who can go with me, help me get there."

Gigi Beaumont, what a fool you've been.

Her eyes were wet with tears as she read his message. It contained nothing more than three simple words.

They are married.

Gigi squinted at the line again, the bold, beautiful line.

They are married.

Oh. My. Oh very, very my. What glorious news. She all but danced a jig about the office. Robert, you dear, sweet man.

This, *this* was her scoop. The one that would put her back on top of the pseudo-news-tabloid world.

"Oh, thank you, Lord, thank you, thank you. You didn't forget your little ole Gigi, did you? Not like those long nights when my daddy was out drinking. Thank *youuuuu!*"

Back in her chair, Gigi hit Reply and studied the screen.

A story like this needed some corroboration, but the salaciousness of it alone was a moneymaker, enough to run it on hearsay. Robert could be her "palace source."

If it turned out to be untrue, she'd print a subtle retraction, buried in the back of the *Post.*

But she'd face the wrath of Corina, such as it was for that sweet, demure girl with little fire in her bones. The toll of Carlos's death continued to demand payment.

But wait a minute, if she was married to Prince Stephen, what was she doing in Melbourne? How long had they been married? Why hadn't the world heard of this?

A secret royal wedding? Oh, this was too good to be true. Trembling, Gigi clicked Reply and typed her own simple message.

How do you know? Deets.

Once the message was off into cyber space, Gigi paraded through the bull pen, suggesting an evening barbecue at her Tortoise Island home, perhaps drop the jet skis and paddleboats into the river. After all, it was the weekend.

The staff responded with an enthusiasm that pushed back the sluggishness of a Friday afternoon. They were *all* in.

Gigi called home, instructing her staff to prepare for the party. Then she sashayed to the tea cart. She still had it, baby, she still had it.

TWENTY-SIX

*A*t 8:54 in the evening, a soft light hovered over Cathedral City. The stratus of twilight scooped low and blended with the amber glow of city lamps.

Corina stepped out of the lift and onto the deck of the Braithwaite Tower, and into the breeze, the cloudless evening, the muted music of city life, and her memories.

And she was glad she came. Glad she'd texted Stephen to meet her here. The idea came to her as they drove home from Dunwudy Glenn. Meet on top of the Braithwaite.

She'd debated the idea all morning, considering it a bit melodramatic. But by teatime, she'd texted him, asking him to meet her here at 8:54.

When the nine o'clock chimes rang out, she'd hand him his freedom. She would end their marriage the way it began.

The Braithwaite was a glorious, above-the-city park with a small garden in the center, potted trees clustered between picnic tables and park benches.

The historic tower was the coveted location for surprises, for victory celebrations, for announcements, birthdays, and weddings. For blind dates and marriage proposals. For good-byes.

Cutting through the garden, Corina made her way to the

forward wall and propped her arms on the railing where the view squared off with the Rue du Roi. In the distance, she could see the northern edge of Stratton Palace.

Forty stories down, the streets moved with traffic. Pedestrians snaked along the sidewalk, moving in and out of the shops, the park, on and off the busses.

From her vantage point, everything looked so small. Manageable. Sometimes all one needed was a change of perspective.

The wind driving up the side of the building played tug-of-war with her hair. Corina dug in her messenger bag for a hair tie.

How different tonight was from six years ago when she stood here with Stephen, wearing the Diamatia, her hair piled and curled on top of her head, sprayed and pinned into place. Not even the Braithwaite breeze could topple it.

Her heart overflowed with human confidence in those days, so self-assured by her abilities, youth, beauty, and wealth. On top of it all, she'd captured the heart of a prince.

Life was hers to command. Until it commanded her and drove her to her knees.

Now as she waited to meet Stephen on top of the historic tower, she had nothing to hope in but Jesus himself. The purest example of loving well.

All day she anticipated his response to her "I love you," but he let the confession go without a word. Perhaps it was for the best. She'd been obedient to God's whisper, "Love well." The rest was up to him.

She turned at the sound of the lift bell. The doors opened and Stephen stepped out, making her heart flutter, still, as he made his way toward her with his uneven, booted gait.

"Hey, you," she said, meeting him at the garden's edge. "Thank you for coming."

"Why wouldn't I?" His eyes drifted over her. "You spent the

afternoon in the home of a stranger for me yesterday." Despite his casual demeanor, he was guarded. His cloaked gaze gave her no access to his heart.

"Want to sit?" She motioned to the perimeter tables.

Stephen walked her to a table in the front corner. Not far from where he proposed. Did he remember? "The old Braithwaite. Eyes on the city." He propped his arms on the guard rail, leaning into the breeze. "You can see every corner of the city from up here."

"Stephen." Corina dropped her messenger bag to the table, reaching inside for the annulment. "I leave in the morning, so let me do what I came here to do."

He returned to her, sitting on the tabletop, feet on the bench seat. "All right."

"First, thank you for telling me about Carlos. I have made up my mind to tell my father. I'm sorry, but I feel I must. But I promise I won't tell anyone else. You have my word."

He nodded, the wind jerking his dark locks from side to side.

"Second . . ." She'd rehearsed this moment over and over, but going through with it proved harder than she imagined. "Here." She handed him the white legal envelope that contained their *end.* "All signed. You came through on my demand, so I'm following up on yours."

He hesitated, then reached for the envelope. "T–thank you."

She sighed, brushing a thin strand of hair from her eyes. "I didn't want to sign it. I hated the language of the annulment. It says our marriage never existed. And you checked the 'Mistake' box." She looked at him, but his gaze was averted. "I don't think any of it was fake or a mistake."

"I had little choice. The 'death of my wife's brother' wasn't an option. Otherwise, I'd have to file for a divorce, but I don't think either of us wanted that, Corina."

She leaned against the edge of the table next to him, willing the full force of her confession on him. "I don't like that you decided my heart for me. What I would or would not think, feel, or want. You had no right."

"You had no right to demand answers of me about Carlos's death." He only held her gaze for a second. "But I yielded to your demand."

"Did you want the annulment signed that much? To break the law, deliver classified information?"

He held up the envelope. "Would you have signed it if I didn't?"

"Probably. Eventually. But I meant it when I said 'I love you.'"

He didn't respond, simply stared at the envelope. Corina weighed her next confession. One she'd thought a lot about, prayed about, considered as important as 'I love you.'"

"S–Stephen?"

He glanced up.

She drew a deep breath. "I forgive you."

"W–hat?"

The tears . . . oh the dratted tears. "I–I forgive you." Were there any more pieces of her heart to break? But each pulsing, shattered piece affirmed her proclamation. "I–I forgive you. I don't see my brother's blood on your hands."

His shoulders shimmied as he looked toward the edge of the Braithwaite.

Corina stroked his hand. "For what it's worth, you should forgive yourself too."

"Is that why you brought me up here?" He adjusted his position on the bench, moving slightly away from her. "Show me up? Be the bigger man, as it were?" The question, laced with accusation, stung.

"No, I just wanted us to end on a good note. Who knows if our paths won't cross again."

He was silent, jaw tense and taut, then, "Last night . . . I couldn't stop thinking about Bird and how he had a child on the way, Corina. A son. You didn't know Bird, but a wife, a family? All he wanted in life. And to play rugby on weekends." The comment was not random, but filled with calculated emotion. "If he'd had known, would he have acted differently that day? I'd be dead like the rest if he'd not fallen on me."

"Stephen, what's the point of this? Stop being the living dead. You're as bad as my parents. You were saved for a purpose and I don't think it was to live in perpetual regret, perpetual mourning." She held her fisted hands at her side, shaking. "Bird chose to protect you. He might not have known about Baby Bird, but he sure as heck knew about Agnes. He gave his life for you. Why don't you choose to honor him by living it?"

"Instinct." He shook his head, refusing to face her. "Bird moved on instinct. If he'd hesitated like me, he might have run for cover. But no matter what, I can't shake the reality that I robbed Bird, Carlos, the others of their lives."

"No, *you* didn't." She moved in front of him, hands on his legs, ducking her head to see his face. "Stop with this reflective guilt. Asif robbed them. Not you. His anger and bitterness." Oh, the picture of forgiveness just became clearer to her own heart. "You keep on this path and not even the pitch can save you. One day, Stephen, you'll be too old to play. What if your ankle doesn't heal—"

"It will heal." His eyes locked with hers and she saw beyond the cloak into the depth of his pain. "It will."

"Then heal *you*. Let go. It's been five and a half years. Don't chain yourself to the past. What's your instinct telling you, Stephen? Right here, right now? You said hesitation caused you to falter. So don't hesitate."

His hand grazed her hip and her passions pulsed, aching to be in his arms. But his answer was soft. Passionless. "Carry on. One day at a time."

Disappointment burned in Corina's chest as the first cathedral chime rang out, a second cathedral bell following. At nine o'clock they were bold and resonating, but a dissonant, uncoordinated sound.

One...

Two...

Three...

Corina determined not to lose this moment. She slipped her hand around his neck and drew him toward her, pressing her lips to his. Tentative at first, then with the full force of her heart, leaning against his leg, pressing toward his chest.

Four...

A kiss to remind him of their love, of the kiss that began it all that day on the pitch in Cathedral Stadium.

Five...

Her kiss deepened with the memories of their wedding night, the heat and sweat of making love for the first time in that small quaint cottage on Hessenberg's shores.

Six...

He held off at first touch, almost pulling away, then his arms slipped around her waist and he drew her onto his lap. They embraced, their bodies pulsing.

Seven...

Then she broke away, smoothing her hand over his chest where his heart kicked against her palm.

Eight...

"Corina—" His breath was hot against her skin.

Nine...

"I love you." She anchored her hands on his legs and tapped her forehead to his, the flutter of the annulment envelope brushing against her arm. "I just do."

Stephen woke Sunday morning, drenched in sweat. He'd dreamt of Corina again, but this time she was in his arms, swaying to the music of violins playing Chopin, the feathery white of her gown pure and spotless.

Forgiven.

With a growl in his chest, he kicked out from under the bed linens and made his way to the bathroom. At the sink, he doused his face with cold water, cooling the emotions that flamed against him.

"You've done it, mate." He stared at his reflection. "She's gone now. It's what you wanted."

He touched his finger to his lower lip, where the buzzing hint of her presence remained. He splashed his face again and tried to rub the buzz from his lip. When he snatched the hand towel from the bar to dry his face, the sensation of her touch had not diminished but intensified.

Forgiven. The word strafed his heart.

Stephen tossed the towel into the hamper and made his way back to his room. He wasn't worthy of forgiveness. Not from himself or Corina. Especially not from a God to whom he barely spoke.

The white annulment envelope beckoned from his dresser. Snatching it up, Stephen walked to his office. This was what he wanted. Not the lingering passion of her kiss nor the resurrection of their memories.

He was free, right? So why did he feel so bound?

Tossing the envelope to his desk, he made a note to carry it over to the King's Office in the morning. By Monday afternoon, it would all be official.

The idea emptied him as he sank down in his desk chair, head in hands. *God, could you love a man like me?*

From down the hall his mobile rang. With a jerk, he pushed out of the chair and skip-walked back to his room. His left ankle throbbed and pinched.

More physio. He must remain determined. Maybe he could entice Darren out on a Sunday afternoon for some exercises.

Corina's number flashed on the small screen and he sighed. Was she still in the city? With his pulse thick in his veins, he answered.

"Hey," she said, low and southern, full of sweetness.

"How are you?"

"Good. At the airport."

"It's cliché, you know. A sappy airport good-bye."

"Guess that's why you're not here?"

"Y–yes, that's why I'm not there."

After their Braithwaite kiss, she waited for him to respond, to relent, perhaps to say he loved her, too, but his heart remained locked.

She laughed. "Smart. Because who likes a sappy airport scene? Especially with a prince involved."

He sobered. "Corina, please, I cannot let you go home with any sort of hope. I'm sorry to speak with such frankness, but I want to be clear. I did you a great disservice with five and a half years of silence. I won't do it again. The annulment goes to the King's Office tomorrow morning."

"Then you should know I meant what I said. I love you. And I meant that kiss last night. We're good together, you and me. What happened in Afghanistan should draw us together not push us apart."

Did she hear herself, really? "You say that now, but in five, ten years, you'll regret waking up next to a man who cost you so much. Can I be so bold as to say 'Let go'? You must move on. Don't hold on to anything for me."

"What about you? Will you move on?" The tentative tone in her question made him think she didn't want an answer. "I–I guess I'll have to prepare to see you with someone else."

"Don't put yourself through this." Move on? How could anyone compare to her?

"Stephen, I've been wondering. If you thought we were annulled all those years, why didn't you move on?"

"Why didn't you?"

"I was just surviving, giving energy to Daddy and Mama. It's so true, the death of a child can break a family if they're not careful."

In the background, Stephen heard the announcement for a flight to Atlanta. "Is that you?"

"First class. That's me."

He grinned, pressing his finger against the sting of tears. "Indeed, love, that's you."

"So, I guess I shouldn't ask you to call or write."

"It's best we break away clean."

"What if I'd been pregnant?"

He swallowed. Grateful she had not been. "Corina, let's just stay on this plane."

"I just wondered—"

"Can you do me one favor?"

"What's that?"

"Forget about me."

"Five and a half years so far and I'm not very successful."

"It's all over now. We know it. The conversation has been had, the stories told, the papers signed." Another call came to board flight 781 to Atlanta.

"All right. I'll move on. But Stephen, that doesn't change one simple thing."

"Corina, don't—"

"I love you."

She said her good-byes and he hung up, crashing down to his bed. She was killing him. He smoothed his thumb and finger over his eyes, squeezing out the shallow wash of tears.

This was it. The last, last time he'd cry for her. Then it was over.

After a few moments, he collected himself, dried his face, and called Darren, who declined a physio appointment because he was heading to the shore with his family.

"Take a respite, Stephen. Rest. Do something with your family today."

"Have a good time, Darren. See you tomorrow."

Robert came in declaring the breakfast buffet was ready. Stephen thanked him and jumped in for a quick shower, where a nagging idea began, finding life among the heat and steam.

Talk to Archbishop Caldwell. The retired archbishop lived in a cottage along Hessenberg's northern shores. Stephen felt sure he'd read that somewhere.

He wondered if the old chap was up for a visit.

"Robert, I'm going out for the afternoon," Stephen said, coming down the stairs, finding his butler waiting for him in the foyer.

"This came for you." Robert met Stephen in the kitchen. "By special courier from the Galaxy via the King's Office."

"On a Sunday?" Odd. "I didn't purchase anything at auction. Who sent it?"

"Not sure." Robert held up a hammer, ready to open the crate. "Shall we?"

"We shall." Stephen motioned for him to open it, helping lift the lid when it was free, then sliding the painting from inside, breaking away the packing paper.

He knew what it was without looking. The Pissarro. Setting it against a chair in the living room, Stephen stood back, and the magic of the golden gas lamps reflecting off the rain-stained Rue du Roi made his hunger for Corina burn.

"My, sir, what an exquisite painting. Camille Pissarro is one of my favorites."

"Mine as well." Corina. This was her handiwork. In the painting's muted brown, rust, and gold colors of the Rue du Roi, he was with her, walking along the avenue arm-in-arm among the other lovers. Her kiss on his lips awakening his heart.

You love her.

Stephen glanced at Robert as he exited the room. "Send it back."

"Send it back to whom, sir? I–it's a Pissarro. Are you sure you don't want it for your collection?"

"What collection, Robert?" Stephen faced him, holding his arms wide.

"Perhaps one day you'll start a collection, sir."

"Perhaps. But I'm not starting with this piece." Was she trying to break him? "Return it to the Galaxy. Better yet, donate it to a museum. But it's not staying here."

You love her. He pressed his hands against his ears, starting for the kitchen. He'd confront this archbishop, this man of God— "Why did you marry us?"—sort out this love business, and be done with it.

"There's a note on the back." Robert's voice roped Stephen to a halt.

Stephen glanced down the curved staircase at his butler. "Bring it here, please."

Robert handed him the greeting-card-sized envelope and Stephen removed the card. The butler-valet-aide went on his way as Stephen sank down to the nearest chair and read.

To say I love you is more than mere words.
'Tis a truth in my heart.
I love you, my darling, and you've married me.
And we will never be apart.

The words were distant, but he knew them. From the card he bought at the shop the night they married. He crumpled the card in his big hand, dropped it to the floor, then smashed it with his foot. Now she played dirty. Unearthing tender memories he only planned to review as an old man, gumming his breakfast, mumbling of a love no one knew about, and they'd think him senile. The babbling Prince of Brighton.

Stephen glanced back at the painting. It was beautiful. But what were her intentions, sending him the Braithwaite painting? Did she intend to torture him, remind him of what he could never have? His heart palpitated at the idea of hanging that painting, her *memory*, in his apartment.

Shoving to his feet, he returned to his room for his walking boot, phone, and wallet. Twenty minutes later, through the light Sunday morning traffic, he parked his motor at the south bay and caught the morning ferry to Grand Duchy of Hessenberg, the island nation south of Brighton, just as she pulled from the docks.

TWENTY-SEVEN

*C*orina peered out the cab window as the driver turned down the long driveway toward her parents' home, exhausted. She tried to sleep during the long flight home, but the moment she drifted away, the fullness of Stephen's embrace jolted her awake.

Then she realized she wasn't in his arms, so she tried to sleep again. But rest never came.

She hadn't planned on coming back here, but she'd miss her flight home to Melbourne. She needed to talk to Daddy anyway, tell him the truth about Carlos face-to-face.

She was grateful for the light traffic and quick drive from the airport to Marietta. For the driver who didn't ask too many questions. For when he pulled past the front gate and down the long, live-oak-shaded drive of home.

She was even more grateful for Adelaide and Brill, her guardian angels, if not in reality then in theory, who said good-bye with sad looks on their angelic faces.

"I told him I forgave him, Adelaide. And I meant it. I—I think that's the core of loving well, don't you?" she asked, wanting truth, wanting confirmation that she'd succeeded in her mission.

Adelaide caressed Corina's arm. "Indeed I do."

"Maybe I should stay? He might come around."

"Leave it to the Father, lass. You needn't fret so. You're in his gracious hands."

"Adelaide, I wish I had your confidence."

Then the taxi arrived and there was no time for more discussion. She was going to miss those two. Whoever they were.

Adelaide and Brill watched her go in the thin light of dawn, and Corina captured the image of the old inn with its single-pane window filled with gold light and the odd and ancient proprietors waving good-bye.

Halfway over the Atlantic she realized she'd not taken one photograph of them. She pulled out her laptop and journaled her thoughts.

The cab driver curved around in front of the veranda and stopped. He popped the trunk as Corina stepped out into the early afternoon heat. Mid-June promised a sweltering summer.

Had it only been a little over a week since she was here? It felt like a lifetime.

"Here you are." He set her suitcases by her feet.

Corina paid him and he bid her a good day. She picked up her luggage and started for the house. She missed Stephen. If she'd stayed longer, could they have started over, fallen in love again, and repaired their annulment?

She wondered if he'd let her know when he received the Pissarro. She wondered if he'd keep it but well, that was up to him. She'd done all she could to remind him of who they were. Who they could be.

She swished up the porch stairs through pockets of cool shade, her stomach rumbling for home cooking, for some of Ida Mae's chicken and dumplings.

At the door, she tried the handle and the front door eased open.

"Hey y'all." She deposited her suitcases in the airy grand foyer then crossed toward the kitchen. "Anybody home?"

"Hello?" A masculine voice boomed from the foyer hall.

Corina spun around. "Daddy!"

"Welcome home, Kit. How was Brighton?"

"It was . . ." She sighed. "It's a long story. You're home. I'm glad." Corina fell against the man who'd been her first prince, her rock, her harbor.

He kissed her head. "I came home to check on a few things." He was somber, and when he motioned with his folded paper for her to sit in the formal living room, dread coated her joy.

"Daddy, what's wrong?" She sat on the edge of the sofa while he perched on the arm of the wingback chair.

"I'm going to live in the Atlanta condo for a while."

"Daddy, don't do this."

"Your mom and I need some space."

"Daddy, you don't need space. You need to come home. She needs to *leave* home. You two need to go back to being Donald and Horatia Del Rey."

"Darling, I'm not sure we can ever find those people again. By the way, our accountant called. Said you took ten million out of your Del Rey trust."

"I bought a painting. A Pissarro."

He looked impressed. "Well done."

"I left it there."

He regarded her for a moment, then nodded. "Are you planning on going back then?"

"No, I don't think so." If she told him it was a gift, then he'd ask for who and she didn't want to tell him like this, when she was tired, when he was telling her about moving out. But none of this surprised her. "Daddy, are you and Mama moving toward divorce?"

"At the moment, no."

"Because you know this is not what Carlos would want."

"He'd not want to be dead either, but he is."

"But you and Mama are one of the great love stories." Corina heard Adelaide's sweet, "It's a gift." "How can you not be there for each other?"

"We are, Corina. In our way."

"What way? From a distance? By letting Carlos's death drive you apart? Drive us apart? What about me? I'm out here all alone. It's like I died too." One sob broke loose and the tears followed. "Isn't there any hope for true, lasting love?" She shot up from the sofa and paced toward the fireplace. "This ticks me off."

"Corina, are we still talking about your mama and me?" Daddy unfurled his paper. "Or this?"

On the front page, under the Sunday *Post* masthead, was a full-color picture of Corina and Stephen from the *King Stephen I* premier. The headline read:

PRINCE STEPHEN MARRIED!

Gigi!

Corina snatched the newspaper from Daddy's hand. "How in the world . . . Where in the world . . . I'm going to kill her."

Daddy hooked his arm around Corina's and walked her through the living room into Mama's library—her chair was oddly vacant—and steered her to the kitchen. Corina trembled the entire way.

"She's a scoundrel." She slapped the kitchen island. "A news hound if there ever was one. Daddy, I want to sue her."

"No you don't." Daddy retrieved two glasses from the cupboard and started to fill them with ice and sweet tea. "And she'd cop to all of those names. With glee."

"Why can't I sue her?" Corina spread the paper before them. "She just told the world my business. Stephen's going to think I did this. To get back at him. The phones in the King's Office will ring off the hook."

"Corina..." Daddy took the paper away from her and handed her a glass. "Calm down. Forget the press. Tell me about you and Prince Stephen." He sat on the stool next to her, cupping his hands around his own glass. "I take it the headline is true?"

"Was true. We were married six years ago. Before he deployed."

"I knew he was Carlos's friend. Never thought of him as yours." Daddy toasted her with his raised glass. "The prince has splendid taste in women."

"I signed annulment papers yesterday. We're no longer married." She tugged a napkin from the center dispenser and wiped her eyes. "The Archbishop of Hessenberg married us in secret." She recounted the story of the midnight wedding, the secrets, the hidden marriage certificate, and Stephen's surprise trip to Florida. "When he came back from Afghanistan, he didn't want to be married, so I came home. I wanted to be with you and Mama anyway." She yanked another napkin from the dispenser.

"Why didn't you tell us?"

She shrugged. "We wanted it to just be our secret for a while. We didn't feel we could tell you and Mama without telling his parents and—"

"That came with complications."

"A few."

Daddy sipped his tea, leaning his elbows on the counter, being available to her for the first time since he walked off into the dusk after Carlos's funeral. "So why did you go to Cathedral City?"

"Gigi sent me to cover the premier—"

"This is Dad you're talking to, Corina."

"I wanted him back." She ran her finger along the etching of her glass. "I thought God wanted us together."

"But he had other ideas?"

Hearing the hard, concrete fact dried her tears. Surprisingly. But Daddy's voice carried a certain tone of authority and comfort.

"Pretty much." She turned toward him, shoving her tea aside. "He was with Carlos when he died, Daddy."

Daddy took a long sip, averting his gaze. "Yes, I know."

"You know?" Her eyes followed his broad back as he went to the fridge for a refill.

"I've always known, Kit."

"Then why didn't you tell us? I thought you hit an information desert at the Pentagon."

"I found a way around it. Had a connection in Senator Smith's office." Daddy returned to the island, this time sitting next to her, adjusting the open collar of his Polo, his eyes glistening as he looked into hers. "He put me in touch with the Joint Coalition, who told me only under the condition of utter silence, after they investigated me for six months."

"Considering what happened, I don't blame them."

"I only learned the news last year. I didn't tell you or your mother because it wasn't prudent. First, I had to get clearance to tell you. Second, it didn't comfort me to know he died saving Prince Stephen's life. How would it comfort you or your mother?" Daddy's dark gaze locked onto hers. "They looked into you, too, Kit. Never came back that you were married."

"I told you, it was in secret."

"Hats off to the Archbishop Caldwell." Then, "How did you find out Carlos was with the prince that day?"

"When Stephen came here telling me about the annulment, I wouldn't sign it. Since he was also with the Joint Coalition, I demanded he use his influence as a prince to find out about Carlos."

"Did you know they were on the same crew?"

"No, I just figured he was the brother of the king, he ought to be able to do something besides host charity functions and cut ribbons. It was just too strange to me we didn't have details—that you couldn't find out anything."

"Did he tell you the suicide bomber was a mate of his? From uni?"

"Yes."

"And that based on Stephen's recommendation, he was assigned to their unit as an interpreter?"

"It's why he blames himself. He said he's not worthy of the lives given for his."

"For the longest time, I agreed with him. I didn't consider him worth my son's life."

"For the longest time? What do you mean? Did you change your mind?"

"When I read the article in the *Post* this morning, I pondered if Prince Stephen was the kind of man worthy of my daughter. Would he love her and treat her kindly, be faithful, and be a good father? Then I realized he was the man my son willingly gave up his life to save."

Corina lowered her head to his shoulder, curling her arms about his strength, a blend of weeping and sobbing.

"There, there," Daddy soothed, his hand over her head. "It'll be all right, Kit."

"I still love him, Daddy." She raised up, reaching for another napkin.

"The heart wants what the heart wants." Daddy's smile seemed a bit brighter, but still, the sadness haunted his eyes. "It's good to have someone to share this with now."

"Are you going to tell Mama? Speaking of, where is she? Where's Ida Mae?"

"Your mom left the house right after breakfast. Ida Mae scooted out of here a half hour ago, said she had to go to Publix." Daddy finished his tea and set his glass in the dishwasher. Multimillionaire or not, Ida Mae did not abide anyone leaving dishes in the sink when the good Lord gave them hands to load the dishwasher.

"Work it out, Daddy. It's worth it."

"Give us time, Corina."

"Daddy, I bought the Pissarro for Stephen. For him to remember. That's what you and Mama need to do. Remember who you were when you fell in love, when we were all together, happy and loving life." Corina drank down her tea and stowed her glass in the dishwasher.

"How did you get so wise, Kit?"

"Listening to my father."

Daddy laughed, and Corina heard a small echo of the man he used to be. "What about your job?" He reached again for the *Post*. "I hear she's having financial struggles."

She sighed, looking over Daddy's shoulder. With an objective eye, it was a fantastic scoop, and Corina rocked that Melinda House dress even if she said so herself. But Stephen? Oh, he was a prince of a man, rugby strong, smoldering, and handsome. "I don't know. I haven't had time to really think about it. My gut says to quit. Gigi broke that story with no regard for me."

"When Carl Hatch read the story, he called." Carl was Daddy's lawyer and partner in the golf courses. "He said Gigi wouldn't risk a libel suit unless she was desperate. So he did some digging, made a few calls. She's in trouble. If you're interested, we can buy the *Post*, relaunch the brand, and—"

"Daddy," Corina said, patting his hand. "I love you for believing in me this much, but I just started back into the workforce, learned the truth about my brother's death, and got an annulment. I think I'll lay low for a while. Get my bearings. Besides, I'm no Gigi Beaumont, conqueror of media empires."

"Could be fun, Kit. We can hire the best in the business."

"Like Gigi?"

"Sure, why not?" Daddy's dark eyes danced a little. He was lean and handsome for his fifty-nine years, without grey in his hair or a spare tire around his middle. "She can stay on as news director. We'll hire someone like Fred Kemp as CFO. He'll have the *Beaumont Post* in the black within a year."

"Oddly enough, Gigi gave me some wise advice once. She said, 'Don't confine yourself to a life of insignificance.' I think that's why she runs so hard through life, trying to be significant. I don't want to mimic her. I want to mimic . . . Jesus." She cleared her throat and peeked at Daddy. Did she sound corny?

"Now that's the best plan of all."

"Have you come back to the faith, Daddy?"

"Not as far as you, but I'm making my way."

"Well hurry up." Corina started out of the room, tossing her papa a glance. "Who knows what First Baptist will look like in another year without you."

Daddy laughed and she paused at the door. "I love you, Daddy."

"I'm sorry about your prince, Kit."

She leaned against the doorway. "It's not easy to catch a prince, even harder to keep one."

"Seems you didn't lose him, darling. He chose to walk off."

"Either way, my love for him wasn't enough to conquer death." She shoved away from the counter. "But then you and Mama already know that, don't you?"

"Kit . . . ," Daddy said.

"Right, give you time. What does Mama think about me marrying a prince?"

"She never said. All I heard was a gasp from her library. Then she was on the phone and, I don't know, ran out shortly after breakfast. Haven't seen her since." Daddy tapped the newspaper against the kitchen counter. "Shall I fly to Brighton and have a talk with your young man?"

She laughed. "It's too late. But thank you for asking."

"Shug, if he really is your prince, don't give up."

Corina stopped his line of thinking with a flash of her palm.

"I just spent a week trying to love well, and what I got was an annulment. But I did forgive him, Daddy."

"That sounds like loving well to me."

Corina jerked her thumb in the direction of the stairs. "I'm going to fix my flight home for tomorrow and take a nap. Tomorrow I'll quit my job, then spend a week on the beach plotting my next move."

"I know a few movie people if you need some help."

"Hey, now you're talking. We can get Clive Boston to star in the movie version of *How to Catch a Prince*. And lose him."

"Don't laugh, Kit. It can happen. Sounds like an Oscar winner to me. But don't you think Clive's a bit long in the tooth for such a role?"

"Don't let him hear you say that." Her laugh mingled with Daddy's, and for the first time in five and a half years, Corina felt a little piece of the way things used to be. "Daddy, I know losing Carlos has been hard on us all, especially you, losing your son and heir, but don't let it destroy us."

"You're my heir, Corina. But you're right." He nodded, but she could tell he still wrestled with his heart. "I'll work on it as long as you promise me that the next time you get married, I walk you down the aisle. I've been looking forward to that since the day you were born." He waved the newspaper at her. "I felt a little cheated when I read this."

"I promise. And you know I wouldn't have it any other way."

"Your Highness." Archbishop Caldwell stepped aside for Stephen to enter his seaside cottage. A cozy abode with a clutter of books and papers stacked around the small living room. "To what do I owe this pleasure?"

"I hope I'm not disturbing you." The place felt like home

the moment Stephen walked in and sank into a plush, deep-red sofa.

"No, no, not at all. This is my wife, Lola."

"Your Highness." She curtsyed. "Would you care for tea?" She picked up the magazines and books by Stephen's feet and stacked them on an end table.

"Thank you, kindly. Tea would be lovely."

"I've baked blueberry scones. Would you care for one?"

"Again, thank you." Now that he was here, the tension eased from his gut and his stomach reminded him he'd walked out on his breakfast. "But please, don't go to any bother."

Her laugh bubbled. "Pshaw, 'tis no trouble a-tall. Mack, I gather you'd like some tea as well."

"As long as you're serving the prince." Archbishop Caldwell removed his glasses, setting them on the table next to his chair. "It's good to see you. It's been a number of years. I heard your service in Afghanistan ran into a bit of trouble."

Stephen sat forward, rubbing his hands together, warming away the chill of nerves. "Some, yes. Lost everyone on my crew but me."

"Do you care to talk about it? Is that why you're here?"

"No, I'm here on another matter."

"Whatever it is, I can see it troubles your soul."

Mrs. Caldwell returned with the tea and scones, giving the men and the conversation a moment to breathe. Gain direction.

Stephen stirred his tea, his spoon clicking against the china cup. He peeked at the archbishop, who drank his tea with a look of contentment, offering nothing to Stephen but the space to speak.

Which he didn't exactly know how to fill. Setting aside his tea, he stretched his legs and cramping ankle. Lately the pain seemed much more intense. He was starting to believe the injury would be with him the rest of his life.

He regarded the spiritual leader. "Sir, may I ask you a question?"

"Isn't that why you're here?"

"Why did you marry us? In secret? Corina and me? We woke you up in the middle of the night, asking you to break Brighton royal law." Six years ago, the archbishop was a servant of the House of Stratton and the Church of Brighton, avowed to keep the nation's and God's laws.

The sister island nations were hobbled together by a hundred-year-old entail until Hessenberg discovered their own long-lost princess last year and established themselves as a sovereign nation once again.

"You tell me," Mr. Caldwell said.

"Why you married us?"

"Yes, why do you think I agreed to your request, keeping quiet all these years?"

"Because I'm the prince? Because you . . . I don't know . . . wanted us out of your hair so you could go back to bed? Leave me to sort out my own mess?"

The man laughed. "I've said no to kings and queens. Do you think I'd have any qualms about denying a young prince his seemingly impetuous request?"

Stephen sat back, holding his teacup in his palm. "Her twin brother died. In Afghanistan. I was there."

"Ah, I see. Is that why you've been apart?"

"Yes."

"And what does she think of this arrangement?"

"She says she loves me. She only recently learned the entire truth and why I cannot be with her."

"Can't be with her? Are you still married?"

"She signed annulment papers."

"And it's bothering you?"

"A little. I want to know why you married us."

"Why did you want to marry Corina a month before you deployed?"

"I just wanted to be with her. Not just for a night, not to . . . you know . . . and then leave. I wanted to give her my name, a title. I wanted to spend my life with her. I love her." He set down his tea, having no desire for it.

"And she loved you?"

"Yes, she loved me. She says she still loves me."

"There's your answer. Why I married you. That night, when you knocked on my door rousing me from sleep, I was a bit irritated. Then I opened the door to two people very much in love. I saw my reflection in your eyes. The way I felt about my missus when we married forty-five years ago. Otherwise, don't think I'd have hesitated to send you back home. Prince or not."

"You see, sir, when I look at her, I see . . . her brother . . . bleeding and dying. I've had a dream of her walking among the dead, wailing, her white wedding dress splattered with blood." Stephen gripped his hands together, squeezing, cleansing away the invisible stain. "I did that to her, to those men."

"You are somehow responsible for their deaths?"

The old man was trying to understand the details Stephen could not speak. He'd trusted him with a secret six years ago, but he could not betray the Defense Ministry's classified files again. He was the Prince of Brighton, after all.

"Indirectly, yes."

"A wrong decision?"

"Indirectly." Asif appeared to be a stellar choice at the start. But . . .

"You cannot tell me more, can you?"

"No, I'm sorry."

"I've enough to understand, I believe." The archbishop reached for a scone, then settled back in his chair. "Would you care for one?"

"No, thank you." He thought he did, but the conversation had filled his empty belly.

"As I see it, whatever transpired over there has left you feeling responsible, perhaps guilty, and you cannot face Corina."

"Not as my wife, no." A soft, blue word slipped from his lips, but he didn't apologize or wish it back. "Her brother, the others, did not deserve to die, not for the cause that spilled their blood."

"You alone survived?"

He nodded, dropping his chin to his chest, his eyes filling, a peppery heat trailing along his emotions, burning his thoughts. "I'm not worthy. I–I hesitated. They died."

"And this hesitation makes you responsible in some way."

"Yes, precisely. And betrayed by someone I'd once considered a friend."

"Quite a sticky wicket."

"Quite." Slumping forward, Stephen crashed his head into his hands. "I dream of them, their suffering."

"And you can't forgive yourself, can you?"

"Never!" He fired to his feet, leaning on his wounded ankle, pain striking his bones, spiking down through his foot. "I am not worthy."

"No man is worthy until Christ makes him worthy."

"Don't you see? They died in vain."

"Did your Lord, the Christ, die in vain as well?"

"Pardon? I don't follow. The Christ had nothing to do with my men."

"He has everything to do with you, and your men. If he counted you worthy of his death, then you were worthy for those men. No greater love is this than a man lay down his life for his friends."

"Stop!" Stephen pressed his palms to his ears. "Lie. It's a lie."

"But you count yourself as unworthy, and therefore not worthy of a woman like Corina and unworthy of Christ's love."

"Because I am unworthy. I may be a prince on the outside, but on the inside I'm a man like every other, and war or no . . ." He hesitated, on the brink of sharing too much. "My life is not worth that of another. And I certainly don't compare to Christ. He perhaps is worth men giving up their lives, but not me."

"He was also man. With emotions. He was also betrayed by those closest to him."

"He's also God."

"But he was also a man."

The archbishop chuckled, though Stephen failed to see the merriment, and considered his tea, taking a hearty sip. The old man broke off a corner of his scone, closing his eyes, *hmmmming* his enjoyment, spiking Stephen's irritation.

He should just leave. This was an ill-planned quest.

"What do you want from me?" the archbishop finally said. "You seem set on your answers."

Stephen regarded him. "I–I . . ." What did he want by coming here? "I thought I wanted to know why you married us." Stephen picked at the upholstery threads, feeling his heart and foolishness exposed. "But now I don't know."

"If you could go back, do it all over again, would you? Marriage, deployment, serving with those particular men?"

"I–I don't know."

"What might you do different? Not marry her? Perhaps serve with different men? Make different choices?"

"No, I'd probably be foolhardy enough to marry her." *Face it, you love her!* "And the boys in our crew were the best in the entire squadron. It was an honor to serve with them. But yes, there are a few different actions I'd take."

"In hindsight."

"In hindsight."

"My dear prince, you need a new perspective." The archbishop struggled out of his chair to join Stephen on the couch. "Your worth is not determined by who you are or what you do, even what you *don't* do. It's determined by the work of your Savior. If our Lord bore the cross to declare you worthy, then indeed you are, and nothing—not war, nor death, regrets, injury, broken hearts, or tabloid headlines—can change it. Only if you choose not to accept it."

"I confess I'm not a religious man, archbishop."

"Then can you be a believing man? One of faith in God? Let him forgive you so you can forgive yourself. Let this matter go to him. Otherwise, your mates indeed died in vain if you confine yourself to a life of regret, bearing a burden that doesn't seem like yours to bear. And not forgiving yourself for it." He spoke in an even, calm tone, sorting through Stephen's emotions with the fine edge of his wisdom. "In the end, you die with them, but only after years of a slow, withering kind of death, fulfilling your own prophecy. They died in vain. That banged-up ankle you sport will seem a welcome respite when it's all said and done."

His words melded with a heavy, oily presence in the room, creating a spicy-sweet fragrance that washed over Stephen. When he closed his eyes, he felt as if he were floating.

"What choice will you make? Your Highness, you cannot undo the past. But you can blanket it in the Lord's blood, not that of your mates, and the Son of God will heal you and ensure your future days."

The declaration rattled him. Disquieted his self-righteousness. He felt the rumble and shift in his chest. He'd believed in God most of his thirty-one years. But after Torkham, doubt and confusion shattered his small faith. "What do you want from me?" His spirit churned, addressing the question more to the One who hovered in the room than the archbishop sitting next to him.

"He wants everything, Your Highness. I'd say he earned it. If you could meet with your mates, somehow in the beyond, wouldn't you give them everything for dying for you?"

"My royal scepter. My crown, my title, my money . . . yes, my everything."

"The Christ will do the same for you. If *you* give *him* your everything. Come to the cross." The archbishop's voice seemed to stir the oil in the room.

Stephen remained planted, shaking so violently on the inside, his hands and legs trembled. He gripped his knees, trying to control the waves coursing through him, but he could not.

"Best give in, lad. The Lord has come for you, and I dare believe he's not leaving until he has your surrender."

"Surrender to what?"

"To him, to his cross, to his love and the fact that you, my boy, were worth dying for."

Worth dying for . . .

The phrase crushed him so intensely, Stephen slid off the sofa, unable to command his muscles, and hit the floor on his knees, weeping, the heel of his hand pressed into his eyes. Humiliating, undignified . . . But he could not stop it.

His chest expanded with each sob, filling with the reality of his own weaknesses and sin. Sin he'd never contemplated, actions and thoughts he'd once delighted in ground him down, further into the unseen presence in the room.

"Lord, forgive him." The archbishop's soft prayer demolished Stephen's last wall.

A wail exploded from his chest, a sound he'd never heard. "Lord, they died for me. An unworthy man." He sucked in a sharp, shallow breath, unable to fill his lungs. "Lord—" The name smoothed over his tongue, and from his lips he confessed. "Jesus, you are Lord and died for me. Forgive me. Let me forgive myself. Please, remember Bird and Carlos, the lads who died. Asif . . . remember Asif. And Corina, my Corina." The words continued to flow as he lowered his chest to the floor, prostrating himself, and letting every hidden thing come to the light.

And moment by moment, Stephen Stratton, Prince of Brighton, became the man he'd always longed to be.

TWENTY-EIGHT

O n a glorious Monday afternoon, Corina marched through the bull pen with an empty printer-paper box in hand, the ping of the elevator behind her, and she remembered. She no longer had a secret.

She'd caught an early flight out of Atlanta, was home and unpacked before lunch. Now she was at the paper, her resignation prepped and ready.

"Oh my gosh." Melissa pounced on Corina the moment she set down the printer box. "How did you keep *that* a secret? A prince? And for crying out loud, what are you doing here in Melbourne?"

"I'm here because I live here, Mel." The lamp was hers, bought the afternoon she accepted the job from Gigi. It went into the box. The pencil canister as well as the hand sanitizer everyone used and the array of squeeze toys were also hers. Corina inspected the stapler. Hers or the *Post*'s? Hers. Too new and nice to be the *Post*'s. But she stored it in the middle drawer. A lovely parting gift for Gigi. "I kept it a secret because it was a secret. Besides, I didn't think we were still married." With a sigh she peered at her friend. "It's not the kind of thing you blurt out. 'Hey everyone, I was married to a prince.'"

"Sure, for most of us, but you're *you*, Corina Del Rey. The kind of girl who does marry a prince."

"Well, we're not married anymore. I signed annulment papers."

"You what?" By the look on her face, one would think Melissa was being divorced. "Why? No, no, no, I want a princess for a friend. And I want my friend to be happy. Do you still love him?"

"That's not the question, Mel. The statement is he doesn't want to be married to me."

"Why not?"

"Mel, I can't go into it." Corina smiled. "Please, just leave it alone."

"Corina, he's an idiot. Can I just say that?"

Corina laughed low. "I know you mean to make me feel better, but the truth is he's not an idiot. He's a very good and kind and decent man." Her voice wavered. "One of the best."

Melisssa tapped the side of the printer box. "Are you leaving?"

"You don't think I'd stay after what Gigi did, do you?"

"Rats, there goes all the cool people."

"No," Corina looked toward Gigi's office. "You're still here."

Through the glass panel, she could see the tip of her blond hair as she worked at her desk. "Do you know how she found out?"

"It's Gigi. She has minions all over the world."

"Yeah, well, it seems she has a minion inside the palace. The article said, 'a palace source.'"

"She could've made that up." Melissa took out the pencil canister and examined the pens. "Can I have the purple pens? I love purple pens."

"Knock yourself out. But she couldn't have made up the fact we were secretly married. She's not that good."

As much as Gigi stepped over the line by running the article, the woman did Corina a favor. She exposed the marriage and outed the secret.

Mama had seemed somewhat changed Sunday evening when she returned home late from wherever she'd gone. Gentler. Kinder.

This morning she came down to say good-bye as Corina and Daddy headed down to Atlanta. She'd brushed a wisp of Corina's hair aside, her eyes misty. "Don't be a stranger."

"What are you going to do next?" Melissa tapped the printer-paper box.

"I don't know. Haven't decided." And she was okay with that . . . for now.

Melissa returned to her desk while Corina packed the last of her things. She'd not been at the *Post* long enough to acquire much. When she finished, she started through the bull pen toward Gigi's office, her flip-flops smacking.

"May I have a word?" Corina said, peeking inside the door, finding Gigi and Mark in a head-to-head convo.

Gigi jumped, startled. "Goodness, I didn't hear you come in."

Mark stood, papers in hand. "Corina, welcome back. How was Brighton? We were just talking about when to run your piece on Clive. Maybe before the American premier. Your article on the Brighton premier was excellent."

"Gigi this is my last minute working for you and Beaumont Media." Corina got right to it. "I'll write the interview with Clive from home and have it to you by Friday. However, the rights will remain mine. I'll be offering the story, with additional pieces of Clive's life, to other news outlets by next week. So if you want a scoop, which apparently is very important to you, you'd better run his story in this coming Sunday *Post*."

"Mark, will you excuse us?" Gigi said, her glance on Corina, steely and unwavering.

Mark leaned toward Corina as he passed. "I didn't know anything about this."

"I'm not suing if that's what you're worried about."

"Oh, thank heaven." The door clicking behind Mark sounded like a sigh of relief.

"He's a peach, isn't he?" Corina said, arms folded, facing Gigi. "How'd you find out?"

"You know I can't reveal my sources."

"So the source keeps his or her privacy while mine and Prince Stephen's get splashed all over the front page, stirring up the entire Brighton Kingdom?"

"The question is why did I have to get it from a source when you sat not thirty feet from me for the last six months?"

"It was none of your business, Gigi."

"What? We're family."

"No we're not. Family wouldn't do to me what you did. Besides, my parents didn't even know. They found out in *your* paper "

"Now *that* is not my business. That is yours."

"How did you find out?"

"You can't ask me that, Corina. Is it not true?"

"It was true."

"Then I'm sorry, but when the Prince of Brighton marries, in secret, it *is* my business. It's the world's business. It's what I do." She smoothed the palm of her hand over a new addition to her office. A marble pelican. "I'm lawyered up, in case you're wondering."

"I told you, I'm not suing. I don't need your money. Why didn't you tell me the paper was floundering?"

Corina caught the edge of Gigi's surprise on her expression. "How did you find out?"

"You know I can't reveal my sources, Gigi."

"Ah, touché. Your father?"

"I'm leaving now, but I want to say thank you for giving me this job, for bringing me out of my fog. But I do not thank you for running that story. You wonder why I didn't tell you? Why didn't you have the decency to talk to me?"

"Turn my back on the scoop of the decade?"

"Good luck with everything, Gigi." Corina reached for the door. "And you might want to check with your infamous source. The Prince of Brighton is no longer married."

Hoisting the printer-paper box on her hip as she exited the elevator for her penthouse condo, Corina felt a swirl of sadness and excitement.

Old life passing away, a new life ahead of her. She was pressing on. On the ride down U.S. 1 for home, she had a hankering to talk to Adelaide, reclining in her comforting wisdom.

In the lobby, Captain was on duty and came around his desk to greet her. "A delivery came for you while you were out. I escorted the courier up to your apartment. It was a rather large box and I didn't want to leave it down here."

"A large box?" Stephen. He sent her the Pissarro. "A wooden crate? Perhaps containing something like a painting?"

Captain thought a moment. "It was wooden. Square. I suppose it could've contained a painting." Captain popped a smile. "Did you purchase a painting, Miss Del Rey?"

"Yes, but not for me." Really, did he despise their time so much he didn't even want the Pissarro? "Thank you, Captain."

"Anytime, Miss Del Rey." He touched his hand to the brim of his hat. "Is it true? What the paper said? You're a princess?"

Corina pushed the elevator button, clinging to her dignity, not willing to break down in the lobby in front of Captain. "No, I'm most definitely not a princess."

The doors pinged open and she almost longed for the slither of remembrance that used to cross her soul when she heard that sound. That she had a secret. That she'd caught a prince. That she'd been wildly in love.

The elevator arrived and she stepped in, pushing the 9th floor button. Her prince did not want her, nor her gifts.

She fell against the side of the car and let her tears go. Now that their secret had been exposed to the world, she'd lost her connection with him, how the slightest ringing, tinging sounds took her back to their love. If he truly returned the painting, then that was the end. They'd have nothing left between them.

She'd not intended to cling or manipulate. Only to bless him. And yes, perhaps, remind him. But . . .

Oh Lord, loving well is so very, very hard.

"There you are, Corina." Neighbor Mrs. Putman scooted down the corridor in her robe and slippers as Corina stepped off the elevator.

It was five in the afternoon, but Mrs. Putman often wore her bed clothes for days. The widow of a former Harris Corp executive, she spent her mornings drinking coffee and reading, her afternoons watching the Soap Network. "A very large package was delivered for you."

"So I heard. Captain told me." Corina adjusted the printer box on her hip as she unlocked her door.

"A crate of some kind. The kind used for expensive things." She crossed arms and raised her delicate chin. "Did you buy yourself something expensive?"

"No, I didn't buy *myself* anything expensive."

"Someone did. Perhaps . . ." Mrs. Putman leaned toward her. "Your prince?"

Corina laughed. What else could she do? Besides, the woman made such a comical face. "Mrs. Putman, I do not have a prince. I'm not a princess and my life is not a soap opera script. I'm just a regular, ordinary, run-of-the-mill American heiress."

"But the story in the *Post* said you'd married a prince. In secret!"

"We're not married."

"It was a lie?" Her eyes narrowed in skepticism.

"Let's just say it's not true." Corina crossed over her threshold, dropping the printer-paper box to the floor. Mrs. Putman peered inside, her nose raised, scanning the foyer for the box.

Corina eased the door closed. "Have a good evening, Mrs. Putman."

"Not so fast." The woman pressed her hand to the door. "I want to know what's in that box."

"As do I." Corina leaned on the door, inching the woman further into the corridor.

"You let me know when you open it. My husband sent me a box like that once and it contained a lovely portrait of our daughter."

"What a very special gift. I'll be sure to let you know what it is." The woman was like a dog with a bone.

"Why can't I watch you open the crate?"

Corina sighed. She felt for Mrs. Putman. Widowed and alone, her children scattered across the country, busy with their own lives. "Tell you what, come for tea tomorrow at ten. You can see what's in the crate."

"Tomorrow at ten?" The woman pinched her expression. "Won't you be at work?"

"No, I won't. I resigned. Tomorrow at ten?"

"Yes, t–that would be lovely." Mrs. Putman's glossy eyes reflected the truth. She was lonely. And she was grateful.

When the door was shut, Corina faced the box leaning against the foyer wall. It was a painting crate all right. A bit deeper than she'd have thought, but no doubt, Stephen had shipped her the Pissarro.

How he managed to get it to her so quickly was a feat for princes and kings.

Worse, *why'd* he returned it. Her tears surfaced again. Did she want the Pissarro? All those memories hanging on her wall instead of her heart?

Digging the hammer out of the kitchen junk drawer, Corina

laid the box on the floor, questions pounding her heart. Did she want to open it? Was she fortified enough to fall into the imagery and sensation of the Rue du Roi?

Whispering a prayer, she aimed the hammer, prying open the lid. If nothing else, the Pissarro would remind her of the night atop the Braithwaite when she caught the heart of a prince.

She'd regale her grandchildren with her story.

When the lid lifted free, Corina anchored it against the foyer wall. She expected to find a mound of bubble wrap but instead found layers of packing and tissue paper.

Kneeling beside the crate to discover what lay beneath, she gasped when the white sheen and feathery beauty of the Luciano Diamatia emerged.

"Oh, Mama." Corina lifted the gown from the crate, new tears rising. A pink envelope dropped to the floor by her feet. Reaching for it, Corina found a simple note inside.

Corina, please forgive me. Your loving mama.

A laugh bubbled over Corina's tears as she hurried to her room, Diamatia's voice, with all of his inflections—rolling *r*'s and slurred *s*'s—paraded across Corina's mind.

At their first meeting, the renowned designer walked around her, musing aloud.

I see a swan. A glorious swan!

Standing in front of her bedroom mirror, Corina held the gown against her, aching to try it on.

Please fit, please fit.

Mourning and grieving wreaked havoc on a girl's body.

Corina spread the gown across her bed, found her phone in her purse, and dialed home. Ida Mae answered with a curt, "I'll get your mama." Bless sweet ole Ida Mae.

"So you received the gown?" Mama said with more emotion in her voice than Corina had heard in years. She drank from her tone as if she pulled a cup of water from a deep well.

"Thank you so much, Mama. But what made you go after it?"

"The story, in the Sunday *Post* . . . about you and the prince."

"Oh, I see." How to tell her the marriage was annulled? "Mama—"

"Your father told me the rest of the story. I'm sorry, Corina. I truly am. Nevertheless, when I read the article I realized what a lovely, capable woman you are and how lucky any man would be to have you as his wife. Especially Prince Stephen. So, I hunted down the dress and hired a special courier to deliver it to you. Besides, you were right, it wasn't mine to give away."

"I don't know what to say." Corina stood at her bedroom window, the subtle hues of the fading sun soaking the June evening, a sense of enrichment swelling in her.

"Say you'll wear it. And soon."

"I married Stephen in that dress."

Mama was silent for a moment. "I'm sorry I wasn't there to see it."

"I'm sorry you weren't there, too, Mama."

"But I'm sure it was all terribly romantic."

"Terribly."

"I'm trying, Corina, I sincerely am." Mama's long sigh brushed Corina's heart. "Be patient with me."

"Always, Mama. Always."

They said good-bye, and Corina fell back on her bed, lying next to the gown, exhausted and exhilarated.

Thank you, Lord. Thank you. Being loved well felt rather grand.

Corina soaked in his presence, feeling his descent the moment she raised the dress from the crate. She didn't always understand the invisible brushes against her arms or the gentle taps against her forehead that made her blink, but they were him. Her God. Breaking in and reminding her he was there, watching and waiting.

If one wanted to love well, learn from the Master. Corina

understood that life was a journey and if she'd trust him, Jesus would carve out her way through the wilderness. Be her light in the dark.

Tears streamed down her temples, gathering in her ears. She was a rich princess tonight. Not because of Daddy or Prince Stephen.

But because Jesus was her King.

After a moment, a gurgle of joy blipped across her spirit. Corina sat up, wiped her eyes, and brushed her hand over the gown.

"Let's see if you still fit." She shimmied from her shorts and T-shirt and with a trembling inhale, stepped into the silk and glory of the gown.

Raising the gown over her hips, and fitting the skirt just below her waist, she smiled. It fit. As perfectly as the day Luciano delivered it. The strapless bodice clung to her with satin tenderness and the flowing, feathery skirt flared out from her hips, floating, like a swan on a pond of sunlight that pooled on the bedroom floor. The hem just kissed the tips of her toes.

Oh, oh, oh, so very glorious!

Corina turned in a small circle, arms wide, her heart exploding in her chest, freedom firing through her. She'd shed her grave clothes. Gone from death to life.

She was so grateful to the pain of her journey that brought her to this moment in God.

I want to love you well, love you well . . .

When the doorbell chimed, she jumped, hand over her pulsing heart, her healing moment with God interrupted. Who could that be? She didn't want to leave this place of peace and promise.

Corina leaned out her bedroom door. "Hello?" She waited, listening. "Mrs. Putman? I'll see you tomorrow at ten." She waited another moment. "Okay?"

The doorbell chimed again. With a bit of attitude this time. Oh for crying out loud. Corina started across the hardwood, her bare feet thudding. a flash image of her lonely neighbor crossing her mind.

Well, there was no reason they couldn't have tea tonight. Corina was a bit overdressed . . . She laughed as she reached for the door. She in a rare designer gown, Mrs. Putman in her robe and slippers.

"Ta-da!" Corina swung the door open. "What do you think—" But it wasn't nosey ole Mrs. Putman waiting in the corridor. "Stephen." Her legs buckled with hot, surging adrenaline. "W– what are you doing here?" Her Stephen. Was on her doorstep. His countenance as bright as a full moon.

Without a word, his gaze fixed on her, he crossed the threshold, scooping her into his arms, kicking the door shut behind him. "I've missed you." His warm, sweet breath brushed her cheek.

Corina shivered and fell into him, her hand resting on his chest as she drank in his presence. "W–what are you doing, Stephen?"

"I came for you." The mischievous glint in his eye beamed ten times brighter than she remembered. She couldn't look away. "You said something to me that I didn't respond to properly. I want to do that now, Corina."

Tightening his embrace, he cupped his right hand along the curve of her neck, brushing her shoulder with his firm, warm hand. His eyes searched hers.

Fire coursed through her. "What? Stephen, please . . . What are you doing here?"

He bent toward her, his lips whispering past hers with a barely there kiss. Corina moaned and melted into his thundering heart. "I just wanted to tell you—" He swallowed hard to catch his next breath. "To tell you that I, um . . ." He brushed her lips again, a half kiss that drove her past her final fears.

She gripped his shoulders, holding on, losing herself in the power of his persuasion. She didn't need to know why he was here, just that she was in his arms and the power of his passion spoke for his heart. She responded in kind. Raising on tiptoe, she pressed her lips to his, finishing what he'd started.

I love you, Stephen!

He answered, hungry and eager, falling against the foyer wall, bringing her with him.

When he raised his head for a breath, his blue eyes like the summer sky, his smile brighter than the night stars, he brushed his hand over her hair. She thought he might speak, but he drew a breath and kissed her again with the pleasure of a man satisfied.

The skirt of her dress swayed, brushing the tops of her toes with delight.

The kiss thawed into a hug, Stephen cradling his face against her. "I love you, Corina." His baritone confession was luxurious. "I love you so much."

Corina tipped her head back to see his face, brushing her hands over his delicious hair because she'd been aching to do it since he came back into her life. He was hers. All hers. "What happened to you Prince Stephen of Brighton?"

"You happened to me. I have so much to tell you. Let's start with this," he walked through the foyer, pointing to his left ankle. "Healed. Miraculously. Haven't worn the boot in two days."

"You're healed?"

"Miraculously."

Corina leaned in for another kiss because she could, because she was thirsty for him again. Would she ever fill up?

"I went to see Archbishop Caldwell and—"

"And you came to God?" Corina's heart jumped at the prospect of Stephen being God's man. All the way. Emptied of his pain and bitterness.

"No," he said, kissing her hand. "He came to me."

"How? And why did you go to see Archbishop Caldwell?"

"To ask him why he married us that night."

"And what did he say?"

Stephen chuckled. "I'm not really sure, love, but I found myself on the floor, weeping, repenting, being washed and healed inside and out. My ankle stopped hurting, and all the locks on my heart opened. I fixed to fly here as soon as I could." There in the foyer, he bent to one knee, pulling a ring from his pocket. "Marry me. Please. Again."

A sputter of joy tickled her lips as she knelt in front of him, as he slipped the diamond and platinum ring on her finger. She regarded him for a moment, then kissed him with the kisses of grace and peace. "Yes, I'll marry you again. And again. The ring is beautiful, Stephen."

"A jeweler friend of Nathaniel's opened his shop yesterday for me. I wanted to ask you more properly this time. And I wanted a ring that was just yours and mine." Stephen walked her into the living room, falling into the recliner, pulling her along with him.

"I love it, but babe, aren't we already married?" Corina draped her legs over the arm of the chair and cuddled against Stephen.

"I filed the annulment papers."

Corina reared back. "Y–you filed them? Then flew all the way here to propose?"

"I'm serious. I want to do it proper this time round. I want to start over, have an engagement time with parties and press conferences. I want to marry you in a big fat royal wedding with you in a white gown every lass will want to model," he fanned the feathers of her dress, "and me in my uniform—"

"You'll put on your uniform?"

"Yes, I will. I want the families of the lads in the front row. I want my parents and yours in attendance, our friends and family. What we had before, Corina, got bruised and broken. We need to end that chapter of our lives and start over." He swept his hand over her cheek. "But this I know, you are the only true love for me and if you give me another chance, I'll fight every day to put our marriage first and make us the couple God meant us to be."

Tears were sometimes the only sufficient answer. Resting her head on his chest, Stephen held her close. So very, very close.

There was no place more like home than in his arms.

TWENTY-NINE

Brighton Kingdom

October 12

Once again he found himself standing in the warm wings of the *Madeline & Hyacinth Live!* show. The still air created a sting of perspiration down his back. He adjusted his collar, then his shirtsleeves.

But he never let go of her hand.

"Are you all right?" Corina looked up at him with those amber eyes of hers that made his heart skip a beat.

"Just a bit stuffy in this spot, don't you think?" Stephen kissed her forehead, then glanced at Thomas, who shook his head, cocking a sly grin.

Since his Florida proposal, Stephen felt swept off his feet, by God, by Corina, by the power of love and forgiveness.

He'd arranged for Agnes and Baby Bird to receive Lt. Mitchell "Bird" O'Connell's death benefits and set up an education fund for the five-year-old, as well as for the children of the other men who died that day.

Even Asif's.

One weekend a month he ferried down to Hessenberg to spend a night and day with Archbishop Caldwell, learning what he should've learned in Sunday school catechism but had not.

His heart nearly brimmed with the growing reality of a loving King as his Savior.

When he'd injured his ankle on the pitch that spring day seven months ago, he'd have never believed what kind of life awaited him. He was unworthy. On his own. Jesus made him worthy and that was a sacrifice he could accept.

Stephen pressed his hand to his chest, to the swirling rise of emotions.

God, I praise you.

In the past three months he'd made an open book of his life, confessing to the press about his secret marriage, annulment, and now re-engagement. If that was a word. How he'd gone dark after events in Afghanistan and how God had wooed his wounded heart to him through the love of Corina.

At one time, Stephen clung to rugby and life on the pitch as his only salvation, afraid to wander away lest he crumble. What he counted as freedom was his prison.

But now that he knew true salvation, and true freedom, his possibilities were endless. He was free to be Prince Stephen again. And since their engagement, he'd been sleeping like a baby. The night terrors had ended. Such a good, good God.

The stage manager passed by. "Sixty seconds."

The show crew quickly changed the set from bright lights with tall director's chairs to a living room aura with plush cream-colored love seats facing one another and a faux fireplace.

Stephen squeezed Corina's hand. "Ready?"

"Ready."

Madeline and Hyacinth took their positions, standing before the cameras as they came out of the commercial break.

"Madeline, we've had some amazing shows this year," Hyacinth said, starting things off. "But this afternoon we have probably one of the best shows we've ever done, or will do."

"I'm so excited about our next guests," Madeline said, reading the cue card. "We surprised you with him before, so we're surprising you with *him* again, along with his fabulous fiancée. Ladies and gentlemen, please welcome the Prince of Brighton, Prince Stephen, and his fiancée, Corina Del Rey."

Stephen led Corina into the wall of applause, their strides together and even. The former beauty queen was perfect for him. The limelight neither frightened nor fascinated her.

After a round of cordial hugs with the show's hostesses, Stephen and Corina sat together on one couch, Madeline and Hyacinth on the other. As if friends sharing tea.

"Let me start off by saying congratulations," Madeline said. "We are so grateful to have you on the show."

"We're pleased to be here," Stephen said with a glance at Corina, who glowed.

"We have a lot to talk about, but first things first. Corina, we've heard a lot about your Diamatia gown these past few months, but nothing on your wedding dress." Hyacinth wrinkled her nose at the future princess. "Can you tell us anything? Just a hint."

Corina's laugh was classic and musical. "I can tell you it's being designed by Melinda House. I really love her work, and she's been a big support to me during this season."

"Well, we cannot wait to see it." Hyacinth smiled like Corina's answer was enough, but Stephen knew she ached for more.

"We hear estimates of five hundred million viewers around the world for the wedding," Madeline said. "Corina, do you think of that at all?"

"So far, I'm in the throes of planning a wedding like every other normal engaged woman." She peeked at Stephen and he loved her confidence. "I'm not focused on the watching world."

Indeed, she was going to make a lovely royal.

Madeline and Hyacinth prattled on with more wedding questions and observations, announcing again to the viewing audience that the big day would be held at Cathedral of David, October 19 at noon, with an afternoon reception at the palace and a private one that evening.

"Why the Braithwaite for your private reception?"

Corina fielded that one. "The Braithwaite has a history and meaning with us, so we wanted to go back to that place to celebrate where we are now and the start of our lives together."

Where it all began, it ended. Now it would begin again, new, fresh with a sense of holy approval.

"Prince Stephen, the King's Office informed us you have an announcement to make." Madeline read from her cue cards.

"I do," he said, tightening his grip on Corina's hand. "Even though my ankle is in the best shape it's ever been in—"

"Is it true you experienced some sort of miraculous healing?" Hyacinth did not hide her skepticism.

"I did, and as a result a lot has changed in my life—"

"Indeed, you were coronated as Prince of Brighton last month," Madeline said. "What a lovely ceremony."

"And with the coronation, I became patron of the War Memorial. The memorial needs some attention, and there is much to be done for the families of our military men and women, so today I'm announcing my full retirement from professional rugby."

A tangible, forceful gasp rose from the audience.

"This is such a sad day for Brighton rugby." Hyacinth leaned toward Stephen, cue card in hand.

"Corina, what do you say? Do you support this?" Madeline read from her cards. "You said in an interview last month that you first fell in love with the rugby player not the prince."

"I said I fell in love with him on the rugby pitch. I fell in love with the man. I had to accept the prince part that came with him."

The audience laughed with a soft sprinkle of applause.

"Will you be starting a family soon?" Hyacinth said.

"Tell you what, Madeline, you'll be the first to know when a baby's born," Corina said to the delight of the audience.

Stephen tucked back his grin, but he could not be more proud of his soon-to-be wife. She was going to do fine in the circus that followed his family.

"I'm sure the Eagles will miss you, Your Highness," Hyacinth said. "Will you miss the sport? You've been quoted many times over the years saying rugby was your life."

"I love rugby and it's been very good to me. I'm grateful to Coach and the lads on the team. I couldn't have achieved what I did without them, but they've several wingers coming up who will far outshine me. And good for them."

They bantered about rugby and Stephen's triumph in the Number 14 wing position until commercial.

"Having a good time?" Stephen whispered to Corina.

"Yes, because I'm with you." Corina kissed him, the audience approving with a corporate sigh.

The studio light came up as the show returned from the commercial break. "We're back with our very special guests, Prince Stephen and his fiancée, Corina Del Rey," Hyacinth said. "We are just so excited to have you both."

"Hy," Madeline said, breaking in, "I just have to ask this." She bounced in her seat. "Corina, Prince Stephen has been touted as one of the world's most eligible bachelors, and certainly one of the most sought after. Though he was so focused on rugby he didn't notice."

"I think I'm liking rugby more and more," Corina said.

"So you can imagine how floored we all were to hear you two were married. I'm sure the women in our audience are dying to know, how did you catch the prince?"

Corina released his hand, sitting forward, clasping her hands at her knee. "I'm not really sure. We met in a postgrad class at Knoxton and—"

"Can I answer the question?" Stephen sat forward. He was the only one who really knew how this incredible woman won his heart.

"Please do," Madeline said.

Corina swiveled to face him. "Oh no, babe, what are you going to say?"

"Babe? Is that your nickname for him?" Hyacinth loved the nitty-gritty.

"One of them," Stephen said with a wink.

"Oh, I want to hear more about that in a minute," Madeline said. "But just how did American Corina Del Rey catch the heart of our Prince of Brighton?"

Stephen reached for Corina's hand. "She loved me well. She loved me well."

THIRTY

Cathedral City

Cathedral of David

October 19

Under a crisp blue Brighton Kingdom sky, Corina held fast to her father's hand as they rode in an open-air, gilded black-and-red carriage, drawn by four gleaming chestnut-colored horses and accompanied by ten footmen, through the city streets swarming with well-wishers.

"The roar is so loud I can't hear myself think," Daddy said, laughing, his heart beating in his eyes.

Corina drew on his strength and waved at the crowd, a nervous laugh in her chest. "Their rugby prince is getting married. And it's a national holiday."

"Nervous?" Daddy squeezed her hand.

"Worse than the Miss Georgia pageant when my shoe broke." Corina leaned against him. "But I'm so excited."

"I'm proud of you, Kit." He cleared the emotion from his

voice. "Carlos would be proud but reminding Stephen he's getting the greatest girl in the world and to treat her as such."

She exhaled. "I feel blessed to have him, Daddy. I never stopped loving him. Even in the dark days when I thought our marriage was annulled."

The carriage turned down the wide Rue du Roi, passing under the two-hundred-year-old royal oaks, ablaze with fall's reddish orange.

The Cathedral of David, where Stephen was coronated officially as Prince of Brighton a month ago, awaited them, watching the avenue with its spiral peaks.

"Thank you for loving and accepting him, Daddy." Stephen had properly asked Donald Del Rey to marry his daughter. And he'd asked forgiveness for his role in the death of their son.

A deep healing began that day in the Del Reys. They weren't the family they used to be, but they were on the journey to the family they would become.

"What choice did I have, Kit? You loved him and Carlos gave his life for him. Plus, he's the Prince of Brighton." Daddy winked. "Your mother had breakfast with the Queen Mum. And her daughter is going to be a princess." Daddy laughed. "She was born for this world. It's like the mother ship has called her home."

"She and Queen Campbell have several friends in common."

"She's healing, Corina. I'm healing." Daddy's voice choked up and he tapped the end of her nose, an affection that started when she was a baby. "You've brought us all healing and love again."

Love well.

The carriage pulled up to the cathedral, the *clip-clop* of the horse's hooves fading to a stop. At the red carpet, two footmen opened the carriage door.

Corina descended the carriage steps, holding on to Daddy, pausing to wave at the crowd, taking the time to focus, see their faces. After all, they took time out of their busy lives to celebrate with her.

At the nave entrance, matron of honor Daisy and bridesmaid Melissa waited with the royal wedding director, Tama.

"Queen Campbell and Princess Susanna are seated, and your mother just went down the aisle." Tama handed Corina her wedding bouquet with a small locket containing a picture of Carlos, laughing, resting among the lilies. "We're ready for you in thirty seconds . . . as soon as the music changes."

"You look so beautiful," Daisy said with a light embrace, tears in her eyes. "And my dream came true. You are a princess."

"You're beaming," Melissa said.

"It means everything to me that you're both here."

In that moment, the music changed and "The Bride's Rhapsody" began, a piece composed especially for Corina and Stephen. The stringed melody rose into the high, arched nave ceiling with notes of joy and celebration.

If she had had any reservations, it was too late now.

"Remember," Daddy said, offering his hand, "everyone here is for you."

Corina placed her trembling hand on Daddy's, her heart's beat resounding through her.

But she'd had this date with destiny for a long time.

As she glided down the aisle with her hand cupped over Daddy's, her gaze locked with Stephen's. His smile trembled, and even from her distance, she saw the glisten of emotion in his eyes.

He was dashing and handsome in his dress blues, a bank of medals over his heart, and the gold royal braid around his shoulder.

Halfway down, among the *oohs* and *ahhs*, Corina slowed, pausing to notice Adelaide and Brill sitting on the aisle end of a long, polished pew.

Adelaide's eyes overflowed and Brill puffed out his chest, smoothing his hand over the tuft of grey hair sprouting from the crown of his head. Then he extended his hand, producing a single rose.

Tears captured Corina's eyes, and she broke rank to reach for the beautiful bloom. "You?"

Brill beamed, winking.

"Better keep moving, Kit," Daddy whispered.

But Corina leaned to kiss the old man, if indeed he was a man, on the cheek. Then Adelaide. "Thank you for everything."

"Our honor. Just remember, you've the tiara, never forget to drink from the cup."

"I won't, I won't."

"Kit, shug, we best keep going."

"Those are my friends, Daddy. The ones I told you about."

Daddy, such a southern gentleman, shook Brill's then Adelaide's hand as the music soared over and among them with the glide of violins and cellos.

As they started again down the aisle, Stephen stepped down from the altar, moving toward them.

In long, even strides, with no hint of a limp, he approached. Were it not for his smile, she might collapse to the floor. *What was he doing?*

"Mr. Del Rey, may I have the honor of walking my bride the rest of the way to the altar?"

Daddy checked with Corina. She nodded, melting with tears, and whispered to Stephen. "You're going to mess up my makeup."

"Sorry, love, I just want to do the honor of presenting you to the Lord myself."

Daddy kissed Corina's hand and backed away. "I love you, Kit." He shook Stephen's hand. "You take care of my girl. I trust you with her life."

Corina breathed in, her emotion swelling. Stephen, right there in the middle of the aisle, with millions watching, broke into tears, resting his forehead on Daddy's shoulder.

"It's all right, son, it's all right." For a long moment, Daddy held his son-in-law in love and comfort.

"Psst, shall we get going?" Tama, flushed and wide-eyed.

Stephen raised his head with a laugh. "I suppose we'd best get on with this wedding." He brushed his cheeks with his fingers and moved in beside Corina, replacing Daddy. "

"You do know I'm crazy about you, don't you?" She couldn't take her eyes from him. He was so brilliant and bright with the light of love.

"Not half as crazy as I am about you."

Corina prepared to walk forward with him, but Stephen looked around the grand nave. "Esteemed guests," he said, the orchestra bringing down the volume of the rhapsody yet keeping the joy and celebration in each movement. "Thank you for being here. I married this woman in secret before I deployed to Afghanistan. Then when I came home, broken from an intense battle, I felt I wasn't worthy of her. So I sent her away."

Corina caught the silky trickle of tears at the edge of her chin.

"For over five years, she dealt with her pain alone, but through a series of rather divine events, we came together again." Stephen clapped his hand over his heart, his gaze now on her, full of blue persuasion. "She loved me when I showed her no regard. When I rebuffed and rejected her. She loved me well. She loved me to Jesus, where I finally discovered what it meant to be a man of worth. So I want the whole world to know I love this woman!" His shout rose to the rafters and rained over them.

The guests cast off decorum and cheered.

Stephen walked her the rest of the way down the aisle to the altar, past their smiling and glassy-eyed friends and family, where the Archbishop of Brighton began the traditional ceremony.

And then the world knew her secret. Corina Del Rey loved the Prince of Brighton.

EPILOGUE

Three days later

"Love, I've an idea." Stephen roped Corina into a kiss as she contemplated what to pack for her honeymoon. They were leaving in the morning for an undisclosed place and Stephen's only hint was, *"Pack your bathing suit and knickers. That's all you'll need."*

"An idea?" She stared at the pile of clothes on her bed. One with beach wear. Another with mountain wear. "Stephen, babe, come on, where are we going? What should I pack?" She turned in his arms and shoved him down on the bed, kissing him as they tumbled.

"I told you, bathing suit and knickers." He laughed. Which he did every time he said that, so she had no idea how serious to take him.

"Fine. I'll pack things that go with bathing suits and clothes that fit over my knickers." She tried to shove away from him, but he held on, rolling her over and kissing her neck. "Is this your idea from a minute ago?" She laughed softly, unable to resist his wordless overtures.

"No, 'tis not." He raised up, hopping to his feet. "Let's pop round to the Manor, say hello to Adelaide and Brill. We've not given them a proper thank-you for their part in our relationship."

Over the four months of their engagement, Corina detailed her strange and seemingly holy encounters with the old proprietors. She'd visited them twice when she'd been in the city for wedding planning. But her last visit had been over six weeks ago.

"Babe, now that's a great idea. I didn't get to spend much time with them at the wedding other than to say hi." Corina took a sweater from the mountain honeymoon pile and slipped on her ankle boots, looking forward to heading out on this crisp, cool Brighton October evening.

"Same here," Stephen said, tugging a jumper over his head. "I looked for them at the reception but couldn't find them."

Downstairs, they informed Nicolas, Stephen's new butleraide-valet, that they were going out.

"Very good, Your Highness."

Stephen took Corina's hand as they walked toward the garage. He ventured out more and more on his own, without Thomas, to places he could trust.

"I'm still sad about Robert," he said.

"You did the right thing."

"But you should've seen his face when he confessed he'd eavesdropped on Nathaniel and me, then informed Gigi Beaumont about us . . . He was in tears. Said he didn't know what possessed him. Who ever dreamed a palace servant would've ever been entangled with the likes of Gigi Beaumont?"

"But he has a good place now at The Wellington, right? As for Gigi, never underestimate her."

"Well Nicolas was thoroughly investigated. Robert was one thing, but I also don't want another Asif—"

"Hey," Corina stopped, turning him to her. "That's it. No

more guilt, regret talk. It's over, forgiven, and we are moving on. And we are safe, babe."

"Right, right." Stephen kissed her forehead. "See, this is why I need you in my life." He opened the Audi passenger door for her.

Before slipping into her seat, she peered into his eyes. "I love you, Your Highness."

"Same to you, Your Royal Highness Princess Corina, Princess of Brighton."

She sighed. "I'm not sure I'll ever tire of hearing that."

Stephen chuckled and gently pushed her into her seat. "Let's go. I want to grab a late dinner on the way home."

They cruised across town, their hands entwined, resting on the console. At a quarter to six, the sun was already drifting toward the west, tracing golden-orange hues across the last of the fall day.

For Sunday evening, the city center lacked the noise and chaos of the week, but the streets flowed with theatre and dinner traffic, and the park was alive with families out for the evening.

Stephen approached the Manor from the south, weaving through back streets, finally pulling along the curb.

"Here we are . . . looks rather dark." Stephen leaned past Corina to see out her window as he cut the engine. "Let's get out and see what's going on."

Corina squinted at the darkness between Gliden and Martings, where the warm, holy glow of the Manor used to be and stepped out. Stephen came around to join her, muttering to himself. "What's going on?"

Where the Manor once stood was a narrow, shadowed alley.

"It's gone." Corina ran down the cobblestones, turning back to Stephen. "Do you see what I don't see?"

"I see an alley and no Manor." He stood back, staring between the two giant department stores.

"Did someone tear it down?" Corina battled a sense of sadness and loss. "Who would do this to sweet Adelaide and Brill?" She cupped her hand around her mouth and called. "Adelaide! Brill!" Across the street, the rising lights of the park sparked an idea. "The park. Maybe they're in the park." She started to dash around the car, but Stephen caught her arm.

"Love, I doubt they'd have moved the Manor to the park."

"Then where? Where are they?" She ran back to the alley. "This is unbelievable." She swerved toward Stephen. "Clive Boston gave me a ride home from the interview and he said he saw nothing but an alley. I thought he was mocking me."

"Now that you mention it, Thomas admitted he never saw the Manor either. He found it rather scary that we did, but all he ever saw was an alley."

Corina pressed her hand to her middle, her skin hot with the sense of descending revelation. "Then what did we see? I lived here for a week, Stephen. Slept in a bed, talked to Adelaide and Brill. Showered, used the Internet, ate food."

Across the road, in the shifting light of sunset, Corina caught a glimpse of a woman. The woman in white. She ran to the curb. "Stephen, there's the lady . . . the one who sent me to the Manor. Hey! Hello? Where are Adelaide and Brill?"

The woman looked up but kept walking between two park lamps and disappeared in their light.

"What lady?"

"In the white coat." Corina pointed. "She was right there, on the edge of the park. You didn't see her? She's gone."

"Gone?"

"I'm starting to feel like a *Doctor Who* episode." Corina slumped with disappointment and walked with Stephen back to the dark alley.

Then, from behind them, a beam of light layered past, spotlighting the side of Martings and a plain polished box at the opening of the alley.

"Adelaide's box." Corina dropped to one knee and gently opened the lid. "The tiara."

"From the premier," Stephen said.

"Yes. Adelaide said it belonged to the Manor. She watched over it."

The light shifted, dropping lower, sparking off delicate blue china cups. Corina laughed, reaching for the nearest one. "Adelaide served me tea in these cups. She said King Stephen I had them made for him and Queen Magdalena."

"I never heard of these cups." Stephen picked up the second cup. "Things like this are kept in the royal archives." Turning his cup over, he whistled low. "Corina, the crown and the sword . . . the House of Stratton cipher."

"She said King Stephen I and Queen Magdalena served the people with a set of these."

He made a face as he studied the blue-and-white cup. "Funny thing . . . it feels perfect in my hand. As if I've held it a hundred times."

"There are so many 'funny things' about this, Stephen." Corina looked toward where the Manor had once been. She missed the warm golden light of the front window. The sense of beckoning, "Come to me."

"The Manor is gone, but the tiara, the cups remained," Stephen said. "I feel as if I've stepped into some divine wrinkle in time."

Corina laughed softly. "Our own fairy tale."

"What do you think it all means. A tiara and teacups?"

Suddenly all of Adelaide's diatribes about true love converged into a single truth. "That if we want to be royals and have all the benefits and authority, to be respected, then we must be willing to drink of these cups, to serve the common man. Be like Jesus. Lead through serving."

A sober-faced Stephen rose up, holding his cup. "I feel as if we should pray or something, you know? Thank the Lord. Seek his guidance." He held out his hand to Corina. "If we've been given a gift. To know what he's asking of us. Honor the One who honors us."

Corina slipped her hand into his, tears sweeping across her eyes. "I feel rather undone."

They stood together in silence, heads bowed, in the middle of the sidewalk under the Cathedral City sky.

Then, as Stephen began to pray, "Teach us how to be royal and humble, Holy Spirit," the cathedral bells began their six o'clock cadence, their call to prayer pealing through the delicate, crisp fall night.

THE LIBERTY PRESS
1 December

The King's Office announced today that a rare diamond tiara, lost from King Stephen I's era, has been found.

"We're delighted to have a return of this treasured family heirloom," said a spokesman for the palace. "Princess Corina discovered the rare piece while touring an old inn in the city and returned it to the family jewels. The royal family is thrilled to have Queen Magdalena's crown safe where it belongs."

The palace has reserved the tiara for use by the new Princess of Brighton, HRH Princess Corina.

Well, how do you like that? Corina smiled as she folded the newspaper, dropping it beside the bed, as she reached to turn out the light. She paused with a sigh as thick snowflakes fell past the window through the palace lights.

Adelaide, Brill, wherever you are, thank you for watching over me. Over us.

Stephen had called Nathaniel and declared a snow day tomorrow, mentioning something about a snow fort and snowball fight.

Oh, there was so much to learn and love about him.

She snapped the lamp switch and burrowed under the covers, curling against the strong body of her warm, gently sleeping husband.

DISCUSSION QUESTIONS

1. Corina has a pretty amazing secret. But it's overshadowed by a tragedy. We all respond differently to hardship. How would you have responded if you were Corina?

2. Not only is Corina's joy brought down by immense sadness, her family falls apart. Corin felt she needed to be there for them. What about you? Would you put your life on hold for five and a half years to "be there for your family." Is there a limit to how much we give to others to our own detriment?

3. Prince Stephen is dealing with the pain of Afghanistan by forgetting who he really is — a prince. He spends his time on the rugby pitch. In dealing with disappointment, it's easy to run, or get angry. How have you learned to deal with disappointment, or devastation?

4. A lot of times we don't like the identity we've been born with, or even marry into. Stephen struggles to step into his identity as a prince. Is there some aspect of your life you struggle to identify with? How can you be more accepting to the roles God has given you?

5. Corina's family is wealthy but her father made her work for her money. Then when she wants to splurge on the

painting for Stephen, she has the cash she needs. How fun is that? Even if we don't earn a lot of money, we can live in a way that allows us to have extra, to be givers. What about you? Do you live in a way you can "give?"

6. In the midst of her sorrow, Corina hears a God whispers to love well. Doesn't it seem to be the opposite of what we want or expect from God when seeking comfort? But it's exactly what she needed. A mission. A holy command. Talk about a time in your life when God spoke life to you in the midst of sorrow.

7. Adelaide and Brill are unusual characters, no? To me they symbolize God's interaction in our lives. Talk about a divine moment in your life—even if it seemed rather ordinary at the time.

8. This is the third book I've talked about the Brighton pastry "puffs." Don't they seem delicious? What do you envision them to taste like? What's your favorite pastry?

9. How about that dress, the Diamatia? Then Corina's mama donates it for charity and turns Corina's room into a quiet room. She is trying to keep her son alive by changing nothing of his. Do you see where she's coming from and how she might inadvertently treat Corina like she was gone too?

10. What does the Manor symbolize about Corina's spiritual journey? If you could "show" your spiritual journey in the physical world, what would it look like?

11. Stephen has a pretty dynamic encounter with the Lord at the archbishop's house. What was the significance for him in that moment? Have you had a similar experience?

12. After Stephen has his "come to Jesus" meeting everything changes. It's so true of scripture that He makes all things new. And for Stephen it freed him to be who he was called to be. How can you have a moment like this in your life?

13. In the end, Stephen and Corina have their happily ever after. Did the story end in a satisfying way for you?
14. What was your favorite part about the book?

ACKNOWLEDGMENTS

This book, in some way, has empty spaces. I have empty spaces. Ones that only the Holy Spirit can fill.

I found myself in a physical battle while creatively struggling with this story. Not a good combination. Yet through it all, by God's grace, I maintained my writing goals until my deadline, climbing to my office every day after a weak night of sleep, facing the page and writing despite my feelings, despite physical weakness.

As I prayed over this book, I felt the Lord would fill the "empty spaces" for each of you, telling you His own unique story to your heart. So ask Him. "Lord, what do you have for me as I read this book?"

God loves story. And He loves to speak to us through every aspect of our lives. So, see what He has in store for you as you read!

The good news is the physical struggle I faced has subsided and I'm back to myself. Prayer and the Word do work for all areas of our lives. Sometimes it requires a bit of warfare, but God is so very willing and able.

Special thanks to:

My publisher, Daisy Hutton, for her graciousness and understanding. We had to push the release out three months, a first for me, but it was needed to regroup. Thank you so very much, Daisy, for your friendship and partnership. I'm honored to work with you.

My editor, Becky Philpott, who was the first to get the call, "I'm not doing very well." This being our first book together, I'd have chosen a different scenario, but I couldn't control the extenuating circumstances. Becky, you graciously stood with me, cheered me, and read a very, very rough manuscript, returning to me with both praise and suggestions. You bless me, friend. Thank you so much for being all an editor can be.

To the entire HarperCollins Christian Publishing team, thank you! What a joy! Marketing Director Katie Bond, we're going on seven years together, friend! What a joy.

To Karli Jackson, Elizabeth Hudson, Becky Monds, Amanda Bostic, Kerri Potts, Jodi Hughes, and Kristen Vasgaard.

And to the amazing Jason Short, Ayannah Mers, and your team for all the great work you do on behalf of the authors. Thank you!!

Susan May Warren, my writing partner, for being on the other end of the phone so many times. Especially one Thursday evening when I called so boxed up I wasn't sure I could write another word. Ever. You set aside your family dinner and hammered out the romantic journey with me, encouraged me, and reminded me almost daily, "You can do this. The Lord has got this!" I've always been honored and grateful for your friendship and partnership, but that night, you were a lighthouse on a dark, stormy sea. I'm so thankful to the Lord for you, friend!

Beth Vogt, my other lighthouse, who got the call, "I'm on page two hundred and the hero and heroine haven't met yet!" This is never a good thing in romance world. You brainstormed the story with me on a Saturday night, lending me your doctor husband's medical expertise on high ankle sprains. Thank you so much, Beth and Rob.

My agent, Chip MacGregor, for your support, wisdom, and friendship. I appreciate you so much.

Jean Bloom, my line editor, for your suggestions and insight.

To everyone who prayed for me in the hard season, especially my church family at Church on the Rock and Freedom Christian Center. Thank you. Prayer changes everything.

To my husband, Tony, for being amazing, for praying over me, for reminding me of who I am in Christ, for challenging me to stand and fight, for loving me. I cannot imagine this life without you.

To my Grandma, mom and sister, and my brothers. Love you all.

To Cara Putman for ideas and help. Thanks, friend.

To the readers who make it possible, and fun, for me to do my job. Thank you!

To Jesus, who partners with me on every book, who gives me ideas, help, and well, everything I need to do what He's given me to do. I write for You!

To everyone who is hurting or finds themselves in a difficult place—physically, emotionally, or spiritually. Know this, He loves you, He's there for you and hears your prayers. There is nothing too big for Him to handle. Just trust. Believe.

Happily ever after begins today.
The honor of your presence is
requested at three spring weddings . . .

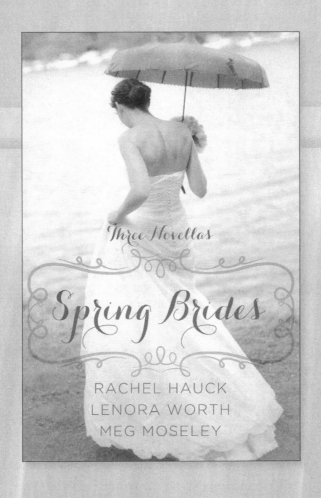

Available in print and e-book February 2015.

The next chapter in
A Year of Weddings begins anew . . .

9780310392187-A

PLEASE JOIN US FOR
RACHEL HAUCK'S
ROYAL WEDDING
SERIES . . .

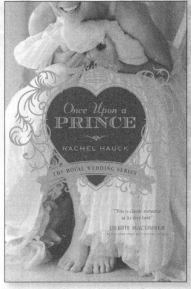

Available in print and e-book

Available in print and e-book

Available in print and e-book

ABOUT THE AUTHOR

*R*achel Hauck is an award winning, bestselling author. Her book, *The Wedding Dress*, was named Inspirational Novel of the Year by *Romantic Times*, and *Once Upon A Prince* was a Christy Award finalist. Rachel lives in central Florida with her husband and two pets and writes from her ivory tower.

VISIT HER WEBSITE AT WWW.RACHELHAUCK.COM

TWITTER: RACHELHAUCK

FACEBOOK: RACHELHAUCK